Given in Honor of

Miss Grace Siewers

by

Mr. and Mrs. Smith Hageman

MILTON
AND THE
ANGELS

MILTON AND THE ANGELS

ROBERT H. WEST

THE UNIVERSITY OF GEORGIA PRESS

ATHENS

Contents

v

49415

Preface

Twenty-odd years ago Professor Harris Fletcher suggested in passing that "a complete account of Milton's angelology . . . should sometime appear . . ." with "examination of the whole range of Christian, to say nothing of the Jewish, treatment of Angels, from its rise in the Apostolic Age through its complete development by the Scholastics." My essay here is certainly not that "complete account," for it would be entirely beyond my powers and largely beyond my interests. I have, however, tried to give here an orderly and proportioned, though elementary, statement of Christian angelology as it helped to shape men's ideas in seventeenth-century England, and then to show specifically how it shaped some of John Milton's ideas and how he freed others from it. I have written most about those angelologists who were undeniably connected with Milton, either in personal history or in thought. Many of these men — Burton, Scot, Fludd, and More, for instance — have long ago been pointed out to Miltonists and are much mentioned by annotators of *Paradise Lost*. Still, they have not been read in any close comparison with one another, but have rather been treated in isolation, or sometimes tumbled together as though angelology were all one sort of thing. I am concerned with significant differences and relations between them. I have emphasized angelologists of Milton's nation and of his time, not that I suppose them of first authority to him or more likely than earlier writers to have come under his eye, but that they show best the state of opinion in his time — opinion shaped, as his was, by earlier writers. By comparing Milton with them we may see him in place, as it were. For the sake of seeing him so, I write much, too, on angelology after Milton's blindness and even after his death. I do not suppose that Henry More contributed a great deal to Milton on angels, and John Webster's chapters in 1677 certainly contributed nothing. But to know the full flow of currents of opinion that did influence Milton's composition and also his readers' understanding of him, these men and others are essential.

vii

The speculation on angels did not have a name of its own in English in Milton's time. The word *angelology* had not yet been picked up from the Latin, and the related word *daemonology* was applied rather to the worship of daemons than to the study of them. But that the speculation had discrete existence is clear from the number of special treatises on it and from the fact that it was a formally acknowledged division of both theology and philosophy. With this much to go on I have as a matter of convenience used the words *angelology* and *angelologist* freely. I have now and then, too, referred to the "science," by which I mean to emphasize the difference between direct speculation on spirits and the casual treatment of them in folklore and fiction. I do not intend to imply either that the seventeenth century spoke of angelology as "the science" or that angelology is a science in the sense that genetics and astro-physics are so. Still, as a branch of theology and philosophy, angelology unquestionably is "science" in the elder sense of a deliberately assembled and rationalized field of "knowledge."

I hope that in the heat of my interest I have not forgotten how peripheral a virtue familiarity with angelology is or how much more important than to know angelology many other qualifications are for a critic of *Paradise Lost*. Angels are, nevertheless, prominent in the poem, and no estimate of it that includes serious misreading of them can be quite just.

All my references to Milton's works and my quotations from them are from the Columbia edition, for the use of which I have the kind permission of the copyright holders, the Columbia University Press.

I have to thank the editors of various publications for permission to use, largely in paraphrase, parts of four articles and three notes that I have published in the last five years. Specifically, *Studies in Philology* for "The Names of Milton's Angels," *The Philological Quarterly* for "Milton and Michael Psellus," *SAMLA Studies in Milton* (University of Florida Press) for "The Substance of Milton's Angels," *Studies in Shakespeare* (University of Miami Publications in English and American Literature, University of Miami Press) for "Elizabethan Belief in Spirits and Witchcraft," *The Journal of the History of Ideas* for "Milton's Angelological Heresies," *Modern Language Notes* for "Milton's Sons of God" and "Milton's 'Giant Angels,'" and the Vanderbilt University Press for "Terms of Angelic Rank in *Paradise Lost*," in *Essays in Honor of Walter Clyde Curry*.

I am deeply indebted to the staffs of the University of Chicago

Libraries, the Widener and Houghton Libraries, the Huntington Library, the Folger Shakespeare Library, the Duke University Library, the Emory University Library, the Vanderbilt University Library, the Columbia Theological Seminary Library, and especially of the University of Georgia Library and to Miss Vivian Branch in particular for her cheerful and able help with interlibrary loans.

I owe special thanks to Professor T. J. Stritch of the University of Notre Dame, and to Professors Roosevelt P. Walker and Calvin Brown of the University of Georgia for reading my manuscript or parts of it and making many helpful suggestions; to Professor W. C. Curry of Vanderbilt University for suggesting my subject and for much stimulation and encouragement; to Professor S. I. Feigin of the Oriental Institute of the University of Chicago for indispensable help with the Hebrew of some angels' names; to Mrs. A. M. Scudder of Athens for making me a working translation from a chapter of Robert Fludd; and to Professor Arthur Kaplan formerly of the University of Georgia for checking my readings of various authors in Latin and advising me about a Hebrew word or so. I am grateful, too, to many others who have helped in innumerable small ways.

Financial help that was not small — in proportion to the project at least — I have received from the Carnegie Foundation and the University Center in Georgia to enable me to visit various libraries; from the University of Georgia itself, which at the intercession of Dean George Boyd of the Graduate School and Chairman E. M. Everett of the English Department, has allowed me much time free; and from Mr. Leroy Michael and the late Mr. David Michael of Athens, who are the generous donors of a yearly research award to a faculty member of the University of Georgia. The University of Georgia and the University Center in Georgia have provided grants in aid of publication. Needless to say, none of these institutions or persons has any responsibility for what I have written or may have omitted to write.

R.H.W.

Athens, Georgia
March 11, 1955

Chapter I

Angelology in the West

In every period of history, even the most positivistic, probably some at least among thinking men have sustained an unabashed conviction that forces which may broadly be called *daemonic* are active in men and things. God does not work only through the mechanism of nature, these thinkers seem to say, but also by a kind of dynamism whose units resemble the mind of man, and whose manifestations suggest personal will and purpose distinct from God's and perhaps opposed. From Newton's time or before, such an idea has seemed to a dominant majority of intellectuals to be either nonsensical or embarrassing, but always it has had its candid spokesmen; in England's age of reason, for instance, the Boehmenist, William Law, and in France's the Boehmenist, Saint-Martin; in Victoria's matter-of-fact times Madame Blavatsky and even, privately, Mrs. Browning. Near the end of those times, while Andrew D. White to great applause was sabering superstition, Arthur Edward Waite, a man certainly no less in stature, was writing seriously upon some thinkers whom White deplored as mystagogues and upon some of their ideas that White called manifestly absurd.

White undoubtedly spoke according to the intellectual proprieties of his time and Waite did not. No discourse could be quite proper in that time if it seemed outside the clear light claimed for reason and science, or if it seemed in that light to advance a fruitless hypothesis. Whatever pragmatic utility characteristic Victorian thinkers may have been willing to allow to conventional religion, they certainly allowed little or none to the notion that beneath God hidden personal forces work in events and glance through the temper of the men who lead in them. Since Victoria, however, we have had two world wars. During such paroxysms the clear light of science may seem after all rather tiny; a suspicion of powers in the dark beyond may come to life in many to whom it is a shock. At such times serious talk of occult energies in men and nature

1

may take on propriety and may turn from virtually private con-
versation among those with a special disposition for the topic to
a public discussion with new interest and standing and, especially,
a fresh impact. Daemonism may become, then, material for the
artist in a serious and at least quasi-literal way and, less freely, for
the speculative thinker.

In our own time when the idea of invisible personal forces has
been scarcely an accepted part of most religion, much less of
philosophy, the sudden suspicion that a demon screeched through
Herr Hitler's throat and that the wrath of God is in his angel of
the Bomb, may have a very powerful effect. Such apparitions are
entirely unpredicted by the calm fabulists of atomic physics and the
social sciences; the thought of two and a quarter centuries that has
culminated in logical positivism and in such reportorial literature
as the novels of James T. Farrell has left many of us extremely
unready for the new plausibility in the old apocalyptic affirmation.
Out of our very amazement that affirmation may gain potency.

Since World War II Aldous Huxley has been able to make
meaningful literary capital out of the fancy that the atomic disaster that is to end our civilization may seem to its survivors manifestly the work of Belial, and Thomas Mann has narrated against
a background of Germany in flames how some devilish force possessed a composer's soul. Among philosophers, the late C. E. M.
Joad, at least, turned with the war to an emphatic conviction not
only of God but of evil. Other writers, too, of many sorts have
spoken in one way or another of daemonic theory or phenomena,
and their words seem, perhaps, to have a new soberness, seem free
in a way they could not have been fifty years ago both of the ob-
tuseness that goes with eccentricity and of the tacit disclaimers
clear in such fantasies as Anatole France delighted to write about
spirits and sorcerers.[1]

Huxley's and Mann's books are novels, it is true, and in them
Satan and Belial do not quite materialize or have an unequivocal
separate existence, however omnipresent they seem in the action.
Able modern authors do not, usually, quite say that disembodied
spirits are in the air about us; perhaps their sense of the proprieties of our day prevents it. C. S. Lewis gives us the letters of a
devil actively recruiting Satan's kingdom, and Denis de Rougemont gracefully exposes Satan's own hand in our misdeeds without either of them implying that he could ever, like Luther, really
have a demon as target for his ink-pot. Still, they do intend a
seriousness not merely moralistic behind their lightness. The devil

lives, they seem to say. And when Lewis passes into the pure fiction
of his interplanetary novels he takes good and evil angels for his
characters as directly as Milton did — not as ornaments for costume
romance, but as present beings whose history helps to explain
man's history.[2]

Thinkers who do not express themselves in fiction are naturally
more at a loss than Lewis is to describe with any directness the
non-human wills that they may suppose invisibly rampant in the
world. Joad does not declare for apparition or any Faustian relations of man and devil nor even discuss such things. The Carmel-
ite Fathers who in 1948 published boldly and seriously on Satan
do not commit themselves positively to the materiality of his activities, and the fascinating innuendoes of the Rev. Montague
Summers that a witches' conspiracy is what sickens the world never
crystallize into an explicit diagnosis.[3] Even Giovanni Papini in his
recent fulsome account of Satan sheers off a little from treating the
physical phenomena of daemonism. This hesitation in current
statement on the daemonic, this unlighted center to what is said,
dignifies the speculation to the modern mind and certainly height-
ens its shock for the modern imagination. If after reading Mann
and the Carmelites we look again at the frightful errors and dangers of our world and consider whether after all such powers as
the angels of God and the devil may be abroad, we are indebted
to our authors for little more than a hint — a hint all the more
electrifying because it does not proceed to any bald details or
vulgar rationalizing.

Twentieth-century outcroppings of wonder, then, about some
secret and separate purposiveness suspected in men and things is
not joined very sympathetically to the thought on such energies
in our Christian past, because its most striking features are first,
the shock of it, and second, the indefiniteness in it that goes far
to sustain that shock. In periods when daemonism was received by
theologians and philosophers they rationalized it strongly. The
traditional Christian doctrine of spiritual powers has no major
surprises for us and is quite definite in its central articles on
spirits' existence, history, and purpose. It both narrowed and
steadied the image men had of the spiritual world. The terms it
put upon the beings it envisaged — *angel, daemon, genius, spirit,
cherubim* and *seraphim, incubus* and *succubus* — were worn
smooth by use, and the concepts of such beings' activity in this
world and the next were commonplaces and, to a degree, still are
so. The modern reader, therefore, whose hair may rise as he goes

through Mann's *Dr. Faustus* or the *Satan* of the Carmelites will find in the explicit spiritism of *Paradise Lost* only a stately succession of well-worn conventions. Milton has himself transmitted those conventions to us more largely than anyone else in literature, and in a work so often combed as *Paradise Lost* anything may come to seem tame.

The fact about the work itself, however, is that Milton composed it in a time as convulsed as ours and in many ways more sensitive to the idea of daemonic powers. The civil war capped with an official regicide made the past lurid and the future ominous for a people who could not escape judging most events out of an expectation of hell and a hope of heaven. The prevalent doctrine of spirits, though it steadied the image men had of the spiritual world, filled their imaginations with its projections. Familiarity with its ideas did not divest them of excitement in the seventeenth century, for the sense men had of mystery around them was too keen for the supernatural to lose its effect simply because preachers and poets had a traditional scheme in which they might clothe it. This traditional account of spirits was itself frightening enough if taken entirely to heart, and it was always at war with others more chilling yet because they were unfamiliar, or perhaps because they were more intimate. In the 1650's one John Pordage, for instance, combining the qualities of a puritan minister with those of a disciple of the German mystic, Jacob Boehme, dispensed a Boehmist "enthusiast's" account of spirits he had personally met. In his house, wrote Pordage, the "Dark World" and the "Light World" showed themselves to the "internal sight" of the godly community he led. A dragon had flamed at him, and his guardian angel had stood beside him. Spirits often drew the curtains of his bed at night, and demons of hell imprinted past erasure dreadful pictures of their habitation on the bricks of the chimney and the panes of the windows. Dr. Pordage was just barely able to save himself from conviction as a necromancer and was still remembered as a wizard years after his death when John Dryden lampooned his son in 1682.[4] All over England phenomena, real or fancied, of the century's dark nights and witch-ridden countryside [5] gave an edge to the supernatural which few but the most matter-of-fact could wholly turn. Imagination — or perhaps it was the time's special spiritual sensitivity — was always ready to break bounds. Divines might insist, as they did against Pordage, that miracles had ceased with the establishment of Christ's church,[6] but certainly, as a sceptical nineteenth-century scientist noted, apparitions, at least, continued frequent in England until the invention of gas light. To the mid-seventeenth-century reader, then, any story of spiritual beings might possess a power that we do not now find in it.

Of such stories those that had pretensions as literature usually tried not only to sustain the effect of the supernatural, but to do it in at least token accord with some theological or philosophical theory on spirits. This last was not in itself an exacting requirement, for many venerable theories were current, and even the most ancient or pagan might be serviceable to a poet. New ones, too, with the spice of novelty were not lacking. Scripture was the authority most available and most assured, of course, and beside it stood its interpreters among the Fathers, the Schoolmen, and the Reformers. Platonists and Rabbis too had their places, particularly in the speculations of Renaissance occultists and mystics, who helped to keep fresh the daily consciousness of spirits. The lore of angels in Milton's time was a spacious as well as a still living study. It had many turns, many conflicts, many overlaps, many follies — and perhaps in essence and in sum more sense to it than we normally recognize now.

II

Christian angelology was an adaptation of a Graeco-Oriental inheritance highly serviceable to one of theology's basic enterprises: the attempt to discriminate what is "done" in the world (and by whom) from what "happens" in it without personal agency. The essence of Christian angelology was insistence upon agents for certain events to which theologians did not suppose God to condescend and to which man was not equal. Unpredictable bad turns of battle and of disease and of weather and of other incalculables seemed often too much like malice to ascribe directly to God, and the equally unpredictable good turns too much like caprice. What was predictable seemed, on the other hand, too confining to be the direct work of the great Illimitable. Even the grand tasks of controlling the stars in their steady courses and the normal growth of seminal forms and the rest of nature's order were too every-day for God's direct attention. Does God manage these things, then, by blind machinery? If the malice and caprice of it are part of an impersonal, self-moving order that God does not interrupt, then either he has built them into it, or it is in some way beyond his power; but these cannot be. On the other hand if God habitually interrupts his order, then he has been moved by it in a sense, and this too cannot be. The design of the world seems to need intelligent administration, and the evident admixture of willfulness in it to show personal will. Something, therefore, which God moves, himself unmoved, may stand between him and the world. God manages in part, certainly, by his visible agents such as kings and priests; why not invisibly, then, by invisible agents?

To explain as acts, yet not God's acts, the events of nature, both the ordered and the random, the internal and the external, Christian theologians had available the Jewish and pagan concepts of rational agents above man and beneath God, who out of obedience or revolt or innate impulse invisibly controlled the events God left to them. Since early Christian theology found such providential agents plain in its scripture and prominent in its time's opinion, it had at least to account for them. Actually, it accepted them, with certain revisions, as indispensable to the description of God's providence in his corrupted yet still functioning creation. The meaning both of nature's regularities and of its vagaries was man's reward and punishment, his testing and tempering — a job to be performed, surely, by rational beings.

Since angels thus engaged primarily on moral grounds in the daily ordering of the universe, the account of it that included them tended to show it moved more commandingly by final causes than by material ones, so that the very existence of angels was a refutation of atomists and other materialists, who explained every change as mechanical. The activity of fallen angels cleared both God and man of originating evil in the world, without impugning the omnipotence of God, who gave all angels their errands but was unstained by their faults. Exalted vastly above man in power, but the creatures and servants of God, angels showed the state and glory of the supreme king and absorbed into their ranks every deity and demiurge that could offer to rival the One. In the long history of Christian angelology these things persist.

Between Epicurus, whom Christian angelologists never ceased to complain of, and Hobbes, whom some of them thought Epicurus's own son, comparatively few mechanist philosophers raised their heads, but angelologists had many serious troubles with the non-mechanists upon whom angelology built. Particularly the Peripatetics were too sparse in what they had to say about spirits, and the Platonists too free. Plato's doctrine of separable forms and the myths about superior beings, which he delighted in, spawned eventually more kinds of invisibles than the scriptural idea of angels could accommodate or a monistic religion tolerate. On the other hand Aristotle's rejection of separable forms and disinclination to allegorize led some of his followers to discount separate intelligences so severely that in the seventeenth century Henry More could put Aristotle among those "not even believing in daemons (as Pomponatius and Vaninus, his sworn disciples to their great satisfaction have taken notice of)" and most Protestants agreed as to a commonplace.[7] Catholic angelologists often tried to exempt Aristotle himself from such censure, but usually listed the ancient Peripatetics among those hostile to the idea of angels.[8]

One direct service, nevertheless, Aristotle did for the Christian effort to show the acts of God's invisible agents. He confirmed Plato's ascription of moving intelligences to the spheres of heaven, a point of belief that lasted under his authority to Galileo's time. Plato had stressed heavenly order as evidence of intelligence in celestial bodies. If the sun and the stars, says the Athenian Stranger in the *Laws*, "had been things without soul, and had no mind, they could never have moved with numerical exactness so wonderful. . . ." All who understand the primacy of mind must acknowledge that each heavenly body does move "by an intelligent will accomplishing good." [9] Aristotle's view was for angelologists, at least, very close to Plato's. The spheres have movers, Aristotle argues, because their perfect circular movements must each "be caused by a substance both unmovable in itself and eternal," since the heavenly bodies are eternal in their motions and so could be moved only by what is itself eternal and unmovable. He does not say that these substances, "themselves . . . without magnitude," are persons, but he does say that we must not think of the stars as "mere bodies . . . entirely inanimate," but rather "as enjoying life and action." [10] This was enough to prompt Christian angelologists up to the middle of the seventeenth century to cite Aristotle as believing in at least the angels of the spheres.

Plato himself did not, perhaps, go much beyond Aristotle in conscious contribution to an angelological way of thinking. His insistence on separable forms, however, gave every object a spiritual principle easily translatable into a personal spirit. Perhaps he did not intend any such translation; his "Ideas" were timeless essences of thought and were a different class of existence from the eternal personal beings he called "souls." But such followers as Apuleius and Plutarch identified souls, which in Plato's myths sometimes seemed indistinguishable from the beings he called genii or daemons, with the daemons of animistic religion, beings between gods and men, often conceived as human souls detached from bodies. The soul became the idea or form either of a fleshly man or of some more tenuous being who was clothed in an invisible body — in "mist," as Hesiod had put it — by means of which it was active in the world. To these beings were ascribed all events not directly done by deity or happening out of matter's blind recalcitrance and tumult. Plato, says one of Plutarch's interlocutors, has served philosophy well in discovering the principle of matter, the thing upon which forms impress themselves, for it helps to evade the extremes of those "who make out the Deity to be simply the author of nothing at all" and of those who make him author of "all things universally." "But to me," the speaker goes on, "those men appear to have solved more and greater difficulties who have made out a family of *Daemons,* intermediate between gods and men, and after a certain fashion bringing together and uniting in one the society of both." The daemons, says Plutarch in another place, are under God the "presidents, ministers, and guardians of this said natural constitution" of the universe.[11]

Plutarch supposed that this invaluable theory of daemonic powers might have come into Greece from Persia or Egypt. Certainly the east did contribute to the empire an oriental profusion of psychic intermediaries betweeen man and God — aeons, archons, angels, daemons — so that in the popular imagination, at least, earth and sky were aswarm with them. In graded hosts they infested both nature and the afterworld; they guarded or tormented the human soul in life and in death. For any Christian project of distinguishing what was done in the world and by whom they were superabundant. Their multitude and their ubiquitous activity might seem to squeeze out of man's consciousness not only impersonal order but even the fiat of God and the fact of man's own will. Gnostic superstition urging endless spells to control and propitiate these rulers of matter and sentinels over the soul distracted the Christian from his Saviour and turned him toward worship of false gods.

The Fathers of the church, who had to use and to control Christianity's pagan heritage, confronting cults and heresies as they did so, could measure their angelology very safely by the Old Testament, which encouraged only a spare doctrine in narratives that were essentially testimony to God's glory and to his concern with man. Angels attended the prophets, vexed the guilty, and oversaw the fortunes of nations to the advantage or the correction of the Chosen. In the common interpretation, at least, they stood to man's dazzled eyes for God himself whenever, as in the burning bush or on the plains of Mamre, he showed his will to man more directly than usual. Satan's, in the common interpretation, was the guilt of the first fall and so of general imperfection. The relation of angels to both God and man was predominantly personal. The good were the retainers of a great king, obedient to his will, watchful of his dignity, and the overseers of his children, whom they encouraged or rebuked according to their conduct. The evil were God's foes, resistant to his will, rivals of his glory, seducers of man to pride, envy, and insubordination. For man and for angels the royal compulsion in the world was neither a chain of mechanical causes nor an impersonal, inbred ideal or function, but God's commands. Obedience or disobedience was the chief cause of all truly important effects. The deliberate pious or impious conduct of men and angels and the consequences that followed from it were the things that were "done"; most of the rest of the world's events might be thought to "happen" as background to the moral drama under God's general polity.[12]

In Rabbinical legend this concern with the angels chiefly as showing God's state and the importance of Israel, results sometimes in reducing angels' dignity — though not their prominence — until they seem servile creatures hardly superior in place, at least, to animals. Those angels who protest Adam's advancement God ruthlessly flings into the pit or totally exterminates with fire. Others, far from being deathless Powers, are ephemeridae who are created, cry one word of praise, and pass into non-being. On earth when great Rabbis sit to expound the Torah angels cluster invisible, thick as gnats overhead to listen.[13]

The Fathers never, perhaps, so debased angels, but they did put firmly into Christian theology the Jewish emphasis on their moral rather than their natural activities. Though the Fathers accepted much from Greek philosophy on the power in the world of separate intelligences and something even on the moral nature, they kept foremost always the fact of personal will in both God and his angels. To Neo-Platonists a good daemon was a spirit (or perhaps a superior stage of emanation) that became one with a man's natural virtue, with his native tendency toward the aboriginal light; it was a kind of right energization in an organic universe that was like a single animal. Christian theologians, for their part, certainly did not deny the alliance with a man's natural virtue of those spirits who ministered to the heirs of salvation nor the complete organization in God of all created things. But always to them the good angel was obeying God's instructions, not just its own nature. To Neo-Platonists the evil daemon acted merely in natural accord with his remoteness from the emanating Source; and similarly the Christian theologian allowed the illusory world of sense, remote from God, to be the dominion of the devil. But he added that the Adversary was deliberately resisting God, not simply exemplifying the poverty of matter. The Neo-Platonists thought every creature exactly equipped for its place and totally responsive to its place. Just so the Christian held that those beings God created to do his will perfectly were created able to do it, whether in heaven or on earth; but the Christian did not admit an original evil nature to any, nor any immutable original virtue.[14]

In the adjustment of pagan demonology to Christian angelology, the theologians achieved valuable economies by absorbing into the ranks of the fallen angels the gods and daemons of the pagans. In this process they discredited the polytheistic religions not only by transforming their gods into devils but by crippling a widespread tendency to identify daemons with the souls of the dead. Thus they damaged the pagan's concept of personal immortality and the cycle theory of the soul. Daemons, held most Fathers, were incarnate never, and the soul but once; neither was without beginning, as Plato's followers had seemed to say, but both were created in time.

In these economies the theologians did not, it is true, win a clear-cut victory before the later Middle Ages; and in the Renaissance, of course, the pagan notion of daemons kept raising its head. Some Fathers asserted miscegenation between daemons and men. Lactantius, for instance, though he affirmed the Christian contention that gods and daemons were fallen angels, yet admitted a class of *daemones terreni,* offspring of fallen angels and the daughters of men; and after him Augustine supposed that fauns and satyrs were, perhaps, a kind of spirits.[15] Michael Psellus, eleventh century Byzantine Platonist, is unclear in his famous dialogue on demons whether they are fallen angels or another genus, and slides into a doctrine not unlike that of the Talmudists, who distinguished demons as a genus half-way in nature between angels and men, with which latter they shared the necessity to feed, beget, and die.[16] The Renaissance astrologer, Jerome Cardan, seemed to think demons mortal creatures distinct from angels, and Paracelsus had his semi-material and non-angelic sylphs and undines.[17] In seventeenth-century England Henry More, reviving Origen's idea of the pre-existence of the soul and the classical terminology of "genius" and "daemon" for the soul out of the body, emphasized its likeness to those spirits never destined to enter a terrestrial body.[18] John Pordage, the English Boehmist, thought angels bodily creatures and distinct from a superior class he called "simplified spirits." [19]

Closely linked with these stubborn survivals was the difficult question of the angel's relation to body. Everyone acknowledged that angels could control bodies; but everyone asked, too, how they could do so unless they were themselves somehow united with matter. The Platonists had usually supposed that daemons and the lower gods, being directly active in the world and subject to passion and perhaps to death, vitalized "simple vehicles" of tenuous matter as man did his compound body of gross matter. Many Fathers retained this view or something kin to it; but others, moved by the scriptural passages that called angels "spirits" and by the Platonic tradition of separate forms and by the insistence of many pagan writers on the impassibility and pure spirituality of the higher gods, contended that angels were wholly intellectual beings. A considerable ambiguity in the use of the word $\pi\nu\varepsilon\tilde{\upsilon}\mu\alpha$, spiritus, makes it hard to know just what stand many Fathers took. Sixteenth and seventeenth-century angelologists often acknowledge that Augustine himself spoke on both sides of the question and left his answer uncertain.[20] In the earlier Middle Ages interest in the problem seems to have been slight. Anselm, for instance, hardly touches it at all, and Bernard only with the notation that although angels undoubtedly must have some kind of body for apparition, he does not know what kind nor need to know.[21] As medieval thought grew in system, however, it examined the Fathers more strictly on angelic substance and reached a general conclusion stated by Lombard and followed by Albertus and Aquinas, and most Scholastics after them, that angels are pure intelligences not naturally united with bodies, though with a natural power to control the local motion of bodies and so to shape materials for apparition.[22] Against this denial of essential corporeity, humanists and reformers largely rebelled, and their revived Platonistic and Patristic views were continued in Protestant countries into the seventeenth century. Most Christian angelologists of all times and persuasions were ready to admit, however, that the question of angelic substance was not critical for salvation, and that what really mattered was not so much how angels existed and acted in the world as that they did exist and act under God.

Despite such admission, however, Christian angelology as a notable part of the prodigious medieval articulation of doctrine went more and more into the details of angels' substance, powers, and offices, always with the dominant purpose of showing their creaturely abilities and limitations in service or enmity to God and man. An ancient pagan tendency to make too much of spirits showed itself in various magical-minded sects, and the contrary tendency to doubt their existence or at least to look irreverently on some of the wonders attributed to them must have been close to the surface in even the most believing age.[23] The orthodox theologian was under pressure, then, at once to keep the doctrine of angels in check lest it give rise to a false worship and to elaborate it in a way to prove its solidity and reasonableness. Between these two impulsions Aquinas put together his rational scheme of angels, a scheme that by answering every question lucidly, cut the ground from under the magician, who profited by mystification in the doctrine of spirits, and from under the sceptic, who profited by confusion in it. Aquinas showed with perhaps more cogency than anyone before or after him how angels might be supposed to do much in nature without having complete sovereignty in it. He showed lucidly, too, that only evil angels served men's willful appetites, and that any deliberate summoning of them amounted to sinful worship. The Church allowed, however, a minor kind of worship to good angels as acknowledgment of their superior place in the scale of creatures, and this provision Cornelius Agrippa and some other Platonistic theorists of the Renaissance took as opening the door to such theurgical practices as were described in the famous *Egyptian Mysteries* attributed to Iamblichus and translated into Latin by Ficino. The magic-minded Renaissance Platonists magnified extremely the part angels had in the world and the means of man's access to them. Without quite returning to the entire Neo-Platonic theory of daemons, they very much disordered the accurate scholastic rationale, particularly by a shadowy but insistent humanist contention that man could come inevitably to God through angels by a sort of resistless, graduated identification of himself with each member in turn of the rising chain of the Dionysian orders. This system obscured orthodox theological emphasis on obedience to God's will and showed the angel again in something of the Neo-Platonic style as a being determined by his place and responding almost of necessity to suitable stimulus.[24]

Against such paganizing tendencies the orthodox could only urge attention to the great scholastic system with its fixed distinctions between a pious regard for angels and a dangerous curiosity about them. But the very fullness of this system and the care of its distinctions exposed it to the effective attack of Protestant theologians, who did their best to sweep away all angel-worshippers at once by damning the elaborations of both Platonists and Scholastics. Protestants minimized angels along with all other intermediaries between God and man, and did it largely by boasting their unabashed ignorance about the details Scholastics and Platonists had labored with. We must not claim, says one Protestant theologian after another, to understand clearly angels' nature or the means of their action, for these things are obscure in Scripture. Lambert Daneau, one of Calvin's contemporaries and supporters, complains bitterly against the influential Jesuit angelologist, Maldonat, "a man, as you perceaue of euyll name," who had disputed "curiously of these matters, proposing this theame openly, and publishing a Book, wherein he professeth that he will intreate of Deuilles." Daneau rejects "these vayne babling proofes, and curious disputations. . . ." He abhors devils and will not try to say what they are like or how organized or of what colors, or any other such trifles, which "by them is more exquisitely and diligently handled, which would be accompted of the more subtil sort among the scholastical doctores. . . ." "I enuie not at it," says Daneau, "and I easily yield them the knowledge of such oglie matters." [25]

In their elaborations on angelic rank particularly, the Catholics found themselves at a disadvantage in the Renaissance because Erasmus and others had signified with good reason that their basic authority, "Dionysius the Areopagite," was spurious.[26] John Calvin could say with a show of objective judgment: "No man can deny that the same *Denyse,* whatsoeuer man he was, hath disputed many things both subtely & wittily in his Hierarchie of heauen: but if a man examine it more nerely, he shal finde that for the most part it is but meere babbling." More temperately, Peter Martyr notes that Dionysius is not believed to have been the Areopagite by those of truest judgment and that he is too circumstantial for credit.[27] Jerome Zanchy, the greatest of Protestant angelologists, recites the evidence against Dionysius' being the Areopagite and asks scornfully why he selects only nine names from Scripture as those of angelic orders when many others would do as well or better.[28] The Dionysian system, Protestants generally agreed, was overly detailed and a pious fraud.

This did not mean, however, that Protestants denied either angels or their ranks. Angels, both good and evil, exist and act as God wills and, like all his creatures, are in good order. Though Calvin rejects scholastic particularities, he admits that we must

rehearse the lore of angels so far as Scripture gives the means, because if we are to know God by his works we cannot omit so noble
an example as the angel and because — even more important, he
seems to imply — "it is very necessary for the confuting of many
errors." But, he says, ". . . we must leave those vanities that idle
men haue taught without warrant of the worde of God, concerning
the nature, degrees, and multitude of Angels," [29] and in his commentaries he rarely passes an opportunity to disparage the medieval readings on angels. Above all we must not credit angels with
the deeds that are God's. "Those men do deale wickedly and
peruersly, who feigne that the Angels haue something of their
own, or who make them Mediatours betweene God and us, in
such sort that they doe darken the power of God, being as it were
set far off . . . Therefore we must beware of those doting speculations of Plato, because God is too farre distant from us, we must
goe unto the Angels. . . ." And again: ". . . the whole glory must
be ascribed to God alone, we are to acknowledge the Angels but
his instruments, for otherwise wee should easilie slip into the error
of the Papists, who ascribing more than is meete to them, doe rob
God of his power, to clothe them with it. . . ." [30]

However unjust this may be to Plato and Aquinas, it represents
the emphasis of most Protestant theologians. Their attention to
angels was almost entirely to the moral significance of their activities as told in the Bible, and always with the notation that God
alone is the real author of the miracles that confirm the faith.
"The Angels can doe nothing of themselues, neither doe they
yeeld us any succour further forth than as the Lord sends them to
bee the Ministers of our saluation: Heb.1.14. Let us not stay our
thought upon them then, seeing their office is only to lead us
directly unto God." [31] In Protestant theology more important
things still were done in the universe than happened in it, but the
tendency to refer them to invisible mediators was much curtailed.

Undoubtedly the reformers helped to prepare the way for rationalism by their scornful repudiation of Scholastics and Platonics
as mere weavers of moonbeams, and they helped prepare the way
for the rising natural sciences, too, by their reserve about angels'
regular functions in nature. Protestants were generally unwilling
to assert, for instance, that angels moved the heavens. Such agency,
they were likely to feel, is unrevealed, and to hypothecate it would
be superfluous and almost impious, since God can move the stars
directly or can so order them that they keep place of themselves.
Samuel Purchas exemplifies this Protestant attitude, which was

firmly fixed by his time. Discussing the movements of the heavens, he says: "But I will not dispute this question or take it away by auerring the Starres animated, or else moued by *Intelligentiae*. A learned ignorance shall better content me, and for these varieties of motions, I will with *Lactantius,* ascribe them to God the Architect of Nature and co-worker therewith by wayes Naturall, but best knowne to himself." [32] Such an attitude seemed non-committal enough, but it was a part of the time's growing desire to find God rather in the marvelous normal order of his creation than in striking emergency departures from that order. Most Protestant writers granted that the miracles which were necessary to establish the faith had had few or no successors for hundreds of years, so that the universe runs, as it were, upon an even keel and a generally calculable course. This was the eager contention, too, of the rising mechanist philosophers, who thought that nature could be described far more profitably in terms of impersonal force than in those of purpose.

If we suppose, says Galileo, that God dropped the planets toward the sun, let them fall until they accelerated to the necessary speed, and then turned them into a circular motion, they would of themselves continue regularly in that motion without any further attention.[33] And the same with the rest of nature: God started it so mathematically integrated that all its real events take place of themselves as automatic effects of the events that preceded them. These "real" events possess in themselves only size, figure, number, and motion. In the perception, true, they are much altered; the senses impose secondary qualities such as color, and man as a valuing creature imposes his purposes, his good and his evil. But for Galileo, interested chiefly in mathematical verities, man is no measure of truth;[34] in Galileo's description of the world moral events do not stand first. Sin and the devil exist, and the good angels too; this much certainly Galileo would admit to the Inquisition. But they are not big on his horizon. He confined himself as far as he could to the basic events of nature, and for him these all "happened" — or, at least, he found it most useful to think of them as a fixed succession of causes and effects.

After Galileo and Descartes and their allies and successors had made this mechanist style of thought the vogue in philosophy, angels not only ceased to be serviceable in the effort to discriminate what is done from what happens, but became a positive embarrassment. Plainly if parts of the cosmos were managed by beings invisible and intangible, out of reach of any experiment, or at least not necessarily responsive twice in the same way to the same experiment, then a settled natural science such as Francis Bacon envisaged would be hard to ground. Even if one assumed, as many pious scientists seem to have — Mersenne, Gassendi, and Boyle,[35] for instance — that good spirits simply did not often interpose in the events of nature, still the very fact of the devil and his angels helped to keep conspicuous the presence in the universe of great moral forces for which the new science could not account and of the great problem of evil, which it could not solve. As the seventeenth century moved on toward Deism angels and devils became increasingly inconvenient. By the end of the century angelology was an abandoned science as far as the main currents of thought were concerned. Few men of standing troubled to deny angels or even the "science" of them; but fewer still found much to say about angels or any real use for the "science."

Among the new philosophers perhaps this lack of interest in angels is a near equivalent to doubt of them. They found no clear conception of angels, only defective testimony to apparitions, and in Lecky's phrase, a strong "antecedent probability" that the effects ascribed to angels came from other energies entirely. This modern or near modern point of view is perhaps most pointedly expressed in the seventeenth century by Spinoza to a friend who has asked his opinion of apparitions and referred him to standard demonologies and the standard "proofs" — as that God had created spirits to be more like himself than bodily creatures could be, that the balance and perfection of the universe required them, and that daily experience of specters confirmed them. It is beyond him, answers Spinoza, to comprehend how the universe is the more nearly perfect for having spirits or "how spirits more than other creatures express God." If, he goes on in a Cartesian vein, he had as clear an idea of spirits as of a triangle, he should unhesitatingly affirm them God's creatures. But "as the idea I possess of them is just like the ideas, which my imagination forms of harpies, gryphons, hydras, etc., I cannot consider them as anything but dreams. . . ." As for the accounts of apparitions, ". . . such stories are only attested by the narrators, and thus a fabricator can add or suppress circumstances, as seems most convenient to him. . . ." The whole conjecture, then, about spirits appears to him "false and not even probable. . . ." In a subsequent letter on the theme Spinoza puts himself into the mechanist camp: "The authority of Plato, Aristotle, and Socrates, does not carry much weight with me. I should have been astonished if you had brought forward

Epicurus, Democritus, Lucretius, or any of the atomists, or up-
holders of the atomic theory. It is no wonder that persons who
have invented occult qualities, intentional species, substantial
forms and a thousand other trifles, should have also devised specters and ghosts, and given credence to old wives' tales, in order to
take away the reputation of Democritus. . . ." [36] Like the atomists
he cites, Spinoza doubtless felt that the distinction between what
was done and what happened was difficult enough to make without complicating it with ideas of personal wills between God's and
man's. Unlike the Fathers, he did not find angels necessary to describe God's world.

Such, in broadest outline, is the history of Christian angelology
in the West.

III

In the eighteenth century the attitude usual toward angelology
was that it was an exploded study which might well be dropped
from sight. Most men of intellect viewed it with complete indifference, with amusement, or with contemptuous hostility. They
were not necessarily inimical to angels as a biblical usage and as
metaphor for a kind of man without man's defects, but they did
not permit any metaphysical conviction of angels to disturb the
controlling frames of their thought — their deistic rationalism,
their mechanistic materialism, their urbane neo-classical assumption that the cultivated man was really the peak of creation. Alexander Pope, for instance, respected angels in literature to the point
of disliking the "Quibbles" of Milton's, and he found his own
literary use for angels, naming them cursorily to top place in the
"Vast chain of Being"; but when he spoke of things done by spiritual creatures it was in the mock heroic "Rape of the Lock," for
which he took his satiric machines from the gently ironic "Rosi-
crucianism" of the Abbé Villars.[37] Bolingbroke in his character as
a deist denied angels to be personal creatures [38] and Voltaire's dic-
tionary entry on them is a subtly suppressed mockery. The *Encyclopedia* after its habit is straightfaced in the main entry, wry in
the referred ones. David Hume, though he formally spares angels
in his *Essay on Natural Religion,* does not leave any room for them
in his posthumous *Dialogues Concerning Natural Religion,* and
undoubtedly meant to sweep away the acts of angels along with
other "miracles" in his *Essay on Miracles.*[39]

Among men of religion, of course, angels kept more footing.
John Wesley, in sermons and letters as angelological as any written

by divines of the seventeenth century, flatly asserted their continued work and apparition; he was very conscious, however, of
speaking against the intellectual currents of his time. Swedenborg
had his own elaborate angelology, though it was not continuous
with that of earlier centuries, for he thought of no "angels" but
separated human souls.[40] He too was certainly against the current.
Lesser Protestant thinkers, men with more care than Wesley and
Swedenborg for the fashion or more swayed by the arguments that
sustained it, were apologetic when they spoke for angels. A minister named John Leland takes issue with Bolingbroke's view of
them, but briefly and much less heartily than he assails some other
opinions of the deists,[41] and in 1723 John Reynolds, another minister, who published *Concerning the State and Oeconomy of the
Angelical Worlds,* emphasized in his Preface that he hoped only
to "afford some useful amusement" and did certainly not intend
to provoke "any learned Fights and Skirmishes," such as, he implies, had disgraced the past. In Catholic countries, of course,
ecclesiastics like Augustine Calmet wrote old-style angelology.[42]
But their work was an intellectual backwater; no one, probably,
any longer expected to find angelology in the list of the sciences;
certainly no men of authority any longer named it there as Bacon
and Locke and others more partial to it than they, had done in the
seventeenth century.

Part of the typical eighteenth-century attitude toward angels
was, perhaps, that to speak much of them was to speak barbarously.
By the nineteenth century distance had turned such barbarity to
quaintness; scholars could look into the literature of angels as
folklore, and poets and novelists could use it for romantic shading.
The supernatural in *The Ancient Mariner* and *The Bride of
Lammermoor,* however, is no more an equivalent of that in *Paradise Lost* than Goethe's Mephistopheles is the counterpart of Marlowe's. Much the same difference exists between the romantic
view of spirits and the Renaissance view of them that exists between the purpose of a county society's reprint of a sixteenth century witch tract and the purpose of the original publication. Such
books as Moncure Conway's *Demonology,* Frederic Hall's *Pedigree
of the Devil,* and Arturo Graf's *Il Diavolo* were condescending
antiquarianism or anthropology; they gave no grace to the opinion
angelology had had of itself as a more or less integrated "science,"
and, in fact, no just view of it as a phenomenon of intellectual
history. They tumbled mountains of information together in a
way that ignored its original organization and the intellectual con-

ditions that accounted for at least the conscious face of it. And when in 1824 Samuel Hibbert published his "Philosophy of Apparitions" it was a naturalistic "Attempt to Trace such Illusions to their Physical Causes." [43] In general religious and scientific thought angelology had, of course, next to no place. Schleiermacher seriously examined the concept of the devil to decide that it could have only poetic truth, serve the faith only as metaphor; and Renan thought of what the Bible said of demons as simply its contemporary way of speaking about phenomena that we ought, from our superior knowledge, to name quite differently.[44] Dorner, it is true, spoke powerfully for the reality of the demonic, but his was a voice comparatively isolated in his century.[45] Among laymen Spencer and John Fiske and their sort touched angelology occasionally as an aberration. They felt that they could explain how it came to be and in part forgive it.[46] But they did not respect it enough to defer to even the general idea of angels, as Pope and Hume did, or to abominate it seriously as Voltaire did. Gustave Fechner, as a religious-minded scientist, remembered angels; but it was to wonder at the bootless opinions men had spun of them as attenuate inhabitants of the skies, whereas, he thought, the solid earth itself was evidently an angel, flying through the heavens on God's errand. William James admired this fancy extremely as an instance of Fechner's vision;[47] and no doubt in another time Fechner might have been a Dionysius. The wide difference, on the surface at least, between his vision and Dionysius' is sign of the gulf that separates the milieu that can breed angelology from that which can breed investigative physical science.

The nineteenth century, in short, was likely to think of angelologists as absurd and amusing, sometimes engagingly human, more often horrifyingly inhuman, and as always the purest type of man-in-error-before-the-establishment-of-science. Much of this general view has persisted into the twentieth century, of course; and even in this year of daemonic passions among men and nations and of more than daemonic weapons, it would be hard to deny that the old angelology was a study often absurd, sometimes horrifying, and most evidently erroneous in the mass of its details. Past doubt it was of the very bone of medieval error, and its essential faults persisted in it to the last. It could not shade off, as alchemy is supposed to have done, into a field of modern science.

The fact remains, though, that many able minds and some great ones concerned themselves with angelology, and that their products cannot be well understood now without attention to it on our part. More far-reaching claims than these have sometimes been made for it; but these are enough, perhaps, to justify those who make some effort to stand clear of the scorn and condescension two and a half centuries have poured on it and to examine it with a decent respect for its undertaking and a sober recognition of its influence and even of its achievements.

Chapter II

Angelology in Milton's England

In England, as elsewhere, angelology died of mere disuse some time near the end of the seventeenth century. As beings with almost no function left in nature, angels could no longer claim attention of the able, and the "science" of them passed out of all serious prominence, whether in literature, philosophy, or religion. Angelology's role in literature dropped to such light uses as Pope explains in the dedicatory letter to *The Rape of the Lock,* to the ironic informality of Defoe in his *History of the Devil,* and to poor imitations of Milton such as Sir Richard Blackmore's. In theology Calvin's kind of impatience with angelology had helped breed a larger indifference to it than Calvin could have condoned. As for what happened to angelology among English philosophers and scientists, it appears clearly in a defense that Robert Boyle makes of some of his conclusions in hydrostatics against Henry More. All he attempted in his experiments, Boyle says, was to show that given God's world and its laws, "the explication of what happens among inanimate bodies" is sufficiently made by "the motion, bigness, gravity, shape, and other Mechanical affections of the small parts of the liquors. . . ." He did not intend "to prove that no angel, or other immaterial creature could interpose in these cases; for concerning such agents, all that I need say is, that in the cases proposed we have no need to recurr to them." His practice, he goes on, is according to the "generally owned rule about hypotheses, that *entia non sunt multiplicanda absque necessitate,*" which has been "by almost all modern philosophers of different sects thought a sufficient reason to reject the agency of intelligences, after Aristotle and so many learned men . . . had for many ages believ'd them movers of the Celestial Orbes." Finally, Boyle asserted that More's explanations of the phenomena he had reported were "rather attempts to accommodate the Phaenomena to the Hypotheses, than objections directly levell'd against my Solutions. . . ." [1]

Probably the last serious and seriously received attempt to engage the reason as well as the faith of literate Englishmen on behalf

of a developed doctrine of angels was the very progressive campaign of Henry More and Joseph Glanville to demonstrate the
existence of spirits largely by an accumulation of "well-attested"
data on contemporary apparition. They had support almost to the
end of the century from some able men, such as George Sinclair,
Meric Casaubon, Richard Baxter, Matthew Hale, and even, hesi-
tantly, from Boyle, who corresponded with Glanville on the project and sponsored the English translation of the really very puzzling account of a kind of poltergeist called the demon of Mascon.[2]
Except perhaps for Boyle, these men plainly did not grasp the
extreme difficulty of verifying phenomena that seem supernatural;
certainly they did not master the difficulty in any way acceptable
to physical science. They were, nevertheless, for their day almost
unanswerable because of their able argumentation, their personal
repute, and the link their contentions had with Scripture. Far
more damaging to them actually than the answers of such men as
John Webster and John Wagstaffe, meeting their arguments and
pointing out faults in their data and methods, was the fact that
they went largely unanswered; Newton and Locke and others of
real stature simply had little interest in the question. When the
loyal rally for spirits had died down by the end of the century, the
learned world would attend little indeed to either the phenomena
or the speculation of angels. Such gossiping tales for the guileless
as those which John Aubrey over-titled "Hermetic Philosophy" in
1696 or out-of-fashion devotional speculation based on the Bible
by such aged or provincial ministers as George Hammond and
Increase Mather or a theosophy much diminished in popular
esteem and in the caliber of its writers were about the only vehicle
left for angel lore in its own right.[3]

In the believing days of the middle century, however, when
John Milton was meditating and composing his epic, serious angelological writing abounded. Between 1640, when Milton first
recorded his interest in a drama of the fall, and 1665, when he
put the manuscript of *Paradise Lost* into Ellwood's hands, several
dozen fairly substantial works dealing wholly or predominantly
with angels or containing a sizeable section on them were published in England. This estimate does not include the numerous
commentaries on the Bible, many of which had long passages on
angels, or condensations of Christian doctrine, such as Gerhard's
and Wolleb's, which like Milton's *Christian Doctrine* treated
angels in discussion of creation and of providence, or the swarm
of pamphlets retailing the marvels of witchcraft and astrology. Nor

does it include innumerable works such as George Rust's *Letter of Resolution Concerning Origen,* George Hakewill's *Apologie,* and Sir Thomas Browne's *Religio Medici,* which contain many short passages on angels. It excludes English publications of the works of ancient demonologists such as Plutarch and takes no account of works by foreigners not translated or published in England, though many — for instance, the *De Operibus Dei* of Jerome Zanchy, and the *De Operatione Daemonum* of Michael Psellus — were widely cited in England.

Of the special publications on angels, many of them re-printed several times, more than a fourth are angelology in the complete sense; that is, they systematically expound and argue the theory of angels. Perhaps the most prominent and influential of these was Henry More's *Immortality of the Soul* on the "angellicall condition" of man after death. It was first published in 1659 and re-appeared twice in the century in the *Collection of Several Philosophical Writings.* It expressed in full the advanced doctrine of spirits that More had foreshadowed in his *Philosophical Poems,* 1647, and *Antidote against Atheism,* 1652, and then repeated in half a dozen other works, refined in two chapters of his *Enchiridium Metaphysicum,* 1671, and finally carried into a fruitless controversy against Richard Baxter's *Of the Immortality of Man's Soul,* 1682. Joseph Glanville in his *Blow at Modern Sadducism,* 1668, and in virtually all his other work that touches on angels may fairly be called a disciple of More's. The same is true of Benjamin Camfield, in his *Discourse of Angels,* 1674, and of Henry Hallywell, in his *Discourse of the Polity and Kingdom of Darkness,* 1681.

Much less progressive than More, but very influential among those whose interest in angels was confined by the Bible and largely devotional, were the Puritans Henry Lawrence and Isaac Ambrose. Lawrence, father of Milton's pupil, published *Of Our Communion and Warre with Angels* in 1646, presumably in Amsterdam. It had three English editions by 1652. Ambrose, in his *War with Devils, and Communion with and Ministration of Angels,* 1662, Richard Baxter in *The Saint's Everlasting Rest,* 1650, Robert Dingley in *The Deputation of Angels,* 1654, and most other dissenting divines clear through Increase Mather and George Hammond, whose *Angelographia,* 1696, and *Discourse of Angels,* 1701, are near the tail of the procession, have sober praise for Lawrence's sober opinions. Ambrose himself won equally golden opinions from the same sort of authors and his book was

reprinted three times with his *Compleat Works,* and twice alone
by 1689. Much like the work of Ambrose and Lawrence were the
Ministry of Angels, 1657, of the Presbyterian zealot Christopher
Love, and such sermons as John Gumbledon's *An Angel in a
Vision* and *Christ Tempted,* both published in 1657. The angelology of these "saints" very closely resembled that of earlier
Protestant authors — Richard Sibbes of Cambridge, for instance,
who published *Light from Heaven* in 1638, and who in his turn
was writing in the track of John Calvin, Peter Martyr, Jerome
Zanchy, and other great men of early Protestantism, whose opinions
seventeenth-century divines cited constantly. This Protestant solidarity was particularly noticeable in biblical commentaries such
as those of Henry Ainsworth, Andrew Willet, William Perkins,
and the like. Resembling all these writers in keeping a tight rein
on speculation, and like them often commended by godly angelologists were Milton's enemy, Bishop Hall, whose *Invisible World
Discovered* appeared in 1652, and Joseph Mede, fellow of Christ's
in Milton's day, who printed *The Apostasy of these Latter Times,*
largely an account of pagan demonology, in 1641. Meric Casaubon's dissertation on the word δαίμων, *The Original and Cause of
Temporall Evils,* 1645, is much like Mede's learned treatise. Also
pious but not entirely conformed to the convention was *The
Retired Man's Meditations,* 1655, of Sir Henry Vane, a Puritan
with a mind and, it is sometimes thought, a sect of his own, who
talks much (often incomprehensibly) of angels. Somewhat out of
the pattern, too, in that they are bent entirely to fortifying men's
hearts against Satan and leave alone the sensational matters of
apparition, possession, and so on, are the *Daemonologia Sacra, or
Treatise of Satan's Temptations,* 1677, of Richard Gilpin, and the
sermon "Of a Christian's Conflicts with and Conquests over
Satan," preached by John Smith as one of a yearly series of sermons by divines of Queen's College "against Witchcraft, Diabolical
contracts, &c."

Different from these theoretical and devotional works in purpose of treating angels but controlled by a very similar pious
angelology are a number of the anti-witch tracts of the time, such
as John Gaule's *Select Cases of Conscience Touching Witches and
Witchcraft,* 1646, and his *Magastromancer,* 1652. Gaule was an
opponent of the famous witch-finder, Matthew Hopkins (whose
Discovery of Witches appeared in 1647), but he did not deny the
activities of devils in the world and, like many demonologists of
his time, collected authenticated stories to back his points. In this

he was succeeded by Stearne, Gardiner, Muggleton, Spurstowe, Farnsworth, Bromhall, and Matthew Hale in works well known to the history of English witchcraft. Equally well known, of course, are their opponents, Thomas Ady, John Wagstaffe, and Robert Filmer, and later in the century John Webster and N. Orchard. Many of the witchmongers do not argue angelology directly, though many do, and of their opponents, Webster does at length in his *The Displaying of Supposed Witchcraft*, 1677.

With the highly uncritical collection of "examples" that is his *Treatise of Specters* Thomas Bromhall printed in 1658 a *Learned Treatise Confuting the Opinions of the Sadduces* by an anonymous French author of evident scholastic training and opinions. In 1665 appeared a publication with a far more incongruous appendage, Reginald Scot's famous *Discoverie of Witchcraft* with an anonymous fourteen chapter addition and his bound-in *Discourse of Devils and Spirits* with a second book added. This second book is a particularly light-headed sort of occultist demonology; nothing could be an odder contrast with Scot's cogent and biting rationalism. In its lurching illogicalities it resembles some of the numerous translations made by Robert Turner in the 1650's: *Paracelsus of the Supreme Mysteries of Nature, The Fourth Book of Occult Philosophy* falsely ascribed to Cornelius Agrippa, the *Heptameron* falsely ascribed to Peter of Abano, *The Notory Art of Solomon*, and other such doubtfully lawful treatises, all of them full of talk about angels and of assumptions on them and sometimes of theory. Similarly Faustian are *The True and Faithful Relation of what Passed Between Dr. John Dee and Some Spirits*, introduced for a pious purpose in 1659 by Casaubon, and *John Tritemus of the Heavenly Intelligences*, translated by Elias Ashmole in 1647.

Kin in much of their subject matter to these occult fragments, but more learned, better composed, and altogether more respectable are the *Discourse on the Nature of Spirits* of George Pictorius, translated by Turner in 1655, and the monumental *Occult Philosophy* of Cornelius Agrippa translated by an unknown J.F. in 1651. Agrippa has twenty-two chapters on angels and was probably as influential in England as any other Platonistic demonologist. A native occultist that often quotes Agrippa is Robert Fludd, whose views on angels are scattered throughout his *Mosaical Philosophy*, published in English in 1659, and appear in more concentration in his *Utriusque Cosmi Historia*, 1617-23, his *Answer unto M. Foster*, 1631, and his *Philosophia Sacra*, 1626. Thomas Vaughan, Fludd's successor as chief of English theosophists, had little to say

on angels, but his succesor, John Heydon, had much to say on
them in *Theomagia,* 1664, and half a dozen other pretentious
works.

As extravagant as Heydon and probably as earnest as Fludd was
John Pordage, the "chief of the Behemists" in England, whose
conviction of angels was so strong that it led him to see visions in
his house and to make disturbances for which he was prosecuted
as a necromancer. A Puritan minister, Christopher Fowler, argued
the case against Pordage in *Daemonium Meridianum,* 1655, and
Pordage defended himself the same year in *Innocence Appearing
through the Mists of Pretended Guilt.* His *Theologia Mystica,*
1683, published many years after his death, shows a more formal
sample of Pordage's understanding of Boehme on angels. The long
expository poem *Mundorum Explicatio,* 1661, ascribed to Pordage's son, Samuel, sounds more like the father, and is at any rate
full of Boehmistic theory of angels.

All of these works — occultist, Puritan, rationalistic, Platonistic,
or whatever — were dependent more than many of their writers
cared to acknowledge on the medieval constructions of the Scholastics. The two English books of the century that most faithfully
and fully recorded the scholastic system of angels were *A Treatise
of Angels,* 1613, by John Salkeld, angelologist to King James, and
Thomas Heywood's long poem with long prose commentary, *The
Hierarchie of the Blessed Angels,* 1635.

Finally, the most cosmopolitan as well as the most disorderly of
seventeenth-century English writings on demonology is Robert
Burton's famous "Digression of the Nature of Spirits." Burton tor-
rentially mentions what seems an almost wilful variety of authors
and touches racily on many of the most involved and controverted
questions of angelology. Did he mean any of it seriously? Certainly
he takes sides seldom among his arbitrary authorities and smiles
as he displays them contradicting one another wholesale. But he
had read the hordes of them, and he records them without overt
hostility to them or to their study. Perhaps he could not have done
these things in the 1620's with merely antiquarian interest.

II

In fact, the educated men of seventeenth-century England were
of many minds about angels. Few cared to publish a flat Sadducis-
tic disbelief such as that of the Familists, who held biblical accounts of angels to refer merely to good and bad impulses in men's
minds. But probably many men of intelligence were temperamen-

tally inimical to the very notion of angels' interposing in the world and, like Spinoza, found the evidence of them slight. The great Dr. William Harvey, full of scientific curiosity about witches and devils, presented himself once to a well known witch as a colleague, so the story goes, and on the strength of his "very magicall face" persuaded her to show him her familiar, a large toad, which drank milk with much aplomb. Dr. Harvey contrived to vivisect the toad and was not surprised to find nothing but the milk and such organs as are normal to toads. Surely, concludes the narrator, said to be a personal friend of the doctor, "this for an argument against spirits and witchcraft is the best and most experimentall I ever heard. . . ."[4] This tale may be apocryphal, but Harvey was probably no friend to angelology. He could have found it bothersome, both as a scientific physiologist and as a practising physician. We know, at any rate, that he was the director of a committee of physicians and midwives who examined some of the Lancashire witches in 1634 and made a sceptical report.[5] In his controversy with Riolan he mentions the lore of spirits and says that those who speak like the Schoolmen of good and evil spirits that possess the body have no physical ground for their assertions, so that "nothing is more uncertain and doubtful than the doctrine of spirits that is transmitted to us." [6] He is said, too, by John Selden to have participated with Selden in an ironical cure with a faked talisman, "a Card . . . lapped . . . up handsome in a Piece of Taffeta. . . ." which drove four "devils" from the head of a credulous Person of Quality.[7]

This prank does not involve a flat denial of the existence of angels, but perhaps it does indicate that Harvey and Selden would have been amused rather than shocked by Samuel Butler's couplets:

> For men are never certaine of strange sights,
> Their Senses are so Distressed with Frights;
> Especially of Specters that forbeare,
> Unless it be in darkest night t'appeare.[8]

These verses express the astringent impatience of the sharp and practical man of intellect with weary bugbears and unrelented pietism. With just such impatience, no doubt, Butler's friend, Thomas Hobbes — friend, too, of Harvey and Selden — explained to Aubrey that in the dark he was very practically afraid of robbers, not of spirits as gossip had it. And with a discreet version of this impatience Hobbes's friend, Francis Osborn, expressed his much-praised doubt of witchcraft.[9] The circle of these men, it would appear, did not believe in angels, much less in angelology.

But the circle, of course, was larger than it seems to be if one looks only for signs of scepticism. If Selden, for instance, was an enemy of angelology, he was yet in a sense an ally of some persistent angelologists. Though a friend and confederate in scepticism of Dr. Harvey, he was a patient of Dr. Fludd, the Cabalist, a friend of Archbishop Ussher, who urged the publication of Dr. Dee's spirit sessions and himself wrote some angelology, and an intimate of Sir Matthew Hale, who endorsed the reality of witchcraft from the bench and actively supported the campaign of More and Glanville to prove spirits. Selden himself makes some reference in his *De Diis Syriis* to. Hebrew demonology. True he intimates his distaste for its extravagances; but many a devout believer did as much, and Selden's complaints taken with the corrections he adds seem to indicate his acceptance in some way of a sober demonology applicable to the Bible. Thus he says that the Jewish astrologers nonsensically call Samael the angel that presides over the day of Mars, but actually *Samael* is simply a most notorious name of Satan, the chief of cacodemons.[10] In his essay on the fall of man the fashionable rationalist, Osborn, speculates entirely in the demonologist's manner on why God should punish the serpent if Satan was the whole mover in Eve's temptation, and concludes that Satan infected the serpent with envy of man so that he was a willing instrument.[11] Hobbes himself, the paragon of English materialists in his time, had to give a whole chapter of the *Leviathan* to angels. Hobbes' Aristotelian foe, Alexander Ross, notices in his gamesome *Leviathan Drawn out with a Hook* how Hobbes strains at the biblical texts on angels in his effort to show the materiality of all created things, and how "he confesseth at last, that though in the Old Testament Angels were but fancies; yet some places of the New Testament have extorted from his feeble reason; a belief that Angels were substantial and permanent." [12] Ross jeers that any faith extorted from a feeble reason must be itself rather feeble; and no doubt the faith Hobbes had in angels was weak enough. But to rescue his argument that all is matter, Hobbes had to enter into what was actually an angelological debate in which he took something like the common Protestant position that such angels as were substantial and permanent and seen by men had subtile bodies especially made for them by God.[13]

Even John Locke, whose philosophy is as little like angelology in tone, aim, or result as philosophy can be, felt that he had to touch seriously on the "science," since he acknowledged the existence of angels to be revealed to us and even that some ideas about them came to us by reflection. When he speculated on what man can know and how he knows it, Locke could not leave angels out of account. His conclusion is that since we can hardly have a science of bodies, it is not to be thought that we could have one of spirits: ". . . that there are degrees of spiritual beings between us and the great God, who is there that, by his own search and ability, can come to know? Much less have we distinct ideas of their different natures, conditions, states, powers, and several constitutions wherein they agree or differ from one another and from us. And, therefore in what concerns their different species and properties we are in absolute ignorance." [14] This ignorance did not prevent Locke, however, from repeatedly referring to angels, to "cherubims and seraphims, and infinite sorts of spirits above us," or from an angelological conjecture on "how far short" men come of "the endowments and perfections" of such beings (IV, iii, 333). "We have some reason," he says, ". . . to imagine that spirits can assume to themselves bodies of different bulk, figure, and conformation of parts. . . ." Perhaps, then, "they can so frame and shape to themselves organs of sensation and perception as to suit them to the circumstances of the object they would consider," that is, to give them at need the powers of the microscope, the telescope, or what you will. This "fancy" is, Locke admits, a wild one; obviously he offers it only illustratively. And yet, he finishes: "The supposition, at least, that angels do sometimes assume bodies, need not startle us; since some of the most ancient and most learned fathers of the church seemed to believe that they had bodies . . ." (II, xxiii, 301-302).

The evident fact about Locke, Hobbes, Selden, and the rest, is that they allowed a difference in kind between what they would admit of the remote and authoritative events narrated in the Bible and what they inclined to accept as fact in their everyday world. They recorded a corresponding difference between that part of their official thought which represented their obeisance to the Bible and to ancient authority in general and that which represented their genuine, living interest. Less successfully than Sir Thomas Browne, the "great amphibium," they existed, each of them, in two separate intellectual realms; of one realm angels were necessarily a part; in the other they were at best an embarrassment.

The century's plainest example of a philosopher and scientist embarrassed by his inclination to angels is Robert Boyle. He could feel a simultaneous strong allegiance to the old view and to the new, for he was capable in the new science and yet too genuinely pious simply to ignore the Bible's testimony. Nor was he willing to do as "some divines" claimed Selden did, and give "not his own sentiment" out. Doggedly Boyle tried to give both science and angelology their due. Some men, he says, prefer that he should never write but as a "naturalist," since they themselves esteem "nothing but the laws and phenomena of nature worthy of a philosophical pen: as if because rational spirits are invisible and immaterial beings, all disquisitions about them must be airy and uncertain speculations, and like their objects, devoid of solidity and usefulness." Then he tries to parallel angelology to the respected science of astronomy; other things than "are ground upon mechanical or chemical notices or experiments" deserve attention, as, for instance, the stars, the study of which is costly and to no practical purpose, yet much honored. We should, therefore, "not undervalue the studies of those men, that aspire to the knowledge of incorporeal and rational beings, which are incomparably more noble than all the stars. . . ." Since he has friends who joy in such studies and who press him to pursue them, he will now attempt to gratify them as he has previously presented his other friends with reports of physical experiments.[15]

Boyle did not, of course, by any means balance his scientific writings with his theological, much less with his angelological; but he did compose several thousand words on angels in two or three works. They are mostly given to a sober collection of angelic attributes out of Scripture, prefaced usually by various disclaimers and reservations about angelology and buttressed by the ancient arguments to show that angels do exist. He questions, though, whether philosophy can positively prove their existence and notes the tremendous difficulties of studying them.[16] Scholastics and metaphysicians have written as though they understood all, but their ideas are really quite dim; in spite of their talk, such things as how spirits assume bodies or declare their thought are incomprehensible.[17] But, he goes on, Scripture delivers these things; though we cannot grasp them they are so. Such writers as Paracelsus on sylphs and gnomes are extravagant and we may pass them over; but we cannot pass it over when the Bible names the classes of angels.[18] If we knew the incorporeal world as well as we know the corporeal, we would be certain to see its creatures immeasurably more noble than any of earth. The government of demons, which God achieves, must be incredibly difficult because of the necessary agility, variety, and malice of these beings; the government of them redounds the more, therefore, to God's glory. Probably angels inhabit the other worlds, which advanced thinkers say must exist, for God would not have left these globes destitute of intelligent beings.[19] We cannot know surely whether angels are properly free of matter or have bodily vehicles, and they appear to us seldom. But we are not to suppose them inconsiderable in the universe, for the Bible testifies that they are a vast host. Since they are beings superior even to the rational human soul, the science of them is far nobler than any study of the action and reaction of material masses can possibly be.[20]

Boyle has risen here to a fervor for spirits almost equal to Glanville's in the *Sadducismus*. But in correspondence with Glanville on that work he is uneasy and warns against ill-attested tales.[21] Elsewhere he says that "Naturalists" admit the probative force of apparitions if they could be believed in, but devote themselves only solicitously to show them false, "as I fear most of them are." [22] To the translator of *The Divell of Mascon* he wrote: "I must freely confesse to you that the powerfull inclination which my course of life and studies, hath given me to diffidence and backwardness of assent, and the many fictions and superstitions, which (as farre as I have hitherto observed) are wont to blemish the relation where spirits and witches are concerned, would make me very backward to contribute anything to your publishing or any man's believing a story less strange than this. . . ." [23] But he did contribute and presumably he did believe. He made a deliberate effort to bring into unity his understanding of the world from the Bible and his understanding of it from his own observations and tests.

Not many of the men who found themselves in Boyle's difficulties about angels took such pains as he over the question, but many of them did make seemly acknowledgment of angels, at the same time that they ignored them practically. It was such formal acknowledgment, perhaps, that led the aging John Dryden, canvassing in 1693 the chances for an English epic more successful than Milton's, to find a favorable circumstance in the fact that the Christian doctrine of angels offered a "machinery" not only elegant but "almost universally received by Christians" as true.[24] Or perhaps this is merely Dryden's own formal acknowledgment and was already as vitiated as the "machinery" he sponsored.

III

The pious friends who pressed Robert Boyle to write of spirits may very likely have been his correspondents John Worthington, Master of Jesus College, Cambridge, Samuel Hartlib, that inde-

fatigable catalyzer among men of intellect, and Boyle's brilliant
fellow member of the Royal Society, John Beal, who once expressed the hope that through Boyle's efforts they might "shortly
complete humane sciences." [25] These men were not religious con-
servatives, nor yet "enthusiasts"; they earnestly wanted "a stay for
the light of reason and experience," as Beal put it, and accepted a
promise of such "stay" in the new science. But they saw a soberly
grounded angelology as a reasonable part of that promise, not as
a contradiction of it. They were, moreover, like Boyle, impelled
by the Bible. Joseph Mede, the admired Cambridge tutor of
Milton's time whose works Worthington edited with praise for
their "pious prudence," gives their view: "It is hard to keep a
mean . . . in the Doctrine and Speculation of Angels, whereunto
men were heretofore so much addicted, as they pursued it not only
to vain and ungrounded Theories, but even to Idolatry and Superstition. . . . But we, who . . . have justly rejected . . . these
vain and ungrounded curiosities, are fallen into the other extreme, having buried the Doctrine of Angels in silence, making
little or no enquiry at all, what God in his Word hath revealed
concerning them . . . wherein are so many passages having reference to them, and therefore questionless something revealed
concerning them." [26]

Nothing in this moderate opinion seemed hostile to science. The
apostle of science, Francis Bacon, to whom Beal conceived himself
intellectually allied, had acknowledged that study of "the nature
of angels and spirits is . . . an appendix of theology, both divine
and natural." [27] The great Polish educator, John Amos Comenius,
whom Hartlib had sponsored in England, had written extensively
of angels in a book whose preface was full of praise for Bacon's
principles.[28] To the modern eye, of course, Bacon seems merely
promoting angelology with theology out of the circle of man's
attention, and Comenius on angels seems to commit every idola-
trous offense of the intellect that Bacon had pointed to. But
Beal — who is on record as far preferring Bacon's writings to those
of such an active seeker after angels as Sir Kenelm Digby, whose
subtleties he thought excessive[29]— doubtless overlooked both the
hostility of Bacon's principles to the study of spirits and the Ba-
conian faults of Comenius' reasoning. He and Worthington and
Hartlib commit the same faults themselves when they talk of angels, though Worthington particularly speaks often with deliberate
rational restraint and Beal noted of Joseph Glanville with a superior twinkle that he was a sound man if properly reined in.[30]

In 1661 in a letter to Worthington, Hartlib enclosed an account of "an angelic vision" to a Frieslander who for forty years had prayed to be informed by angels of the fate of certain heretical lands, and who now on the strength of his vision prophesied confidently that God was going to visit those lands with "famine, pestilence, and sword, if they repented not." Could this prophecy, which if sound would be a weapon in the hands of the faithful, be trusted? Beal, "no despiser of the angelicall visits of this last age," thought that it might be, provided the Frieslander was known in his own community as having always "abhorr'd the vanity of lying." Beal is "confident that God will not send a person, infamous among good men for falsehood, on his embassy." He reminds Hartlib, though, that another prophet, one whom Comenius had sponsored, had turned out to be an "exstatick" and so most embarrassingly unreliable. This raised the question: even if the man is honest, he may be deluded, his vision the deceitful work of an evil angel; how, then, shall it be tested? Hartlib favors a test suggested by Otto Faber, a "Helmontian physician" visiting in England: discover whether the angel appeared bearded or not. According to Jean Bapiste Van Helmont no good angel wore a beard. With this opinion Beal agrees: "For long-bearded good angels, or lady angels of true light, they do indeed cross all the old Records of Antiquity, whether Gentile or Jewish." [31]

Upon all this Worthington turns a most judicious eye. The realisation of the prophecy, he says, will be the best corroboration of it, and prophets of the recent past have had poor luck. He will not ascribe deceit to the old Frieslander, but many have erred through melancholy. As for the beard test, he has looked up Van Helmont's opinion and found the reason he gave for it "very much enfeebled, and out of order." Adam, argued Van Helmont, was the first ravisher of virginity and so "had a mark set upon him, viz. a beard, that he might be like to that salacious creature the goat"; no good angel, then, would assume this mark in apparition any more than he would assume Cain's mark of murderer. To Worthington the reasoning is thin. However praiseworthy Van Helmont's "chymical operations" may be, he frowns, this turn of his into inference upon Genesis is odd and extravagant. Van Helmont is dictating "magisterially," which Worthington thinks "a thing very unpleasing to the ingenuous and free pursuers of rational knowledge." Genesis gives us no reason to suppose that Adam was beardless and much reason to think that he visited his wife with the entire approval of God. "As for Van Helmont's inference, (that therefore no good angel ever appeared barbatus) I do as little believe it, as that the good angels are like little plump-cheek'd boys, as the painter makes them."

Though Worthington thus sharply rejects Van Helmont and his beard test, he does not at all reject angelology, but on the contrary practises it then by earnestly retailing two stories — neither of which would stand a moment's examination — of supposed apparitions of angels both good and bearded. He ends by citing not very appropriately the great angelological authority of his time and circle: "You may see what Dr. More suggests in his 3rd book against Atheism, ch. 14, That angels have no settled form, but what they please to give themselves upon occasion." [32]

More himself resembled Boyle and Worthington in that he was, or supposed himself to be, only a hesitant believer in contemporary spirit phenomena; what he published on them he selected with thought and caution as things that a man of responsibility could soberly put his name to. At a report from Beal that he had seen angels around his bed, More wonders smiling what defect in Beal could make him credulous enough to "conceit that no less than 24 grave long-bearded harping Elders should from some part of the inward World rest around the bedside of so young a stripling to give him a fitt of musick in a morning." More analyzed stories of apparitions with the same scientific scepticism that led him to question *a priori* Cardan's fantastic testimony that the Bird of Paradise had no feet. We have, too, a record of his physically tracing at least one seemingly supernatural voice to a natural cause.[33]

But when More had restrained himself thus far, he felt that he had satisfied all the reasonable requirements of what Worthington had called "the free pursuers of rational knowledge"; More did not, like Spinoza, reject testimony to apparition simply because fraud or error was possible. In the preface of his *Antidote against Atheism* More says that in selecting stories of apparition for the book he has been so "cautious and circumspect" that he uses no narration doubtful either from "the avarice of the *priest* or the credulity and fancifulness of the *Melancholist*. . . ." [34] In Book III he gives the "touchstone" for historic miracles: "if what is recorded was avouched by persons who had *no end* or *interest* in avouching such things . . . if there were many Eye-witnesses of the same Matter . . . and if these things which are so strange and miraculous leave any sensible *effect* behind them." He will not himself, he says, "acknowledge that all those stories are *false* that want these conditions," but for any person to reject such as do meet them is mere sullenness (III, i, 88). More never himself testifies to having personally beheld an apparition, but he could believe wholly and immediately from the testimony of others. He might have answered with John Wesley when asked whether he had ever seen a ghost: "No, nor did I ever see a murder." Unlike Boyle, More was able to bridge for himself the gap between what he acknowledged from ancient authority and what seemed probable in the "clear light" of his newly scientific world.

More was perfectly conscious of the gap, however, and of the difficulty that it made for the faith of many men of learning. What he set out to do, then, in his angelology — which was but an adjunct to his arguments for the immortality of the soul and the existence of God — was to bring the angel-world into focus as an everyday fact, not merely as a formal faith or a metaphysical theory or a literary fancy. Some men say they cannot conceive how invisible beings can exist around us and that what is told of such beings comes of our self-fright and morbid imagination and appetite for marvels. Very well; More will show that on the contrary the conception we have of spirits may be clear and reasonable, their connections with us most natural, and the evidence of them among us incontestable.

In his theories of spirits More was as independent as a man so well read in earlier speculation and in the Bible could be. He accepts the Bible wholly, of course, though sometimes with his own special interpretation, but in his philosophizing he often puts it aside deliberately in order to face sceptics on their own ground. He explicitly repudiates much angelology, which he feels to be only an embarrassment to his cause, particularly that of the Scholastics. To desert their opinions, he says, is of great importance "when something more rational and more safe and useful offers itself unto us." [35]

More's "more rational and more safe and useful" theory stood upon a maximum use of the new science. We must "bid adieu to Metaphor" in the inquiry about spirits, he tells Richard Baxter.[36] In his *Immortality of the Soul* he uses some diagrams of physical phenomena whose occurrence he tries to trace to spiritual causes; for instance, he draws a muscle and its activating nerve to show how the soul moves both (II, v, 165-166). Often in his arguments about spirits he relies on the findings or theories of scientists. Thus he uses Harvey's recent study of generation to show that women might have children by devils. Devils are without seed, he admits; however, even in human beings "the Seed of the Male gives neither Matter nor Form to the *Foetus* itself; but like the Flint and Steel only sets the Tinder on fire, as Dr. Harvey expresses it"; and are not devils quite capable, witches testify, of giving women extreme pleasure, which will "loosen the body into a transmission of such principles and particles as will prove in their conflux in the wombe vital and prolifical?" [37]

This up-to-dateness in More seems today merely grotesque; but in the 1650's it might have looked very much like an angelology progressing with its times.

More had great respect, of course, not only for contemporary authority but for many of the ancients. Particularly, he says, he had in his pneumatology "a zeal for the credit of the Platonists, whose imaginative presages I have often observed to hold a faithful compliance with the severest reason." [38] With some "Platonists" of his own time, however, who did not cut their "presages" to the pattern of "severest reason" More and his friends had very little sympathy, as Worthington's impatience with Van Helmont indicates. Such men as Robert Fludd, Thomas Vaughan, Robert Turner, John Heydon, and their great continental predecessors Paracelsus and Cornelius Agrippa, More condemned as "chymists and theosophists," together with several other sorts of men "more palpably mad." He objected particularly to their allowing their thoughts to be "carryed much to Astrology . . . a fanciful study built upon very sleight grounds. . . ." He scorns Paracelsus' pneumatology, largely because of its link with the stars. "That the *Gnomi, Nymphae, Lemures,* and *Penates,* Spirits endowed with understanding as much or more than men, are yet wholly mortal . . ." because they "were the conception and births of the imaginative power of the influence of the Starres upon matter prepared by them. . . ." are "rampant and delirious Fancies. . . ." [39]

To us Paracelsus' fancies seem hardly more delirious perhaps, than many of More's own, and at least some writers of the seventeenth century, too, seem to feel that More went too far in them. Samuel Parker, for instance, in his general attack on Platonists hits not only "our late English *Rosi-Crusians*" but unmistakably More himself (though not by name) as one of those who with "unpardonable Luxury and Wantonness . . . spend their time and study to disclose distant and inscrutable Mysteries and frontlessly to dictate to the world in such Theories as are infinitely remote from Humane knowledge and discovery. . . . As when they confidently take upon them to give the world exact and minute descriptions of Incorporeal Beings. . . . When they define whether the *Apostate Genii* be purely immaterial; and whether they be vitally united with matter; and whether they were made peccable only by union with their Vehicles. . . ." [40]

Between such Platonists and the Rosicrucians, however, Parker puts the big difference that whereas the latter are victims of out and out "Enthusiasme," the former are, after all, "Wise and considering Philosophers" who have merely misused some of their time. In spite of the utmost extremes of his angelology, More undoubtedly had a far sturdier reputation even with those who disliked his pneumatological theorizing than did Robert Fludd, the chief of English Theosophists, whom More himself refers to condescendingly as among "the more discreetly fantastical." [41] So far as angelology was concerned, Fludd was trying, like More — and like Aquinas, for that matter — to make it integral with a larger body of thought. But More, for all his elaborateness, is essentially a simplifier; his elaborations come from his insistence on answering every question thoroughly. He rationalizes, he prunes what leads away from Scripture, or else tucks up stray tags of legend and old wives' tales with Scripture into one neat bundle of ready reference that takes the mystery out of angels. Fludd, on the contrary, spreads mystery like a fog over the whole subject, lights it murkily with esoteric terms and thickens it with a multiplication of concepts. Whereas More is willing to free himself of whatever hampers his sober, limited purpose, of establishing the existence of angels as the parallel that buttresses the similar existence of the thinking, perceiving, eternally responsible soul of man, Fludd never even raises the question of existence but pours out a stream of notions, many of them radical and others obsolete, on the nature and functions of the angels. With Fludd, angelology is not a theological science; it is a developed intuition using scraps of theology. To the question of whether Fludd "believed" in angels he gives no rational response.

Fludd himself no doubt considered his unorthodox opinions on the cosmos to be in the very van of human thought, and he did show some of the signs of his progressive times. He introduced the sympathetic cure into England, for instance, which the enlightened Francis Osborn seemed to think an enlightened act, though he deprecated Fludd's largely angelological defense of it.[42] Like More, Fludd expressly asserted his independence of medieval ways of thought and backed his text with charts and drawings of physical demonstrations he had concocted to verify items of his cosmology. At least one admirer, John Webster — who, like Osborn, has himself been praised for his modernness about witchcraft — links Fludd not only with Paracelsus and Agrippa as a forward-looking thinker but with Galileo, Harvey, and Descartes.[43] We can see now, of course, that Fludd was forward-looking only in the anomalous sense in which the Rosicrucians, whom he defended, were so. They were scholars who had freed themselves of some old bonds; this much they shared with Galileo, Harvey, and Descartes. But their further progress turns out in the light of history to have been simply eccentricity. And so with Fludd's advanced thought. Such eccentricity does not count against his angelology now, of course, when all angelology seems eccentric, but in the 1670's when readers still might discriminate among angelologists, John Webster could gain little with the judicious against More and Glanville by quoting Fludd as his authority on angels.

In his confusion and obscurity and passionate conviction of invisible forces, Fludd is one with the authors of the spate of occult works put into English in the 1650's. Trithemius, Agrippa, Paracelsus, and John Dee were enlightened men of a less disciplined century than the seventeenth, and in angelology they made disorder much of Fludd's sort. Harvey, Hobbes, and Selden must have found their words on angels nonsense, and More and Worthington were hardly more sympathetic. Yet the fact that more translations of them appeared in England during the dawn of science and the rule of Puritanism than at any other time in history is itself some evidence that a good many literate people in Milton's England believed in angels with as whole a conviction as it is possible to conceive, a conviction that swallows difficulties at a gulp because it grants eagerly every requisite assumption.

IV

Although these believing books appeared during the Puritan rule, the angelologists most characteristic of Puritanism were very little in sympathy with them or with any free-reined speculation on angels. Like Joseph Mede they detested excesses in angelology, though like him too, they felt that an understanding of the Bible required some attention to angels. Richard Baxter, the one of them who most delighted in angelology, restrained himself manfully and complained repeatedly of those who, he thought, did not restrain themselves. He cannot understand, he says, how More and Glanville can go to the extremes they do. "I am accused of overdoing of curiosity myself; But I endeavor to confine my enquiries to things revealed." [44] As for the Paracelsans and Boehmenists and others who profess "visible converse with angels" as "you may see in Dr. Pordage and Mr. Fowler of him," he considers their rise part of a Jesuit plot to divide Protestantism.[45] Theirs are "the philosophical whimsies of an over-stretch'd imagination." [46] Nevertheless, angels are not to be left unstudied. For the "true and spiritual use of this doctrine" of angels Baxter refers godly inquirers to "Master Lawrences book (Member of the House of Commons) called Our Communion and War with Angels." [47] This work, its author says, avoids excesses, for it is "bottom'd" upon Scripture; it does all that is lawful to "gratifie and serve the good Angels, who . . . have been too little considered . . ." but nothing to serve idle curiosity.[48] Isaac Ambrose, who makes a third with Lawrence and Baxter, states roundly in his Prolegomena the solid Puritan attitude; he grants "that such as have lately discust of Angels have met with the censure of more curious conjecture, than of evidence in their discourse, reason not reaching to the Subject, and Scripture not speaking distinctly of it." Yet in some things, at least, he believes that "they have brought truth a-bed" so that the effort was worthwhile.[49]

As angelologists Puritan divines felt always a pinch between, on the one hand, their stern intention not to ascribe more things to angels than comported with man's knowledge and God's dignity, and, on the other, the obvious necessity to interpret what was told of angels in the Bible and to find them some secure place in the attention of the contemporary world. They did not want to advertise the angels' ordinary control of disease and weather and other daily events, for to do so was to encourage direct application to them and perhaps to deprive God.[50] On the other hand neither did they want to show angels so remote and inactive that they would fade from the consciousness of the faithful. Consequently Baxter, Lawrence, Ambrose, John Gaule, Sir Henry Vane, and other Puritans asknowledge the general overseeing activities of angels but seem reluctant to be explicit about what they do. They are rulers and governors of the world, says Vane, and Baxter for his part believes that "God's Works in the World are usually by Instrument, and not immediate." [51] Ambrose quotes and apparently endorses this view (pp. 511, 518), and Gaule seems to think that angels are at least more active as God's instruments than the stars can be.[52] Lawrence cautions that "it is an easy and vulgar step from the last effect to the highest cause," so that we tend to look "presently and immediately upon God" as the cause of things,

passing over the angels because their activities are "unseene and
undiscerned" (Epistle). Again he says: "God indeed doth all
things, yet he speakes by men . . . & there is a forme above men,
Angells, which hee useth also . . ." (p. 24). Neither Lawrence nor
the others, however, name any specific use God makes of angels
but that they have "immediately managed" the war for our souls.
It was this activity entirely that interested the Puritans, and in
emphasizing it they tended by implication almost to deny the rest.
They acknowledged that in the prosecution of moral warfare
angels have certain powers over the elements and over the humors
of men's bodies, but never said whether they used these powers
also to manage the routine of nature.

Even the doctrine of angelic ministration to souls had its dangers in Puritan eyes. As the ancient idea of the celestial hierarchy
shedding down God's power was suspect among them because it
might open doors to magic by the ready parallel between the
orders and the celestial spheres and to priestcraft by its traditional
parallel to the ecclesiastical hierarchy, so the whole idea of the
angel ministering to souls seemed dangerous, as setting up a source
of heavenly succor distinct from God. Yet the Puritans wanted to
retain the opposition of the evil angels, who assaulted the soul,
and the good, who assisted it.

Determined, then, to allow the reality of some angelic operation
in the world the Puritans had, nevertheless, to be most circumspect in accounting for it. Lawrence must insist, for instance, that
God always have the credit for what angels may achieve in the way
of conversions, since angels would not be worshipped (p. 41); yet
he must insist, too, that angels are active in the work. Some reader
will ask, he says, "what do we leave now to Christ and the spirit,
if you give to the Angells the worke of teaching and hinting
spiritually things?" Lawrence answers: "What will you leave to
the Angells, if you take this imployment from them . . . ?" Bodily
ministrations? But does not Christ's care reach the body also? No
"division of work" is needed; angels are but ministers; Christ and
the Spirit employ them not for need of them "but because these
are God's ways of administration, his ordinances of which we can
give no account, hee useth this chaine, and subordination of which
one linke toucheth another . . . of which the Angells are a great
part. . . ." If one wants to know in detail, however, what God does
in us and what the angels do, that "were a search more nice than
safe" (pp. 48-49). In all this Lawrence is one with Ambrose, who
notes that we do not deprive the Holy Ghost when we say that

angels "inspire us to good by infusing pious thoughts and impulses . . . for it is the will of the Holy Ghost to . . . communicate himself to us by the ministry of angels, and therefore the Holy Ghost and angels need not clash." The "Spirit of Christ," of course, is always the real origin of holy impulses; but recall Baxter's opinion, Ambrose reminds us, that God's works are ordinarily by instruments (p. 518).

The Puritans usually made no pretense of being "free pursuers of rational knowledge" in the sense that appealed to Worthington, Beal, and More. Baxter did indeed read Gassendi to refute him, but it was in much the same spirit that he would have read Julian the Apostate. Once, too, Baxter looked at the moon "through a tube," and he read Galileo on other worlds [53] with tolerance; but such things seem to have had no prominence on his intellectual horizon, certainly no weight in his conception of spirits. The only use of science that Ambrose shows is in such medieval bits as his analogy that just "As rest is the end of all motion, so the perfection of blessedness consists in rest." After Judgment Day, therefore, "the Angels, being discharged of that charge which they took at the beginning, they have no more to do, but in one choir to join with the saints, and everlastingly to sing hallelujah . . ." (p. 577). If anyone had told Ambrose that rest is not the end of motion, it would certainly have made no change in his angelology, even if he had accepted the new physics. Lawrence, for his part, had no idea of, for instance, the distinction being made in his time between primary and secondary qualities. He uses man's conviction of color to found the authority of sensory knowledge in the physical world; if the senses were ordinarily deceivable, he says, we could know nothing, even that snow was white or grass green (p. 16). Galileo or Descartes would have answered him very shortly that those qualities were as little in the object as the most doubtful show of deceitful apparitions.

The impression Ambrose and Lawrence give in general is that they have certainly little of the mystical yearning of the occultist toward created forms above them nor any of the keen interest in physical and metaphysical understanding and demonstration that moved Beal and More. They had a most determined belief in angels held in a way that was sure to stifle all moving faith in any supernatural; they wanted at once fervor and a rigid control of fervor, an intimate acquaintance and a cool abstention from detailed inquiry. Their belief was one that had a very narrow area of either rational or emotional conviction and was sure not to survive in any real force beyond the imbalanced state of religion that created it.

As a widespread formal acknowledgment, however, their kind of belief in angels outlasted that of either Fludd or More by far. Most of us depend today upon the echoes of it when we read *Paradise Lost*.

Chapter III

Scholasticism and the Puritan Reserve

Near the middle of the reign of King James I an Englishman named John Salkeld came home from Spain and Portugal, where, apparently, he had been trained as a Jesuit, and throwing off the Roman religion yet made use of his training to ingratiate himself with the King by publishing in 1613 a very solid *Treatise* on what is reputed to have been one of James's major interests: the nature and operations of spirits. Salkeld called his book *A Treatise of Angels,* and he covers, according to the title page, the "Nature, essence, place, power, science, will, apparitions, grace, sinne, and all other proprieties of Angels." The title page also asserts unabashed Salkeld's Romanist qualifications for treating his subject: he is "lately Fellow of the Iesuites Colleges in the Universities of Conimbre, Corduba, and Complutum. Assistant in studies to the famous Iesuites Francis Suarius, and Michael Vasquez."

That Salkeld could confidently offer such credentials to his very Protestant majesty and to the Protestant public of England is some evidence of how largely in his subject particularly, Protestant thought still rested on the great scholastic rationalization. Calvin and Zanchy and their like might sneer at its elaborateness and put forward their exceptions to its doctrines, but it was an indispensable foundation to them, nevertheless, and probably a majority of educated Englishmen thought of angels largely in its terms. Most of their incidental allusions to angels, at any rate, seem to suit scholastic ideas, and many English writers explicitly though casually record their axiomatic acceptance of such ideas. Thus George Hakewill expresses in passing his astonishment that no less than twenty-two Fathers contended, as "Mr. Salkeld . . . hath observed," for such an absurd notion as the *"Corporeitie of Angels."* [1] If Hakewill was aware of the approval many Calvinists and Platonists of his own day gave this anti-scholastic thesis, he shows no sign; he assumes non-corporeity as standard and undisputed.

Even Protestants who wrote extensively on angels with a deliberate anti-scholastic bias were likely to use many scholastic articles
and now and then to refer cordially to Catholic authorities. Thus
the Puritan ministers Gumbledon and Ainsworth cite Aquinas
favorably more than once. Henry More, though he rarely speaks
well of medieval scholastics, does countenance such sixteenth-
century advocates of Aquinas' angelology as Jean Bodin and Nicholas Remy. In their "shorter systems" of divinity Protestant
theologians are often so sketchy on the subject of angels that they
may easily be taken in a Thomistic sense. Thus Alexander Ross
reads what John Wolleb has to say of angels' substances in the
famous *Abridgment* as suiting the Thomistic scheme, though the
probability is that Wolleb meant something a little different from
Aquinas' meaning.[2]

The outstanding fact about Catholic angelologists of the sixteenth and seventeenth centuries is their unanimity. To meet the
chaotic surge of Platonizing and Reforming doctrines they closed
ranks almost solidly behind Aquinas. All the Catholic witchmongers — Binsfield, DeLancre, Bodin, Remy, Boguet, Delrio, and a
dozen others — and all the more general writers such as Cicogna,
Casman, Anania, Le Loyer, Maldonat, Michaelis, and Valderama
are single in their attachment to Aquinas on virtually every doctrine that the insurgents challenged and on most others.[3]

In seventeenth-century England Salkeld is the best representa-
tive of their solidarity. Among the authors he relies on are almost
no Protestants except Calvin and Zanchy and only a very few
pagan philosophers. His chapter headings go through the usual
list of scholastic Questions: are angels corruptible? are they compound of matter and form? how are they in place? how do they
move? how do they understand themselves and God and nature?
how do they communicate? what order exists among them? can
the good sin? To nearly all of these questions Salkeld recites the
orthodox Romanist answers, favoring Aquinas and Augustine
chiefly, and, except on the question of the Dionysian orders,
taking almost no notice of Protestant views. He takes little notice,
either, of the Protestant partiality for spareness in angelology, but
after the scholastic fashion goes most into detail in just those questions that Protestant theologians preferred to dismiss as both
irrelevant to salvation and beyond man's comprehension. Salkeld
has five chapters, for instance, on how angels are in place, and
eleven on how they know. He has five long chapters on angelic
substance and apparition.

First, he inquires whether the substance of angels is corruptible and notes that some authorities such as Casman argue that it must be, since only God is absolutely immortal. If, they hold, angels are incorruptible it must be by God's "extrinsecal will," not by the nature of their substance. Salkeld names Cardan, Plutarch, and Hesiod as assenting to this scholastical reasoning. But true divinity, he goes on, teaches that no spirits are subject to natural corruption. Though by God's power they may be annihilated, yet that they should be is "contrary to what their nature doth require, as also to that which euer is to happen." [4]

The second question on substance is whether angels "be compounded of matter and form or be rather pure spirits without any matter" or body. "Bonaventure . . . and Aureolus were of opinion that the angels were made of a most pure fine materiall substance, farre exceeding the matter of all inferiour subiects: and that to this they had united a most perfect form farre also exceeding the forme or soule of man or any other creature. The reason which the Doctors give, is for that seeing the Angels be subiect to change and mutation, as necessarily must be the nature of a creature, they must of necessitie haue some matter, which onely is subiect and cause of all mutation" (p. 30). Of the same opinion, he thinks, are the "Platonicks" and some "Moderne," naming Zanchius. Many of the Fathers also held for some body of air or subtile spirits, though not of flesh, and Psellus agreed (p. 31). These authorities, he goes on, based their belief first on the passage in Genesis about the Sons of God begetting giants on the daughters of men, and second on the fact that devils are punishable by fire, which they could not be had they not body (pp. 30-32).

But, says Salkeld, by Sons of God Genesis means progeny of Seth, and even if we suppose hellfire corporeal, yet by God's will it may burn spirits, else it could not burn damned souls — unless someone claims that they too are material (p. 34). The truth is that angels are "altogether immaterial, pure spirits, without concretion of matter or bodies," for lacking such creatures the world "were not complete and perfect." Dionysius calls them *materia liberos et incorporales,* and Basil, Nazianzen, Chrysostom, and others demonstrate immateriality out of places in the Bible "where the Angels be absolutely called spirits," as in Psalm 104 (p. 33).

How, then, do these supra-sensible beings appear to men? Some say by uniting to matter as our souls do to our bodies (p. 37). But the angel is a substance complete in itself and cannot become more. Tertullian seems to think that the union is hypostatic in the same manner that Christ assumed human nature, with the difference that since angels come not to die they are, therefore, not born. But Christ, says Salkeld, is infinite, and his union is unique (p. 38). The common opinion, then, is Lombard's that the union of the angel with the body by which it appears is that of a mover with the moved. The angel makes this conjunction immediately by his own ordinary power, though perhaps at God's order, out of air so condensed and tempered that it takes all colors and forms as do clouds (pp. 39, 40). This is the opinion of Aquinas and by it he explains most of the marvels that the devil does for witches (p. 51), although noting that spirits may also show things to men by controlling the humors and internal senses (p. 53). But however solid an assumed body may appear, no angel can by it eat, see, smell, speak, taste, engender, or perform any other vital act except in show, for he is not united to this body (p. 55). As for angels' eating, some authorities point to Raphael, who seemed to eat with Tobias, and others cite Augustine, who said that angels have eaten, though not converting the food to their own substance (p. 56); thus Duns Scotus affirms the "true vital eating of angels" (p. 57). But to say so in his sense is a mere "manner of speaking," for if angels cannot convert the meat to their substance, then no matter how they break and consume it in show they cannot be said truly to eat, and so Raphael disclosed to Tobias only that he seemed to eat (p. 58).

If angels move bodies to men's eyes, are they then locally present where those bodies appear? Evidently angels are subject to place in a sense, for Satan fell from heaven (p. 60), and only God can be everywhere at once. "Durand (otherwise a learned schoolman) was of opinion that the Angelicall substance . . . was in every place after the manner that it was in place . . . *and that it was no more in one place than in another*" (p. 65), and Duns Scotus held that an angel is in place by his substance immediately. But Aquinas says that an angel can have place only by "the operation or contact of his vertue, by which he produceth some motion, light, or other effect." Cajetan adds that an angel may be in a place virtually even though he does not operate (p. 70). At any rate, many angels can occupy the same place at the same time (p. 72). But they cannot move from one place to another without passing through "interjacent" space and taking at least a second of time to do it, for if they could they would be able to work, like God, everywhere at once (pp. 75-77).

Many deny that angels move the spheres, and it is not in Scripture. But the Platonists and Peripatetics think they do, and Aquinas and Bonaventure, also, and indeed it seems a prefixed order of God that, as St. Augustine puts it, inferior bodies are governed by superior ones and "the superiour by the spirit of life, that is by some Angell" (pp. 81, 82). Some have protested that as all angels are ministers to the heirs of salvation, none can be deputed to the heavens, but Aquinas explains that we may consider angels either in regard of their "internal mission," which is the illumination of inferiors, by which all angels of all grades are involved in passing the light down to us, or in regard to the "external mission," in which only the lower orders are actually sent, and are hence called *Angels,* that is, *Messengers,* or *Archangels,* that is, *Chief Messengers* (pp. 84-85).

How do angels know themselves and their tasks? Some writers hold with Aristotle that the separated intellect knows itself simply by its own substance, in which exists no passive power: angels are forms and "admit no passion or reception of accidents inherent in their substance" (p. 113). But Augustine, Dionysius, and Aquinas say that only in God are understanding and the act of understanding one thing. In intellectual creatures these writers distinguish *essence, virtue,* and *operation,* of which three *essence* is the radical cause of the other two, and *virtue* the immediate cause of *operation* (p. 115). Angels know themselves, then, by an act that rises from a power of which their essence is a condition. They know other creatures by intellectual forms or species (p. 117), of which the general ones are infused by God, says Duns, but the particular ones received from the things themselves, for the latter are so many that if God had infused them all into each angel, each would know all objects, present and future, contingent and necessary (pp. 119-120). But Aquinas and others contend that all these species are infused at the beginning of the world as perfect forms to be actuated at need by the angel's perfect understanding. As for the future, it is dark to the angel unless God discovers it to him, except, of course that he has great natural understanding of consequences in nature, such as the action of medicine (pp. 121-124). The angel knows himself immediately without species or "any other intellectual similitude," Aquinas holds (p. 127 ff.), and he knows God the same way (p. 132). For natural knowledge, at least, the angel does not require discourse; he knows perfectly what is in the sphere of his understanding, without composition or division of things or inferring one of another (p. 156 ff.).

Does the good angels' knowledge of God compel them to love

him? No, says Duns, for they love God by a supernatural charity infused into them, which if it necessitated love in heaven would also do the same here in us. They may, therefore, at pleasure cease to love God (p. 210 ff.). But Aquinas thinks, says Salkeld, that they are drawn into loving by a sweet kind of necessity when they behold the vision of the Divine Essence (p. 213). The common opinion is, therefore, that though by nature the elect angels can sin, yet by the grace in which they are confirmed they cannot (p. 217 ff.). Still, Duns holds, an angel is not "intrinsecally impeccable" but only so by the "extrinsecall" protection of God, so that "if a man or Angel in Heauen were left to his own will, no doubt . . . but that they might transgresse" (pp. 220-221).

The evil angels, despite Origen's opinion, are confirmed in sin as the good are in grace (p. 349). Unlike the will of a living man, the will of an angel cannot reverse itself (p. 199; p. 222). Some Fathers hold, out of Genesis 6, that the fall of angels resulted from the Sons of God lusting after the daughters of men. But the angels, who have seen the face of God, could not be seduced by the beauty of women. Plainly the Sons of God of Genesis 6 are not angels but the descendants of Seth (p. 324). After the fall the devil kept his natural powers, the "proprietie of his Angelicall nature," as to substance, though darkened by sin. He lost the knowledge necessary to salvation, which is given by grace, but not his knowledge of nature or his power in it (p. 350 ff.). Saved souls will more than fill up the room in heaven of the fallen angels (p. 209).

In addition to his intricacies on angels' nature, Salkeld has some briefer chapters on their history. Particularly he treats the story of the creation and rebellion. Some Fathers held that the creation of angels was long before the world's, though a few think after the world's, since God says to Job, "Behold Behemoth [Satan, in Salkeld's opinion] whom I made with thee" (p. 11). But the "most undoubted" conclusion is that Genesis 1.1 means the angels when it speaks of God's creation of light. So Aquinas and most others (p. 12 ff.). Where were angels made? In the highest heavens (p. 15) — and, says Aquinas, more of them exist than of anything else, since the perfect must exceed the imperfect (p. 23). (But this is not quite a sound reason, Salkeld notes from Durandus, for if it were we would have many Gods and more precious stones than common ones.) How many fell? Fewer than remained, but we cannot, like Aquinas, depend on the Apocalypse, which speaks of one third of the stars of heaven drawn down by the Dragon, because it plainly refers to the last fight before Judgment, not to the original rebellion (pp. 344-345). Lucifer was chief of the fallen, the principal Fathers and Aquinas agree; his sin was pride, and he drew the rest after him by example (pp. 347-348, 335).

In the opinions that he favored on all these questions of angelic nature and history Salkeld agreed closely with Catholic angelologists, Aquinas most often, yet seldom diverged from what Protestants too might accept. Many Protestants, it is true, would not allow the name *Lucifer* for *Satan* because the only biblical warrant for it was a tropological interpretation of Isaiah 14.12 that read what was said of the king of Babylon to apply also to the king of hell. But that was a very small point. Many Protestants, too, took rather uncertain issue with Aquinas about angelic substance, favoring vague Patristic ideas that angels were somehow bodily; but Fathers, Scholastics, and Reformers alike admitted that the question of angelic substance was a very difficult one and that the exact nature of it was not a thing one had to know to escape damnation.

To three points of Catholic angelology, however, many Protestants were outspokenly irreconcilable. The prolific Hertfordshire clergyman, Andrew Willet, lists the three in one of his influential writings against Papistry published about the same time as Salkeld's book: first, Catholics follow the Pseudo-Dionysius on his nine orders and even "charge infidelitie and blasphemie" to those who doubt him, whereas Protestants, though admitting order among angels, think those rash who say exactly what it is; second, Catholics hold that every man has a guardian angel assigned to him at birth, whereas Protestants, though sure of the protection of angels for the elect, doubt individual assignment; finally, Catholics allow a certain adoration of angels, but Protestants forbid all worship of any kind to them.[5]

Of these three snags for a Jesuit-trained Protestant, the last aroused probably the most feeling, and on it Salkeld keeps an almost utter silence [6] that contrasts notably with the outspokenness of other Protestant divines. Jeremy Taylor says flatly that to worship angels as Papists do is highly dangerous.[7] Joseph Mede links angel-worship with saint-worship as an apostate "doctrine of daemons," a renewal of the pagan practise of deifying great men and of worshiping them and intermediate spirits between men and gods.[8] John Gumbledon asserts against Bellarmine that the Catholic doctrine which allows a kind of worship of angels was "invented and maintained meerly to give the Angels and Saints in Heaven, more than their due . . . and in the mean time to rob

the God of Heaven of his whole due, in point of *religious worship*
and *adoration;* for if we give part of this honour to *Saints,* and
part unto himselfe, as the Church of Rome doth, he esteemes it
as if we gave him none at all. . . . If thou *worship Saints* with the
Doulia, which (though the *Jesuits* would have it so) is no ways
proper unto them; thou canst not at all rightly *worship God* with
the *Latria;* thou canst not, because both are his due (though the
Jesuite will not grant it) both the *Doulia* and the *Latria;* and
hence it is that this *distinction* of the *Romane* party (though in
favor as they pretend of *Saints* and *Angels*) is not without just
cause by many of our modern and judicious *Divines,* quite *exploded,* and rightly branded with the *name* of a *simple,* a *counterfeit* and *bold,* a *vain,* an idle, and an halting distinction. . . ." [9]
Among his "judicious Divines" Gumbledon names Jewell, Calvin,
and Peter Martyr. Ussher, More, Leigh, Stillingfleet, Bull, Baxter,
and dozens of other English divines support the Protestant
position.[10]

On the question of guardians, Salkeld rather diffidently favored
the Catholics, citing nearly two dozen Fathers, Greek and Latin,
who had believed that God assigns a good angel to every individual man (p. 251 ff.). He says, too, that in spite of Calvin's scornful
hesitation on the matter many Protestants believe in individual
guardians (p. 252). This was enough from Salkeld to enable the
Puritan Robert Dingley, a determined and forthright controversi-
alist for individual guardians, to cite him approvingly if somewhat
erroneously in 1654 as among "modern Writers (untainted with
Popery) who have eminently appeared for the particular Deputation of Angels. . . ." [11]

On the question of "the Diuers Orders, Subordination, and
Degrees of Angels" Salkeld pulls himself together and largely rejects the Scholastics. Without naming any Protestant authors he
yet gives many of their arguments against the Dionysian scheme,
with copious citation of the biblical passages and patristic commentary upon which they usually relied. Though he has repeatedly quoted Dionysius with reverence on other questions, he now
sourly doubts that we have the "true Dionysius," then speaks
flatly of "counterfeit Dionysius," and finally refers us to a writer
he says has proved that Dionysius is not the Areopagite (pp.
294-302). Must we believe in nine orders of angels in three
hierarchies? The names of the orders, indeed — Seraphim, Cherubim, Thrones, Powers, and the rest — come from Scripture, and
most Fathers assert them to signify angelic rank (p. 292). But then

other Fathers assert other numbers of orders — one hundred, for instance, or ten, or seven (pp. 296-297). Many theologians, therefore, are not so bold as to assign nine particular degrees, though they admit order (p. 302). The whole question is remote from our understanding and we have no firm authority to guide us. Augustine asked why all are called by the general name Angels and yet are also Archangels, Thrones, Dominions, Powers, and so forth? Are they distinct in species and essence as in name? Augustine confesses his ignorance (Salkeld with him) and thinks it no danger to his salvation (pp. 313-314). Aquinas, pretending knowledge, claims that no angels above Virtues are sent to man. But he is without authority, except Dionysius and Gregory, and if the "ministeries of the divine providence . . . be not unbeseeming the immediate concourse of God himselfe, much lesse may it seeme too base for any creature . . . to cooperate immediately . . . in the disposition of things. . . ." We see that Cherubim closed the gates of Paradise and that a Seraph touched Isaiah's lips with a coal. Dionysius claims that this Seraph was actually an inferior angel called a Seraph because of his purging and inflaming ministry; but either Scripture here means one of the supreme order, or we have no place in it to show that this order exists. If "wee will admit the opinion of . . . Aquinas" that the angels who minister before the throne are always there, it must be that "though sometimes they be [sent] in matters of greatest moment" yet they do not cease "from their office of assistance [before the Throne], for seeing they do enjoy Gods presence . . . in every place, they may easily be conceived to execute their office in every place." St. Paul says that all angels are ministering spirits to the heirs of salvation, and that must mean that they enter the world (p. 315 ff.).

The reader's final impression of Salkeld on the hierarchies is that but for reasons of policy he might well have preferred the whole Catholic view. Deviation on this matter was not enough to send a man to the stake, it is true, nor even to hamper a popular literary work — Spenser, Drayton, Jonson, and others used the Dionysian hierarchy, and Heywood framed his whole long angelological poem on it — but Salkeld could no doubt easily have affronted his royal master about the organization of angels. Like most Protestants, James "will not denie that there be a form of order amongst the Angels in Heauen," yet like most he seems impatient of details about it.[12]

Except for the tender points on worship, guardians, and the

hierarchies, plus a general inclination to shake heads at elaboration of the questions on angelic nature, Protestants usually accepted scholastic angelology and often showed themselves impressed by its precision and method, so that Salkeld's standing in
seventeenth-century England was probably better than it would
have been had he lacked his scholastic background.

II

Two typical English writers on angels who at once used and
deprecated scholastic angelology, were Henry Lawrence and Isaac
Ambrose. Though they levy on Aquinas for much and even on
such sixteenth-century Catholic demonologists as Jean Bodin and
Nicholas Remy, they reject them strongly on worship, guardians,
and rank, and they incline to disparage both the aims and the
detail of Scholasticism. Lawrence says in his dedication that he
has tried to keep the speculative part of his treatise under strict
control, and what he means appears when, for instance, he comes
to discuss whether angels have bodies or not. It is, he snaps, a
question "much controverted" between Platonists and Scholastics,
and "the reasons on both sides are not unworthy considering, if
one would amuse themselves in that, out of which the Scripture
gives no issue." [13] Ambrose, too, says that he will not insist on such
a controversial and doubtful article as the exact spiritual nature
of angels.[14] He cites Peter Martyr that "to inquire of the angels
accurately and subtilly" is more for the sake of our curiosity than
of our spiritual health, and he wishes "that the Schoolmen in
their knotty, thorny, and unprofitable discourses had observed
this. . . ." [15]

Ambrose will affirm with Peter, nevertheless, and with Calvin
and Musculus, that it is profitable to know about angels, since
"they are destined to our ministry" and Scripture is not silent on
them. The thing about angels "most worthy of our knowledge"
he holds to be that "which the school-men in all their learning
took the least notice of, and that is of the ministration of angels
in reference to God's people" (p. 480). Lawrence, too, says that
though he must speak something of angels' general nature, he
does not intend "so large a discourse as the thing will beare" but
will treat chiefly of the spiritual warfare for the soul of man,
"keeping neere the Scripture and not departing from our assured
rule, the word of God . . ." (p. 6). Lawrence deliberately gives
almost a third of his book to a semi-allegorical discussion of "the
whole armor of God"— truth, love, righteousness, faith — which

the believer can put on against devils (see The Epistle), and much
of the rest is "practicall Corollaryes" to such unavoidable speculation as he has on the angelic nature. Ambrose allows only about
ten pages out of eighty-five in his work on good angels to the
angelic nature and devotes almost all of the companion *War with
Devils* [16] to retailing the kinds of temptation devils can use against
us. The emphasis of these authors is very different, plainly, from
that of Salkeld, a man who went willingly into the intricacies of
the angelic nature for their own sake.

In spite of this difference, Lawrence especially has many particular points in common with Salkeld. Angels were probably
created on the first day (p. 7), he says; they know by means of
species God put into them (pp. 30, 31), but do not know all
particulars since "there is too much of infinity in that" (p. 32);
the elect angels are confirmed in their bliss (pp. 29, 32) and the
fallen in their evil, for the fall was to them as bodily death is to
man, after which no repentance is practically possible (p. 60);
God can destroy angels, but will not (pp. 12, 17); angels may
control men's fancy (p. 35 ff.); the saints will fill up the room of
the fallen angels (p. 71); God does not need angels, but to use
them is his way of governing the world (pp. 23, 24, 48). These
are all commonplaces of scholastic angelology taken over in outline, if not in their fullness, by most Protestant writers.

On the difficult question of angelic substance and apparition the
characteristic Protestant reserve of Lawrence and Ambrose eventu-
ates in a doctrine which, though vague in details, is yet distinct
from both the scholastic and the Platonistic, although on the
surface it is very close to the former and shares many terms with
the latter. Protestants liked the scholastic insistence on angels as
spirits and disliked the Platonistic notion of them as dichotomous,
so that Lawrence can say flatly that "Angelicall natures as the
soules also of men, are not compounded of matter and forme, but
are simple formes and substances, subsisting by themselves"
(p. 13). Thus far Lawrence has the scholastic doctrine; and scholastic too is the modification of it which he gives in another place:
". . . they are not essences so simple as they are altogether un-
capable of composition, it is onely proper to God to have his being
and his essence, or substance the same; Angels are mutable, they
consist of an act which they are, and of a power into which they
may be reduced" (p. 9).[17]

Protestants found, nevertheless, that as Lawrence notes, "many
of the Fathers adhere" to the Platonistic notion that angels have

bodies, and since Protestants had much rather agree with the
Fathers than with the Schoolmen, very many of them — Calvin,
Zanchy, Peter Martyr, Bullinger, Vossius, Willet, Perkins, Ussher,
Baxter, Vane, and others [18]— shape their characteristically inde-
cisive opinions on angelic substance to include the possibility that
angels do after all have bodies of a sort. And so Lawrence: "But
if they have any such composition as may be called a body, it is
certainely of the greatest finenesse and subtility, a spirituall body,
and therefore not like to be of that grosseness that either the air
is, or those heavens that are framed out of the Chaos, but neerer
the substance of the highest heavens, which seeme to have bene
made at the same time . . ." (p. 9).

What Lawrence means here by "any such composition as may
be called a body" appears, perhaps, in a parallel passage from
Ambrose. Certainly, Ambrose says, angels have no flesh and blood;
yet they are not spirits either "without all composition" in the
sense that God is so; they are not "infinite or immense as God
is, but are terminated in their dimensions, and move from place
to place as bodies do" (p. 475). And so the authority whom Ambrose values "above all, learned and godly Zanchius," [19] "approves
rather of the antients than of the Schoolmen, That Angels are not
simply and altogether incorporeal, only their bodies (saith he)
are not earthly, nor airy nor heavenly as the Stoicks would have
them, for all such bodies were created of that Chaos, Gen. I.1. but
rather as the Empireal heaven is a corporeal substance far different
from these neather heavens visible to us, so the angels made together with that heaven, are corporeal substance, far purer, &
more subtile than either earth, or ayre, or fire or the matter of
these visible heavens. I will not say they are of the same body, but
they may have like bodies to that glorious body of the highest
heaven, or seat of the blessed . . ." (p. 475).

Lawrence and Ambrose end their discussions in identical words
with an ancient formula: ". . . in comparison of God they are
bodies, in comparison of us they are pure and mighty spirits"
(Lawrence, p. 9; Ambrose, p. 476).

This idea that angels are corporeal compared with God and
spiritual compared with man is at least as old in the West as
Gregory the Great; and Aquinas, citing it from Damascene, shows
that he can accept it without admitting that angels have "anything
corporeal in them." [20] Casman, Cicogna, Maldonat, Anania, and
other Renaissance Catholics follow him.[21] In England, scholastic-
minded writers such as Thomas Heywood and William Foster, a

clergyman who wrote against Robert Fludd, use the doctrine to explain away Patristic contentions for body in angels.[22] But Peter Martyr sneers that in this the Schoolmen simply "deuise another shift" to justify their subtleties. He seems, like Zanchy, to take the formula as signifying corporeality of a sort.[23] And so, presumably, do Lawrence and Ambrose.

Even if angels were thus corporeal, they still needed in the Protestant view to assume elementary bodies in order to be visible to men. These assumed bodies, says Lawrence, are "formed of nothing, or of pre-existant matter," or they are natural bodies possessed by the angel as Satan possessed the serpent's (p. 13). "If you aske mee what kinde of bodies they tooke, and whether they were true men or no, in taking human shapes: Answ. First though they appeared in a humane shape, they were not true men, as Christ was a true man, because hee was personally and *hypostatically* united; but bodies were not united to the Angells, as to their forme, as the bodie is to the soule, which is its forme, nor was the humane nature body and soule, united to the person of any Angell, but they tooke bodies to them as garments which they tooke up, and laid downe upon occasion" (p. 14). These bodies are usually elementary, probably of condensed air given figure and color as in clouds. What becomes of them? "The answer is, that if they be created out of nothing, they are reduced into nothing, by the power of God; But if they be formed of pre-existent matter, the works being done for which they were taken up they are resolved againe into their Elements, or Principles . . ." (p. 15).

This explanation of apparition owes a great deal, of course, to the scholastic rationalization, but it carries also the mark of a much older and apparently hastier rationalization, one put together by Tertullian to answer Marcion's contention that the Incarnation was by the same means as the apparition of angels. The angels, said Tertullian, did not merely fake bodies, as Marcion claimed, but for their ministry were indued by God with miraculous true bodies of genuine flesh, and were indeed like Christ in this, except that as their bodies were not to die, they were not born but were created out of nothing.[24] Tertullian's polemical improvisation attracted many Protestants because it piously referred the whole wonder of apparition directly to God. Peter Martyr and Zanchy are writers particularly influential in England who seem to favor Tertullian's views,[25] and Calvin himself uses the doctrine in explaining how angels ate with Abraham.

Most Protestant exegetes, both English and continental, of the sixteenth and seventeenth centuries follow him in this.

> I do not doubt, [says Calvin] that God . . . gave them bodies, for a time, in which they might fulfill the office enjoined them. And as they truly walked, spoke, and discharged other functions; so I conclude they did truly eat; not because they were hungry, but in order to conceal themselves until the proper time for making themselves known. Yet as God speedily annihilated these bodies, which had been created for a temporary use; so there will be no absurdity in saying, that the food itself was destroyed, together with the bodies.[26]

So far as the eating was concerned this was, of course, substantially the scholastic opinion too, although like Salkeld, most Scholastics preferred to say with Aquinas that as angels did not assimilate, they did not truly eat. The Calvinistic stand is at bottom only verbally different, since it admits that angels eat, as Peter Martyr says, only in the sense that they "chawe the meate, or conveyghe it . . . downe into the bellie," not in the sense that they "convert it to the substance" of their own bodies "by concoction through the power of vegitacion. . . ." [27]

With this opinion Lawrence's runs almost verbatim in parts. The angels who appeared to Abraham and others, Lawrence says, "did what they seemed to doe," so that "their coulour, their shape, their eating, their drinking . . . was what it seemed to be. . . . If you aske what became of the meate they eate, for their assumed bodies needed no nourishment? I would aske you what became of their bodies, their meate as well as their bodies was reduced into nothing, or the pre-existent Elements, of which they consisted, as that which Christ eate after his resurrection" (pp. 15, 16).[28]

Protestant divines talk about angelic apparition usually as a part of biblical exegesis; few of them before More and Glanville's campaign show much interest in contemporary phenomena. In fact most, Lawrence and Ambrose among them, say that just as miracles have ceased since the coming of Christ so have apparitions of good angels, and that those of devils are "almost as seldome now a dayes as of the good Angells . . ." (Lawrence, p. 45). The ministrations and assaults of angels, good and bad, go on, but they are almost entirely "spiritual," undetected behind the veil of the sightless substance. As for what work angels did besides their warfare for men's souls, neither Lawrence nor Ambrose show any concern, and in this, too, they are in the pattern of Protestant divinity. Angels may move the heavens and control seminal forms and the weather; Lawrence and Ambrose seem to admit their power to do so. But whether they regularly act in such matters and how they go about it interests the Puritan angelologist no more than it interested the makers of the Old Testament. Angels, good and evil, are God's retainers and his servants for the guidance and punishment of his children. That is all the Puritans know or care about angels, and to avoid the chance of idolatry they are perfectly willing to minimize any other part angels may have in the world and to deny most of man's acquaintance with them that is not through the word of God. Lawrence and Ambrose do not profess to know angels' names or their kinds or ranks or their places in the world or in heaven or how man may get overt contact with them. Many of the parts that made up angelology for the Scholastic, then, Lawrence and Ambrose reject, and they reject nearly all that made it for the occultist. They gave scope to an extent they certainly did not intend to the voices of a sceptical rationalism.

III

The most uncompromising of such voices in the middle of the seventeenth century was that of a man who died before Lawrence and Ambrose were born. When Reginald Scot's *Discovery of Witchcraft* and *Discourse Concerning Devils and Spirits* were reprinted in 1651, 1654, and 1665, they were still a more advanced, as well as a more cogent, statement against demonology than anyone else had published in England or was to publish for fifty years. As a consistent opponent of all the salient doctrines of angelic activity in the physical world, Scot goes far beyond John Webster and even beyond Hobbes. He is, nevertheless, unmistakably Calvinist, and some of his ideas are closely allied to those of Lawrence and Ambrose.

In the Protestant convention Scot makes much play on the difficulty of knowing anything about beings so remote as angels. He pours the usual scorn on all the scholastic doctors who talk as though they had visited heaven. He ranges himself virtuously with St. Paul and St. Augustine and other great men who had expressed reservations, rests with them exclusively upon Scripture, and attends with them only to those things needful for salvation. He repeatedly cites Calvin to justify his general attitude, and quotes him and Peter Martyr and other Protestant authors to support his ridicule of scholastic and Platonistic elaborations. He speaks strongly in the usual Protestant tone against worship of angels, the individual guardian, and the Dionysian orders. Worship he links scornfully to paganism.[29] As for guardians, he says we have for them "not reason in nature, nor authorities in scripture," and

he quotes Calvin on how shameful it is to refer to one angel the
care God has for every man of us (p. 424). As for Dionysius on
the hierarchies, either he "Folowed his own imaginations and
conceipts, or else the corruption of that age"; Calvin makes it
plain how little we should trust him (p. 420). The "schoole
doctors," Scot jeers, pretend that some orders are not sent and
that archangels are sent only about great matters whereas "angels
are common hacknies about evere trifle . . ." (p. 424). These are
"fond imaginations" and "impious curiosities."

Scot takes care to make plain that he himself believes in angels;
he can be indignant against the Sadducees, "impious and fond,"
who say that "divels are onelie motions and affections, and that
angels are but tokens of God's power." For his part, he will "confesse with *Augustine*" that these matters are above his "reach and
capacitie: and yet so farre as God's word teacheth" he "will not
stick to saie, that they are living creatures, ordeined to serve the
Lord in their vocation. And although they abode not in their first
estate, yet that they are the Lord's ministers, and executioners of
his wrath, to trie and tempt in this world, and to punish the
reprobate in hell fier in the world to come" (p. 453).

Like Ambrose and Lawrence, Scot holds that the assault of the
devils and the help of the angels is "spiritual," and in this too he
sounds (as he takes care by repeated citation of great Protestants
to make himself sound) as though he were in received Protestant
tradition. But it is just here that Scot leaves that tradition, for
when he says that angelic activities are spiritual, he means to deny
totally that they are ever in any sense bodily. This is a stand that
Scot never compromises, and with it he totally rejects witchcraft,
magic, apparition, celestial management, and virtually everything
else that comes under the heading of "operation" in the demonologies. He even rejects the article upon which Lawrence and
Ambrose most depend, the angel's ability to handle the humors
and so control a man's fancy internally to tempt and trouble him
or inspire and soothe. When they speak of a "spiritual" contact
between man and angel, they usually mean this secret suggesting.
What Scot means he never says in physiological terms; but he does
not ever concede to angels any kind of physical rule of anything.
Like Lawrence he notes that Paul "biddeth us put on the whole
armour of God," and like Lawrence he interprets the armor alle-
gorically (p. 426). But he does not, like Lawrence, allow that this
allegorical armor has ever to turn a bodily assault. Whatever
biblical references demonologists use to show angels physically

active, says Scot, are either grossly misquoted, as when Bodin
claims that an angel slew the first-born of Egypt, whereas the text
says God did it (p. 434); or are misinterpreted, as when Lucifer
in Isaiah 14.12 is thought to signify Satan instead of Nebuchad-
nezzar, as the plain sense is (p. 421). Genuine biblical references
to spirits are best taken as figures of speech, else we might suppose
that the devil really goes about roaring like a lion, although what
the Bible says of his lion-likeness "is mente of the soule and
spirituall devouring, as verie novices in religion may judge"
(p. 455). If "we have onelie respect to the bare word, or rather to
the letter, where spirits or divels are spoken of in the scriptures,
we shall run into . . . dangerous absurdities. . . . For some are so
carnallie minded that a spirit is no sooner spoken of, but immedi-
atelie they thinke of a blacke man with cloven feet, a paire of
hornes, a taile, clawes, and eies as broad as a bason." Surely the
devil would not be so foolish, even if he had the power, as to show
himself in an ugly form (p. 426).

    But, thinks Scot, he does not have the power to show us any
form. "His essence also and his forme is so proper and peculiar
(in mine opinion) unto himself, as he himselfe cannot alter it, but
must needs be content therewith, as with that which God hath
ordeined for him, and assigned unto him, as peculiearlie as he
hath given to us our substance without power to alter the same
at our pleasure. For we find not that a spirit can make a bodie,
more than a bodie can make a spirit: the spirit of God excepted,
which is omnipotent" (p. 454). As for the testimony of those who
claim to have beheld apparitions or works of witchcraft, "See
whether the witnesses be not single of what credit, sex, and age
they are; namelie lewd, miserable, and envious poore people; most
of them which speake to anie purpose being old women, & children of the age of 4.5.6.7.8. or 9. yeares" (p. 455).

    Scot notices rather vaguely the distinction between the scholas-
tic view that by an ordinary power angels "can assume & take unto
them bodies at their pleasure. Of which mind all papists and some
protestants are . . . ," and the Tertullianesque opinion of "another
sort," less gross, "which hold, that such bodies are made to their
hands." He was here on dangerous ground, since virtually every
great Protestant commentator was of one of these sorts. In a
chapter of hardly half a page Scot just sneers at the diversity of
demonological opinion and quotes Peter Martyr very disin-
genuously to leave the false impression that as Peter criticized
some theories of apparition, he denied apparition itself (p. 433).

Scot rejected flatly not only all demonic apparition in special bodies, but all demonic possession, even that of the serpent by Satan. "Indeed we saie, and trulie, to the wicked, The divell is in him; but we meane not thereby, that a reall divell is gotten into his guts . . ." (p. 430). He reads Genesis to mean not that Satan entered the serpent, but that when it said *serpent* it signified Satan. The Bible, explains Scot, asserts only that the serpent seduced Eve, and that against him the curse went out (p. 451). If it meant that Satan controlled the serpent, who was afterwards punished for it, then it chronicled a great injustice to the snake in very misleading language (p. 452). Obviously Genesis speaks metaphorically: ". . . the divell is resembled to an odious creature, who as he creepeth upon us to annoie our bodies; so doth the divell there creepe into the conscience of *Eve,* to abuse and deceive her. . . ." Though in consideration of our feeble capacities this event is described as a "materiall tragedie," we are not to think that it really was so (p. 453).

Plainly Scot was nothing of a scientific rationalist; but plainly too he brought to even biblical evidence of angels an independent judgment that could confront the angelological tradition more unflinchingly than could that of scientists like Robert Boyle. Scot was not, like Boyle, merely sidling away from angelology because it was unserviceable to a particular kind of worldly inquiry. He was hacking at the very bole of what, like other Protestants, he thought an absurdly proliferated growth, which, unlike others, he believed would best be cut back to the very root.

Chapter IV

The Occult Profusion

A RECENT WRITER on the literature of magic has suggested the ironical probability that the chief effect in England of Reginald Scot's brave rally against demonology was to widen the audience for devil-lore and conjuring forms.[1] The *Discovery* and the *Discourse* indeed contained for their century the most thorough and detailed accounts easily available in English of the names, natures, and control of spirits. In the middle of the next century what Scot designed as a documented exposure of demonology undoubtedly caught the eye of many of its readers because his illustrations of demon-magic seemed to them not ridiculous or repulsive, as he had intended, but darkly fascinating. The second edition of Scot's work appeared in 1651 to a public receptive in the same year to the English translation of Agrippa's *Occult Philosophy* and in the same decade to a gush of other occultist translations. That printers were aware of the off-color appeal of Scot's work, with its Solomonic incantations and Wier's catalogue of demon princes, is plain in the two insulting suffixes to the 1665 edition: to the *Discovery* nine chapters of frankly conjuring prescriptions, and to the *Discourse* a Book II of the most extravagant demonological speculation. The title page blandly lists these as "conducing to the compleating of the *Whole Work.*"

No one knows the author of these rank additions, but he has been designated Anti-Scot, and the term suits. Every quality Scot's work shows of cogent scepticism tempered with piety and of connected, persistent polemic for a rationalist view of spirits had its antithesis in the superstitious, blasphemous credulity and the incoherent asseveration of Anti-Scot. The chasm that separates the two men shows, for instance, in the contrast between Scot's firm insistence that angels are eternal creatures above us so purely spiritual that they can never be conceived to operate in the temporal world and Anti-Scot's carelessly dropped remark (probably following Paracelsus) that "the very imaginations and affection of a Magician, doth create an evil Essence or Devil, which was not

61

before in being," yet which, we gather, answers conjuration in a full outfit of horns and hoofs, and then loses all individual exist- ence "when the force of that imagination is gone which was the cause of their production." [2] Obviously Anti-Scot is wholly at odds not only with the valorous rigor of Scot's scepticism, but with that pious caution of his Calvinism which gave scepticism its purchase.

True Anti-Scot does from time to time himself speak the senti- ments of conventional piety; then he contradicts most of them so plainly and so swiftly that they keep little weight in his work. He concedes once, for instance, in a very orthodox tone that whoever "do at present alledge, that they enjoy familiarity with a familiar Spirit; I say its greatly to be suspected that all such familiars be- long to the Kingdom of Darkness . . .," for "if communication with Angels, or good and holy Guardians be at all attainable, yet such is the difficulty of the attainment, that the examples thereof, if true are exceeding rare" (pp. 499, 500). But before the end of the page he is saying that "Both the *Hebrew Cabalists* and *Heathen Magicians,* as also those addicted to Magick in Christianity, have all of them laid down certain forms of attaining the company of a good or evil Angel. . . ." and that in his added chapters to the *Discovery* "many forms of obtaining the Society of the *Bonus* or *Malus Genius,* are plainly decyphered. . . ." The good angels, he says again in a tone virtuous enough to be Lawrence's or Am- brose's, "are imployed for the glory of God and the protection of mankind" and are not subject to conjuration (p. 495). Yet in his additions to the *Discovery* he has told how they might be con- jured, beginning with an earnest prayer to them (pp. 483-484).

This prescribed prayer to good angels is, of course, not at all the same thing as the *doulia,* the limited worship, defended by Scholastics, though occultists sometimes tried to identify their angel worship with *doulia.* The difference in aim and spirit is great and shows itself in the fact that the Catholic church sanc- tioned prayer by name only to Michael, Gabriel, and Raphael, the three good angels named in its Bible, and explicitly forbade invo- cation of any other by name, whereas the prescription of Anti- Scot requires, like those of all magical manuals, that the angel be prayed to under a name discoverable by occult processes. The Anti-Scot's un-Protestant features, then, do not at all identify his angelology with the strict if proliferant speculations of Catholics. He has, it is true, an occasional article probably derived from Scholasticism (as that hell is always with the devils, no matter what their local place),[3] but in most of his theory as well as his tone he is as remote from Salkeld as from Ambrose and Scot.

The work of Anti-Scot is, in fact, an unholy agglomeration of occult lore, owing most perhaps to Paracelsus and the evilly-designed manuals of spirit magic that claimed Solomon as their originator.[4] Its inconsequent patches of godliness are the protective coloration usual in the manuals, a precautionary attempt at identification with the dominant religion. The rest of its occasional points in common with orthodox pneumatology are but the accidents of a fantastically eclectic theosophy.

Anti-Scot asserts two basic sorts of invisible creatures active in the world: angels, good or evil, and what he calls astral spirits. The latter are beings who, he says, "are of the source of the stars," either the astral bodies of men or any of several classes of elementals (pp. 493-495), which Paracelsus had called Sylphs, Undines, Gnomes, and Salamanders.[5] This paralleling of shadowy human vestiges with invisible non-human beings and this insistence upon rational creatures in the elements distinct from fallen angels were ancient paganizations that theologians had tried to freeze out of Christian pneumatology as unscriptural, extravagant, and conducive to a dangerous misreading of supernatural manifestations. Various Renaissance occultists — Paracelsus most prominently and most originally — had renewed them with very little attention to the theologians or their purposes, and Anti-Scot presents them confidently, and even names the respected Jesuit demonologist, Martin Delrio, as acknowledging that the elementals exist as a kind of "middle spirits" (p. 495). Delrio had in fact declared that nothing could be more impious than Paracelsus' doctrine of elementals or further from the faith.[6]

Like Paracelsus, Anti-Scot divides what he calls the "Astral Spirits separate," that is, the non-human astral spirits, according to the elements of which they are made and in which they live, and he mixes into the classification also a good deal from Psellus and Trithemius. Like them particularly, he is willing to call the elementals *spirits*, whereas Paracelsus had been very forthright in asserting that they were not spirits, but a kind of animal, since they were soulless and so mortal.[7] Anti-Scot agrees with Paracelsus that they are mortal, though long-lived, that they reproduce their kind, and that they require food (p. 495). He does not mention Paracelsus' doctrine that occasionally they co-habit with human beings and have children with the spark of eternal life in them and by the union themselves gain the same spark.[8] Anti-Scot designates the food of astral spirits, by Jean Baptiste Van Helmont's coinages: "the *Gas* of the Water, and the *Blas* of the Air" (p. 495). He is Paracelsan again when he says that in physical matters devils can do little or nothing without the help of these astral spirits (p. 516). He seems untroubled by the fact that he had said earlier that astral spirits, as well as devils, find apparition as difficult as "a man to continue with his head under water," since to appear to us they have to leave their proper element (p. 503).

The reason Anti-Scot gives for devils' unhandiness in the physical world is that their "subtle and spiritual nature" cannot work in the "crude and rough" bodies and possessions of men (pp. 516-517). Devils can, he says, contract and dilate themselves (pp. 493, 527), and perhaps he intends to indicate, according to a doctrine common among Platonists, that by contracting they thicken their substance and painfully make it visible. He mentions this power of contraction, however, only in connection with the numbers of devils, not in connection with their apparition, and speaks so equivocally of it that he may mean that the devilish kingdom as a whole pulses with the creations and extinctions that follow witches' evil imaginations, not that the individual spirits expand and contract their persons.

Plainly whatever corporeity he thinks constant to devils is a very special kind, for he sneers that to suppose that devils "are materially vexed and scorched in flames of fire, is inferiour to any to give credit to, who is thoroughly verst in their nature and existence: for their substance is spiritual," and outward flames could have no effect on their bodies, which "are able to pierce through Wood and Iron, Stone, and all Terrestrial things" (p. 493). Like the elemental spirits, nevertheless, angels have to eat: "As every natural, and supernatural being is upheld, and maintain'd out of the self-same root from whence it had its original, or rise; So the Angels feed upon the Celestial Manna, The Devils of the fruits of Hell, which is natural to their appetite, as trash for swine . . ." (p. 515). This fruitful hell is not a "Chasma or Gulph in a certain place, above, under, or in the Center of the Earth" (pp. 518, 519) any more than day or night is one place, but is simply the darkness of sin, so that locally devils may stay in "the Aery Region." Some, however, by Anti-Scot's account, do seem to be in a place locally distinct, where apparently they are, after all, in spite of the spirituality of their substance somehow exposed to bodily torments. "Excess of cold and heat" is "continually raging among them. Neither is there any light or lustre to be seen within their Courts, but that which comes from their fiery Eyes, as a deadly glancing or glimmering, being sudden fiery flashes and sparkling, as the enkindling of Gunpowder . . ." (pp. 529-530). Anti-Scot's phrase that this hell is a "dark world" founded on God's wrath, hints at Boehmism as set forth in England by the Pordages.[9]

The ranks of good angels and of evil, Anti-Scot says in one place, exactly correspond to each other (p. 518); but later he acknowledges that "As for the Rancks or Orders" of devils "there is some difficulty in the true discovery thereof, by reason that we know not certainly of what Orders they were that *Fell*. The opinion of most men is, *That of every Order many fell*. But those that better know the nature of the Heavenly Hierarchies, have sufficiently proved, *That of any Ranck or Order none can fall unless all do follow*. Therefore with more reason may it be judged, That before the Devils fell, the Hierarchies of Heaven did consist of three Rancks or Orders; to wit, the Order of Uriel, of Michael, of Lucifer; That of Lucifer is totally in *Hell*: the other which is under Michael, is the dominion of Heaven; the last which is Uriels, are more in the dominion of this principle of the *Stars,* having the *Planets* in their dominion, with the influences thereof" (p. 527). The catalogue of devils that Scot reprinted from Wier in the *Discovery* is, says Anti-Scot, "utterly feigned and fictitious" because it gives to its devils the titles Seraphim, Powers, Thrones, etc., "whereas the whole Kingdom of Hell consists but of one only Hierarchy, which is that of Lucifer . . ." (p. 527).

Not only the ranks but the names in Wier's catalogue are wrong, says Anti-Scot. If the list had any certainty "it were to be preferred as the most ample and exact delineation that is extant" (p. 524), but Wier recorded the names merely "from the mouth of Tradition and obscure Manuscripts," and his list "is the rather to be suspected, because of the little coherence it hath with the former received Names of Devils either in Europe, Asia, Africa, or America" (p. 524). Thus he rejects Wier first as depending on tradition and then as not agreeing with tradition.

The truth is, Anti-Scot thinks, that devils kept their Hebrew names from the creation of the world to the coming of Christ (p. 523). Since the coming, they have assumed names to suit whatever work they were about, so that one devil may have twenty or thirty names. Only "it must be granted, that there be some principal kings and Dukes in the Infernal Hierarchy, that have Names established upon them which cannot be transferr'd or altered" (p. 523). What cause he has to think so or why in reason it should be so, Anti-Scot does not say. The implication is that unless some

devils have stable names, conjuration is impossible; and this un-
interesting state of things he simply does not care to face.

Obviously Anti-Scot is not responsible to everyday logic or to
ordinary rules of exposition; no doubt he felt, like most occultists,
that his subject matter did not fit everyday logic and ordinary
rules. He would assert what gratified his occult yearning as the
moment seemed to call for it and persons of vision could understand him. Better that the rest — such crass and irreverent scoffers
as Reginald Scot — should not understand.

II

Not all the occultists read in seventeenth-century England were
quite so disjointed in their exposition as Anti-Scot, and many were
concerned with spirit lore only as a part of much grander fields
of learning. One of the worthier of these — and certainly one of
the more influential — was Cornelius Agrippa von Nettesheim.
The twenty-two chapters on angels in his famous *Occult Philosophy* as translated in 1651 are all of them tied in with his theories
of an elevated kind of magic, a theurgy leading the adept to God.[10]
Agrippa depended very largely on the Jewish Cabala, which, following his noble predecessors, Reuchlin and Pico della Mirandola,
he thought to contain a doctrine parallel to Christianity and illu-
minating to all perceptive Christians. Like Anti-Scot, Agrippa is
often self-contradictory and inconsequent, certainly not strict in
selection of the speculations he reports, and inclined to keep his
piety by him partly as a cloak to unorthodox views. But Agrippa
never sinks to be a simple curiosity-seeker, nor is he one of those
who, in Lambert Daneau's words, study about spirits merely because "there is a most large field thereby opened unto them,
wherein they may runne and wander freely, farre without the true
boundes of fayth. . . ."[11] To Agrippa, writing a hundred and fifty
years before Anti-Scot, the revival of a refined spirit magic had
something of the vitality and promise that the new science was to
have for Galileo and Kepler and their contemporaries.

Long before the *Occult Philosophy* was brought out in English
this promise had failed, and Agrippa's grand magic was acknowledged even by Agrippa to be half impious, half vain. But this
acknowledgment did not cancel the fascination of his esoteric
learning, and the hollowness of his system of magic for the gracious
gifts he had envisioned did not necessarily mean to an Englishman
of the 1650's that Agrippa was misinformed about spirits. Some
think it strange, says Meric Casaubon in 1659, that the spirits Dr.

Dee had talk with seem to borrow their demonology from Agrippa and Trithemius and Paracelsus; but nothing could be more natural, for spirits had taught those men before they came to Dee.[12] The English translator of Agrippa admits that "in his work there is much superstition and vanity." But, he urges, "consider the time of darkness" [13] in which Agrippa wrote and remember that gold does not come pure from any mine.

Theoretically Agrippa was a Catholic, as Anti-Scot, we may suppose, was a Protestant. But like Anti-Scot and most other occultists, Agrippa leaves the reader with little clue to his church. His extravagant admirer, Thomas Vaughan, could insist that he was a secret Protestant, and to modern authority he seems, indeed, "a semi-Lutheran." [14] In his survey of angelology the only partiality he shows is to Platonistic and Cabalistic ideas, which he frequently turns to the Bible to support. Although he often cites Scholastics, particularly when they happen to suit one of his special ideas (as that prayer to angels is permissible), and like nearly all Christian angelologists of his century depends on a scholastic matrix of thought, he is really less attached to scholastic angelology as a system than are Ambrose and Lawrence. Many of its articles considered most important for the preservation of sound religion he ignores.

He ignores most prominently the Papal prohibition against using more names of angels than appear in the Bible.[15] Agrippa's entire scheme of Cabalistic magic depended on the names of God and of angels, and not only does he recite some general principles about angelic names, but he outlines the Cabalistic system for discovering names (pp. 417-446). Though he piously admits the Bible to be the only source of true names (pp. 379, 414), he takes impious latitude in sifting them out of it: "Wheresoever . . . the Scripture speaks of the office or work of any spirit, good or bad, from thence the name of that spirit . . . may be gathered" (p. 418). The anagramatic system of the Hebrew "Mecubals" could thus supply names by the thousands. Agrippa does not himself go into production of them, but he does list several dozens on the authority of the "Mecubals." He notices that good angels' names usually end in *El, On, Jah,* or *Jod* to signify a name of God, by which all angels' names have their qualities. In the names of evil angels *Jah,* which expresses beneficience, has no place, but *El,* which expresses God's power, may appear, "for neither can evil spirits either subsist, or do anything without the vertue of *El,* God" (p. 430). Evil angels may take their names from heathen gods, and either good or evil from men and from places named in the Bible. Thus the name *Uriel* is from that of Uriah, the Prophet, and *Ariel* as the name of an evil demon, is from the city Ariopolis and its idol (pp. 435-436). Only God knows the true name of any angel, but divinely appointed men have the power "to impose names upon Spirits" just as Adam named all things that God had created. Usually names "are put upon them from their works" (p. 414), and of this kind are the names *Michael,* signifying the strength of God, *Raphael,* the medicine of God, and others (p. 415).

While naming angels, Agrippa often gives the cosmic functions of the more prominent, as that Michael rules the east, Raphael the west, Gabriel the north, and Uriel the south. Of these four the opposite numbers among the evil angels are Samael, Azael, Mahazuel, and Azazel. In the elements Cherub rules air, Tharsis water, Ariel earth, and Seraph fire. Agrippa names angels also for the signs of the Zodiac, the mansions of the moon, and the seven "planets" (pp. 414-417).

For him and other "practical" Cabalists this charting of angelic names and offices was a sound part of man's knowledge of God and the world as well as an indispensable preliminary to magic. But to Protestant divines of the 1650's it sounded impious and dangerous. Christopher Love, for instance, calls such lore "the Cabalistical divinity of the doting Jews," and he notes as one of the "bad effects" of the Catholic doctrine of individual guardians that it encourages this assigning of angels throughout nature.[16] More temperately Benjamin Camfield, publishing twenty years after Love, says simply that Agrippa and Trithemius are bold and over-curious in these matters, though certainly angels do have a share in running the world.[17]

The connection of angels with the stars is, in Agrippa's view, very important for a man to understand, since that *"Genius* which is given to every one from their birth" (p. 410) is always from the retinue of some celestial "President" or other and is best able to help his human charge in times and places agreeable to the influences of the planet which his chief rules. This, of course, is itself considerably beyond the Catholic doctrine of guardians, and Agrippa goes on far beyond it to explain that in fact "Every man hath a threefold good Demon . . . the one whereof is holy, another of the nativity, and a third of profession." The first comes after all not from the stars but direct from God; it guides the life of the soul by putting good thoughts into the mind, and when we are purified we perceive this daemon. We may avoid the malignity of fate by worshipping it, so that through dreams and signs it will divert evil fortune and procure good. A man's second good angel, his daemon of nativity, "which is called the Genius," descends "from the disposition of the world, and from the circuits of the Stars, which were powerful in his nativity." Some authorities (ancient believers in pre-existence, Agrippa might have said) think that the soul chooses this preserver as it prepares to descend into the body, and that the Genius then helps the soul into the body and afterwards defends the man as long as he lives. The "Demon of profession," finally, comes from the stars that rule the work a man has chosen; it changes if the calling changes and varies in dignity with the calling (pp. 410-412).

Not only individual angels are connected with the stars but also orders of angels, and each order, Agrippa explains (pp. 467, 468), infuses virtues into men through the stars. The orders he names are those of the Pseudo-Dionysius, which he had given in an earlier chapter as "according to the opinion of the theologians," and which he had backed with analogues from Proclus and Iamblichus (p. 395). Agrippa knew as well as the Protestants who condemned Dionysius' scheme how many competing terms could be drawn from the Bible; but the knowledge did not seem to him reason, as it did to them, to frown on the whole enterprise of ascertaining angelic rank. He rather joys in the profusion, and with Dionysius' scheme of nine matches Athanasius' of ten, and then that of the "Theologians of the Hebrews" with nine (pp. 396-397, 368-369). He has also a chapter on the orders of the evil spirits and gives a classification apparently devised by the later scholastics (pp. 397-399), which Protestants often cited as "an instance of the same curiosity" that produced Dionysius' scheme, "an unsatisfied itch for Knowledge which searcheth into all depths, and spareth neither Heav'n nor Hell in its presumption." [18] Evidently this hierarchy of devils carried some interest to Protestants, for both Thomas Heywood and Robert Burton — writers on demonology who intended at least as much to divert as to inform — list it in full.[19] It is awkward, however, for the traditionally received notion of rank in hell, since it seems to make Beelzebub the highest ranking devil and Satan simply prince of the fifth order, inferior to Beelzebub, Belial, and Asmodeus, and only a cut or so above Astaroth, Mammon, and others. In his table of the number One Agrippa had called Lucifer the "One Prince of Rebellion, of Angels, and darkness" (p. 176). He does not, though, anywhere make specific the identification of Lucifer with Satan.

Agrippa seems to subscribe to the usual Catholic contention
that only angels of the lower ranks are sent to men; but he does
not argue it (he rarely argues anything), and all classes of his
angels he seems to think influential in earthly events, for he lists
all as instruments of Providence in one way or another (pp.
368-369). He has some rather uncertain remarks about the punishments in hell, as that fire burns darkly there (pp. 9, 10), and notes
from Porphyry word for word in Ficino's Latin that the habitation
of evil spirits is a place "nigh to the earth." Agrippa adds as
though it were Porphyry's phrase — which it is not — "yea within
the earth itself. . . ." (p. 394).[20]

On the question of angelic substance Agrippa, like most occultists, is non-committal, though, again like most, he seems to favor
the idea that spirits have a proper body and appear by contracting
it rather than by assuming a body of casual matter. In his chapter
"Of the Bodies of Devils" he starts by mentioning the "great dis-
sension betwixt the late Divines and Philosophers" and by noting
Aquinas' opinion (p. 402). Virtually all the rest of his chapter he
gives to those who assert angels to be somehow bodily. Of these
the one to whom he allows most space and apparently most authority is Michael Psellus, an eleventh-century Byzantine informed
about demons, he said, by the monk, Marcus, who had lived with
them in the desert. After Aquinas and the Pseudo-Dionysius,
Psellus was perhaps the demonologist most cited by sixteenth and
seventeenth-century writers, and he circulated not only in the
original Greek but in a French translation and in several editions
of two Latin translations. Clerical writers, it is true, especially
Protestants, named him with distaste or at least with caution; yet
they felt the weight of his name, and "philosophers" in general
valued him greatly.[21] To the Calvinist, Daneau, he seemed but a
"coulde Christian," [22] and the Church of England controversial-
ists on possession, John Deacon and John Walker, speak of the
"dotages of dreaming Psellus." [23] Richard Baxter thinks his opinions "too grosse." [24] But George Pictorius and Jerome Cardan seem
to rate him as perhaps their solidest authority on demons.[25]
Salkeld opposes his opinions on substance but without disparaging
him;[26] the famous Jean Wier, who tried to help witches by blam-
ing devils, says he cannot wholly accept Psellus' views, yet later
gives many of them as especially worthy of credit.[27] Zanchy quotes
Psellus soberly, though holding that much of what he says shows
him altogether too curious about demons.[28] Scot ridicules Psellus
through two considerable chapters, digesting capably all of his

chief opinions.[29] Mede, Fludd, Cudworth, More, Heydon, and many other seventeenth-century Englishmen of Platonistic leanings speak well of Psellus on demons.

Agrippa, who rarely takes time to discuss his authors, says merely that Psellus was at once Platonist and Christian, and then scatters Psellian opinions through several chapters until he has expounded nearly all the characteristic ones. "Psellus, Platonist and Christian, does think that the nature of spirits is not without a body; but yet not that the body of angels, & devils are the same; for that is without all matter; but the bodies of devils are in a manner material, as shadows, and subject to passion, that they being struck are pained, and may be burnt in the fire. . . . And although it be a spiritual body, yet it is most sensible, and being touched, suffers; and although it be cut asunder, yet comes together again, as air and water, but yet in the mean time is much pained. Hence it is that they fear the edge of the sword, and any weapon." Some devils know lust as incubi and succubi, "yet there is none of the *Demons* (as *Marcus* supposeth) is to be supposed male or female, seeing this difference of sex belongs to compounds, but the bodies of Demons are simple, neither can every kind of *Demons* turn themselves into all shapes at their pleasure; but to the fiery, and aiery it is easie so to do. . . ." (pp. 402-404).[30] Agrippa had already noticed in an earlier chapter that demons "do disturb men with vain fear," "some heightning themselves to the length of a Giants body, and again shrinking themselves up to the smalness of the Pigmies, and changing themselves into divers forms" (p. 400). In a later chapter, treating the problem of how demons speak to men by sliding into their senses and how their own senses operate, Agrippa gives Psellus' explanation, though without mention of Psellus: "For there is a spiritual body of Demons everywhere sensible by nature, so that it toucheth, seeth, heareth, without any medium, and nothing can be an impediment to it: Yet neither do they perceive after that manner as we do with different organs, but haply as sponges drink in water, so do they all sensible things with their body. . . ." (pp. 413-414). Finally, while talking about men sired by spirits, Agrippa brings in Psellus' opinion that "Spirits sometimes cast forth seed. . . ." (p. 453). He acknowledges, though, that Psellus claims nothing more from this seed than the generation of "certain little creatures," animalcules. Psellus does not suggest sexual intercourse among demons, or propagation.

Psellus is not clear, in fact, as to whether this "seed" is really a semen or is a vermin-spawning excrement; he seems to refer to it both ways.[31] Agrippa ignores the possibility that Psellus meant a demonic elimination, and ignores, too, the important corollary that in Psellus' work goes along with the idea of elimination: the need and assimilation of food. Demons are nourished, says Marcus, "by a kind of breath like the spirit that flourished in the arteries and nerves, indeed by a humor." But they do not eat by mouth, as we do, but like sponges.[32]

One other of Psellus' characteristic ideas on the nature of demons Agrippa leaves unmentioned: that they not only change shape somewhat as an earthworm does by stretching and contracting, but that they change color, just as men grow pale in anger and red in embarrassment.[33]

Psellus' account of demonic substance leads into his celebrated six-fold classification of demons as fiery, airy, watery, earthy, subterranean, and lucifugous. This scheme he had from the Neo-Platonists,[34] and from them or from him many Christian demonologists reproduced it. Agrippa does not borrow it whole, for he nowhere mentions the lucifugous demons, and he does not mention the subterranean class with those of the four elements (p. 392). In telling of the subterranean, he does, however, paraphrase Ficino's translation of Psellus or possibly Trithemius' verbatim levy on the same source or perhaps Reuchlin's (p. 400).[35]

Both Psellus and Agrippa are murky on the question of whether these demons of the elements are fallen angels, or as Paracelsus, Anti-Scot, the Talmud, and Cardan would have it, are beings intermediate between angels and men.[36] Angelologists read Psellus sometimes one way, sometimes the other. Thus the Comte de Gabalis, for instance, classes Psellus' demons with the elementals of Paracelsus, whereas the Puritan, Andrew Willet, thinks Psellus' "fables and fictions" are definitely about fallen angels.[37]

Agrippa's vagueness in this and other matters (he never says, for instance, whether he holds angels dichotomous or not) is, like the vagueness of most occultists, a by-product of his profusion. He has so much information to give about the nature and activities of angels, he so joyfully multiplies names, places, ranks, kinds, and functions, that for him to become precise and methodical to the level of the scholastics would have meant keeping much of his music within him. Agrippa was far too generous for that.

III

If Agrippa's work is contorted by the forgetfulness and disorder that may accompany profusion, that of his English counterpart,

Robert Fludd, is positively agonized with them, although Fludd's fault is not so much in careless omissions as in totally undisciplined repetitions combined with a rushing incoherence that by contrast makes Agrippa's style seem placid. Fludd published in his lifetime a dozen titles in folio volumes, some of a thousand pages, and all liberally repetitive and grandly chaotic. His theories of angels have a sizeable place in most of these volumes and are often all but incomprehensible. They are, however, usually positive in statement instead of tentative like Agrippa's, they show much originality, and throughout twenty years of their publishing they are largely unchanged. Fludd wrote in a period and a country more open than Agrippa's to theosophical speculation (though perhaps less convinced of either its worth or its dangers) so that whereas Agrippa was no doubt wise to be tentative and to delay publication almost twenty-five years for fear that he might shock theologians, Fludd voicing equal impieties — many of the same impieties, in fact — seems to have been put into little danger by his heresies and could be as positive and as original as he pleased about angels. He did, it is true, meet some opposition from theologians and much from astronomers and physicists, both to his angelology and to his whole scheme of the cosmos; but perhaps this merely forced him to be more positive and more consistent than he might otherwise have been.

The opposition that caused Fludd to speak most plainly about angels was that of William Foster, a country cleric who attacked Fludd's theory of sympathetic cures by asserting, among other things, that it contained an erroneous idea of the nature of devils.[38] Fludd had a salve to cure wounds by application to the weapon that had made them; he explained the treatment as a work of sympathy between the blood on the weapon and the blood in the wounded body, and he offered as analogical a persisting malignant response he asserted of the blood in a witch's body to that which her familiar devil had sucked from her (cf. below Chapter VI).[39] To this, Foster clamors that Fludd "would leade us into the errour of *Plato* and *Iamblichus,* followed by *Apuleius* . . . who hold that the Divels have *tenuia corpora,* tenuious and slender bodies; for the Doctor who impiously attributed composition to God, dares falsely (though it be a sinne to belye the Divell) attribute corporeity to Divels. The contrary of which, that they have no manner of bodies, is the tenent of the Church" (p. 48). In the margin here Foster cites Gassendi against Fludd.[40]

Fludd answered in the only one of his works to be originally published in English. He explained that if he said "God is in a composition" he meant it "not as a part compounding; but as the sole compounder in composition," as one says that the Word is incarnated (p. 47). He asserted positively (as any Protestant of his time might well afford to do) that angels did have tenuous bodies, and he further asserted in a Platonizing vein with original variations that they were dichotomous, composed of body and soul, or, as he usually puts it, of *internal* and *external* (pp. 48-55). As an incidental datum to back his contentions, Fludd started his whole argument with the drastic, the almost unheard-of statement that angels could assimilate earthly food. "But if indeed Angels . . . were incorporeall, how could meate and drink, a substance corporeal, remaine with the Angels which *Abraham* entertained? if they were incorporeall, or if they assumed bodies accidentally, could they eate and drinke with them naturally? or was Abraham so senselesse to offer counterfeit shapes, meat and drinke? Surely a man so profound in diuine mysteries, would not haue been so absurd, as to haue offered them his food, if he had knowne that it would not naturally haue nourished them. The same absurdity might iustly haue beene imputed unto Lot." Then, as though suddenly conscious that here he opposed the whole of Christian commentary, Protestant and Catholic, on Abraham and his guests, Fludd adds with a hesitancy rare in him: "verily it is aboue the reach of Worldlings to scan rightly, or discouer iustly this doubt" (p. 84).

Fludd grants that "there are some of the Fathers and Schoolemen, who are of opinion, that the Angels are absolutely incorporeal, as *Damascene, Thomas Aquin, Denis*. . . . But there are as many; yea, and more of the learneder sort, who giue a contrary sentence . . . and say flatly that an Angel is a corporeal substance . . ." (p. 48). Among these, he claims, are Basil, Origen, Augustine, Lombard, Trismegistus, and all the Platonists, and he gives some rather untrustworthy readings of Augustine and Lombard to back his claim. Then he says impatiently — and here speaks the real Fludd — "But why should we rely onely (as Master *Foster* doth) on bare Authorities? I will come unto plaine Philosophical proofes to show . . . that Angels haue soules and bodies, or externall and internall" (pp. 49-50).

Fludd's "proofes" begin with a form of the argument recognized by theologians generally that only God can be spirit in an absolute sense. If angels were "identity, that is, of all one simple formall being, they would be all one in essence with God their Creator,

who is called Identitas, or absolute and simple unity. . . ." They
must be, then, and in fact are, "compounded of two: namely, of
light, which is the beame of God, which they receiue, to informe
them and make them creatures, and spirit, which as a polished
looking-glasse, receiueth the glory of that diuine light, they are
called *Alteritas,* or Alterity, that is, composed of two" (p. 50).

Fludd's use here of the word "spirit" for the "external" or bodily
part of the angel, is troublesome to the modern reader but not out
of line with general usage among Platonistic demonologists, who
were often very loose in their terminology about the angelic body;
thus far the reader feels that he can understand Fludd. But immediately, then, Fludd says that "it is evident that the Angel's internall, and as it were his soule, is the brightnesse of Gods emanation: his polished or pure aery internall [sic], is his spiritual
body, which receiueth this light." The second occurrence in this
sentence of the word "internall" seems surely a misprint. Yet
seven years after the publication of the answer to Foster when
Fludd himself, according to his biographer, translated the English
into Latin he kept the statement precisely as it was in the English.[41]
His discussion, which soon leaves pretense of logical "proofes" and
becomes pure revelation, indicates that his conception is far more
difficult than a simple dichotomy of soul or form and a body with
which it temporarily unites. The angelic dichotomy according to
Fludd is like that which in other works he seems to ascribe to the
human soul itself: a part which is God's own essence and a part
which is receptive to that essence. The angel himself as an individual exists only in the personal union of the two. His "spiritual
body" is his "external" with respect to the informing beams of
God's light, but an "internal"— or so Fludd sometimes seems to
say — to the physical world which, according to Fludd's cosmology,
angels themselves inform, as channels of God's light. The universe,
he says, is "composed of an internall or inuisible, which is the
soule or spirit, animated by God's Word, and an externall and
visible earth and water, which is the body" (pp. 50-51). This
"soule or spirit" of the world "animated by God's word" seems
to be a Platonist *anima mundi,* and of its substance is the substance of the angels: "Angels of all kindes haue their externall
from the aery spirit of the World, and their internall act, from
this externall viuifying spirit, in whom is the property of the foure
Windes . . ." (p. 53). The external of the angel, then, is an abstract
"air," that is, the "spirituall created Catholick waters" of Genesis
(p. 51).

Now I conclude thus: If the externall substance of the Angel be ayre (for
either it must be of spirituall water, or else of the substance of God, which
is meerely formall, and not materiall) then wee know by the rules of Philosophy, that ayre subtiliated is fire, and againe ayre inspissated is a vapour, a
mist, a cloud, and so by inspissation, ayre inuisible becommeth a visible substance . . . which being granted, what should hinder spirits, by contraction
of this their externall substance, to appeare when they please visibly, and
organically to talke with a person, as the tempting spirit did to Christ? and
againe by an immediate dilatation of the same externall aery spirit, to become
inuisible, no otherwise than a smoake by dilatation vanisheth, or a cloud, or
mist made of a compacted, and thickened ayre, doth oftentimes without the
appearance of any drop of raine passe away inuisibly? (p. 52).

Finally, then: "It is most certaine, that where there is *rarum* &
densum, thin and thick, there consequently is corporeity either
thinne or thicke. For whatsoeuer is in his substance transmutable
unto a thinner or thicker body, must needs bee bodily, though not
a visible body. . . . Now the externall of Angels, must be created
of the spirituall substance of the higher world, or not at all: . . .
consequently it is bodily, though of a thinner or thicker consistence according unto the dignity of the Angell" (p. 54).

So Fludd concludes triumphantly and groggily against Foster's
attack on his angelology.

In spite of his dissent from Aquinas on angelic substance, Fludd,
like Agrippa, owes much to the Scholastics, including many items
that Protestants thought out-of-date, such as the idea that *Lucifer*
was the name Satan had before his fall.[42] Particularly, in nearly
all his books, Fludd accepts the Scholastics on the orders of the
angels, both the Dionysian hierarchy for the good and the parallel
late scholastic scheme for the evil, which Agrippa too had listed.
The order of the good angels Fludd gives an integral place in the
cosmic scale by which, he says, the soul descends from divine unity
into multiplicity and then may reascend. In this scale *Pura Terra*
is most remote from God as the lowest of the "nine regions of the
elements": earth, minerals, vegetables, sweet water, salt water, and
the three regions of the air. Above these come the ethereal heavens, comprising the celestial orbs from the moon through the
Primum mobile; and finally, next to God, the nine orders of the
angels in the empyreal heavens.[43] Through these nine orders, and
thence through the stars and elements which correspond to them,
God sends his creative and sustaining light into all his creation,
so that in a sense the angels and the stars and the abstract elements
exist intimately in every man and in every act.[44]

These were, of course, Platonistic ideas present to some degree in the Pseudo-Dionysius and detailed in the Cabala, whose nine orders of angels Fludd, like Agrippa, identifies with those of Dionysius. Fludd follows Agrippa and the Cabala in explaining how these orders receive through the names or "attributes" of God the divine emanation which they dispense to the world. Each order has a ruler, titled *Archangel* by Fludd. Metatron (who, Fludd explains, is the same as Michael) rules the Seraphim, or as the Rabbis called them the *Hayoth;* Zophiel rules the Dionysian Cherubim, the Rabbis' *Ophanim;* Zabkiel the Thrones or *Aralim;* Zadkiel the Dominations or *Hasmalim;* Samael the Powers or Rabbinical *Seraphim;* Michael the Virtues or *Malachim;* Anael the Principalities or *Elohim;* Raphael the Archangels or *Ben Elohim;* and Gabriel the Angels or *Cherubim.*[45]

Fludd gives this list without doubt or hesitation or any sign that he realizes how many more questions he has raised than answered. Why does he call the angelic chiefs *Archangels* regardless of the order each leads? Is the Michael who is synonymous with Metatron the same Michael who rules the Virtues? Why are Michael and Gabriel, who are the only good angels named in the canonical Bible, here in inferior orders? What has become of Uriel, their companion before God's throne and like them (according to Agrippa, Fludd himself, and many others) angel of one of the cardinal directions? These and similar questions would, no doubt, have seemed to Fludd simply the narrow obstructionism to be expected of pedantic novices in mystical angelology. He feels himself unfolding awesome realities in the poor words a man can find; the order of heaven is not ruled by our distaste for verbal contradiction, but in fact appears to the fervent understanding through the very expansiveness of contradiction.

Dionysius, speaking in the same tone as Fludd, though rather more tunefully, had indeed tried to explain some similar contradictions of his own. An angel, he said, might properly be named as of any rank below his true one, since he in a sense comprehended all lesser angels; or he might for some uses be named as of any rank at all, since all the angelic appellations were common in so far as all angels had a fellowship in the likeness of God and in the reception of light from him. Michael, he seems to say, was angel of the Jews and so worked in the world in the sense that his power from the supreme order passed down through channels to operate in their behalf.[46] Of such explanations from Dionysius, Protestant theologians thought most poorly, and Fludd's occasional labors at a similar accounting appealed to them no more. Certainly his attempted reconciliations are not very enlightening today.

In Fludd's scheme the four angels of the cardinal directions operated immediately on the world, blowing in healing to men and good weather to their crops by the normal management of the winds, which Fludd thought very powerful in the chain of natural causes. The four good angels were matched by four "standard bearers" in the army of Satan — Samael, Azazel, Azael, Mahazael, the same whom Agrippa had from Reuchlin — who bring pestilence and storm by their routine administration.[47] The wise man who understands both natural causes and the supernatural manipulation behind them might, in Fludd's view, achieve cures and predictions impossible to the uninformed.

Fludd always staunchly repudiated, nevertheless, the character of magician, which his critics sometimes tried to fasten on him, and he was not, certainly, ever a seeker after vulgar apparitions. Instead of communing with spirits in his living room like Pordage and Dee or certifying invisible drummers and the visible dead like Glanville and More, Fludd simply worked with incredible pertinacity to describe the universe in terms that would link the mystical revelations of Cabalists and Rosicrucians to observed phenomena of nature. The angels he speaks of are beings real, indeed, to him, but so imbedded in the telescoped layers of his abstractions that justly viewed they have something of the dignity as well as the incomprehensibility of basic natural phenomena like gravity and light. The engravings of Fludd in his books show him a hot little man with the air of one stuttering indomitably to make himself understood. However he may have failed, no one can say that either his effort or his aim was petty.

Chapter V

Henry More and the Tradition

THE DIFFICULT WINDINGS of Dr. Fludd's angelology undoubtedly contributed something to the disregard of the "science"
in the later seventeenth century among men of sense,[1] but probably it was less such vagaries in themselves that brought on
angelology's decline than the fact that they could persist undis-
mayed by more orderly and orthodox views. Angelology was un-
stable at its soundest, and angelology as escaped from the dis-
cipline of the schools both revived and produced vagrant notions
and hair-drawn distinctions in a conflicting swirl that signified
clearly its intrinsic unfitness to be a "science" at all — certainly
to be a science of the new kind.

The chaotic condition of the study by the first quarter of the
century appears plainly in Robert Burton's celebrated survey of
it, his "Digression of the Nature of Spirits." Burton names more
than one hundred and twenty writers [2] as authorities on spirits,
writers as various as Homer and Kepler, St. Augustine and Cardan, Pythagoras and Bellarmine, and he rattles off their views
with very little discrimination of great thinkers like Aquinas from
devotees like Trithemius or dull pretenders like Pictorius and
Boissardus. Repeated juxtaposition of contradictory opinions without convincing show of Burton's own opinion or any other clear
advantage in his text of one opinion over another leaves an impression of the dubiety of all. For instance, beside the late scholastic view that devils are in nine orders according to sin and
temptation, Burton puts Plato's view — grounded upon Socrates,
"who (he writes) would rather die than tell a lie" — that daemons
are in nine other orders according to a principle of classification
entirely independent of the scholastic.[3] Burton pays no attention
to the historical difference in meaning between the word δαίμων
and the word διάβολος. The difficult question of the angelic substance Burton beats around the compass. He notices that according
to Psellus demons are corporeal and mortal and can suffer pain
and hunger. These notions "our Christian Philosophers explode,"

79

but "*Cardan* confirms and Scaliger justly laughs him to scorn for . . .," yet Augustine "approves as much" and so do "many ancient Fathers . . ." (I. 207). Burton rushes on to cite these Fathers and other men of like conviction without stopping to support Scaliger and the rest of "our Christian Philosophers" or to say whether he means to exclude Augustine and Cardan and those who agree with them from the ranks of Christian philosophers. Bodin, he says, claims that demons have spherical bodies and Psellus that the human eye can see demons; but many will not believe it, and "if any man shall say, swear, and stiffly maintain, though he be discreet and wise, judicious and learned, that he hath seen them, they account him a timorous fool, a melancholy dizzard, a weak fellow, a dreamer, a sick or mad man, they contemn him, laugh him to scorn. And yet *Marcus* of his credit told Psellus that he had often seen them" (I. 209). Is Burton indignant at the abuse of judicious believers or is he giving us a roguish lead as to how to treat visionary fellows? We have no way to tell surely, and probably Burton himself did not know what reliance he put in Marcus' credit.

When Burton has noted from Psellus that devils "use sometimes carnal copulation" with human beings, he says that elsewhere he will himself "prove" it (I. 209). His proof starts with the reservation that "if all be certain that is credibly reported" then "Spirits of the Air" do indeed dote sometimes upon men and women. He gives some stories from Philostratus and Ovid and from "an honest historian of our nation" and ends that he will for his part "subscribe to Lactantius" that the sons of God who polluted themselves with the daughters of men were good angels. "Many Divines stiffly contradict" the whole notion of angelic amorousness, but he will conclude with others that "examples, testimonies, and confessions of those unhappy women who have coupled with devils are so manifest on the other side . . . that it is likely to be so . . ." (III, 49-53). To confirm himself he cites authorities — Sprenger, Erastus, Nider, Delrio, King James, and other such orthodox demonologists — most of whom belong properly with the divines who "stiffly contradict" him, for though they acknowledge incubi and succubi, they deny flatly that demons are drawn to women by lust or by anything but a desire to damn them.

Apparently, then, Burton not only displays the confusion of opinions possible in angelology in his time but is himself confused about some of the opinions he recites. Once he names Zanchy as contending that a devil might cause a true metamorphosis (I. 208) and again as denying it (I. 211). Indeed Zanchy could be read superficially on either side of the question, as on either side of that about angels' "true" eating; Burton merely neglected in his first reference Zanchy's qualification of "true" as here meaning to the eye only. Burton neglects, too, to distinguish Paracelsus' elementals from devils. Many orthodox writers show the same neglect, for they thought the distinction merely a wizard's evasion; but Burton gives no indication that he read Paracelsus with any such reserve. Burton suggests that Galileo was talking about middle spirits when he spoke in the *Sidereal Messenger* about inhabitants of Saturn and Jove (I. 216). That he was does not now seem likely, though many in his own time must have interpreted him so.[4]

The sum of Burton on spirits, then, is a careless and diverting chaos of conflicting opinions and blurred distinctions. Certainly angelology could make a better show of order and good sense than Burton allows it, but glimpsed as a whole it must have seemed to many simply a jungle, a rank growth far easier to abandon than to clean up.

II

Among the Englishmen of the seventeenth century who preferred to clean up angelology, the one who recognized the need most acutely and went at the tangle most confidently and most cogently was Henry More, particularly in his *Immortality of the Soul*. Although More spoke primarily in this book of the souls of the dead, he spoke almost as much, too, of angels, for his demonstration of man's immortality turned upon man's kinship with the angels, and More was desperately concerned to show a plausible picture of the celestial world.

When Samuel Hartlib first read More's *Immortality of the Soul* he wrote to Worthington of the book that "the like I am verily persuaded, hath never before been unfolded upon paper in any language whatsoever."[5] Hartlib does not say just what he considered extraordinary about the book, but perhaps it was the detailed literalness with which More laid out the conditions of the angelic life, and the fundamental resemblance he found in them to some conditions of this life of man. More himself while composing the book wrote to Lady Conway: "This present world is so full of vexations and disturbances, that I am up to the hard eares in computing the certainty of that which is to come, severely demonstrating to myself in dry prose that the soul of man is imortall and that there are enjoyments attainable after this earth." [6] The "dry prose" More contrasted, perhaps, with the verse fancies of his *Philosophical Poems* — which have been called "in some respects . . . the most singular attempt in literature to turn metaphysics into poetry" — and the severe "demonstrating" with such rapturous deductions from Scripture as Robert Bolton's in his *The Foure Last Things* or Richard Baxter's in *The Saints Rest*. More does not speak like Bolton about Heaven's peculiar light and the face of God, nor like Baxter about "an everlasting Rejoycing in the fruition of our God, a perpetual singing of his high Praises," in a Heaven of "spiritual Rest, suitable to a spiritual Nature," [7] but of "enjoyments attainable" very like some of the joys of this world, and he draws for his conclusions not upon Scripture, but solely upon his natural powers.

More's officially announced purpose in *The Immortality of the Soul* was to "take away this objection against the Life to come viz. *That no man can conceive what it is, and therefore it is not at all,* (which is the ordinary Exception also against the Existence of all Incorporeal Substances) by a punctual and rational Description of this future state. Which I exhibit to the world as an intelligible Hypothesis, and such as may very wel be, even according to the dictates of our own Faculties. . . ." [8] His "intelligible Hypothesis," More thought, both refuted Hobbes's formal claim that spirit was nothing, since it was nowhere,[9] and supported waverers like Boyle, who found the picture they had of spirits to clash with both their everyday sense of the world and their intellectual interests. Particularly to accommodate these latter thinkers, perhaps, More seems in the dominating third book of *The Immortality of the Soul* to bring the angelical world down very close over men's heads and to suit it "to the dictates of our own Faculties." He says that the aerial and ethereal angels — *genii* or *daemons,* he habitually calls them — know the same sun and moon and stars that we do, and the same earth and air and fields and streams with the same kind of sense perception that we have (p. 371). He demonstrates from "natural Light, unassisted and unguided by any miraculous Revelation" (Preface 1) that angels and the dead live not in a timeless, placeless, changeless eternity (such as the giddy Sir Kenelm Digby boldly averred out of his own natural light),[10] but in and around this stage where we too play out our parts, and that like us they grieve and rejoice, converse and remember, rest, think, and play, worship God, and travel through his creation to examine and admire it.

This was a strikingly anthropomorphic face to put formally upon the "angelicall world."

To maintain himself in his detailed conjectures of the spirit-life, More tried to adapt to pneumatology the methods and the findings of contemporary philosophy. He was sure, indeed, that he was writing a new kind of pneumatology. He sneers at the "ridiculous fancies" of the Schools not so much for an excessive boldness and groundless detail as for a faulty method and fallacious reasoning. Thus he derides the scholastic question about how many angels "booted and spur'd may dance on a needles point at once" not because he considers it unreasonable to speculate on such a difficult matter as whether more than one angel may occupy a point of space at one time, but because he thinks it error to conclude as Scholastics did that an angel might have place without dimensions (pp. 341-342). More contended on the contrary that all spirit is extended. In this as in many other articles of his angelology he hoped to be to his time an innovator almost as striking as Copernicus had been in astronomy and Galileo in mechanics. As surely as his correspondent, Descartes, he felt himself to be fighting free of a deadening medieval influence and away on a new and fruitful investigation.[11]

In Books I and II through a series of axioms and inferences More developed a general conception of spirits' nature with a certainty which he thought hardly less than mathematical (p. 5).[12] First, he tried to establish that spirit generically is distinguished from matter not by extension, which he claimed common to both, but by the definitive qualities of penetrability and "indiscerpibility," which were the reverse of matter's definitive qualities (pp. 6-24). Second, as regarded individual created spirits, More expounds again the theory that he had already set up in his *Antidote against Atheism* that they are beings distinguished by "Self-motion, Self-penetration, Self-contraction and dilation, and Indivisibility, by which I mean Indiscerpibility: to which I added Penetrating, Moving, and Altering the matter. We may therefore define this kind of Spirit we speak of, to be A substance Indiscerpible, that can move it self, that can penetrate, contract, and dilate it self, and can also penetrate, move and alter the matter" (p. 25).

When he has established these things by his system of axioms, More goes on to what is one of the most important points of his angelology: "I look upon *Angels* to be as truly a compound Being, consisting of Soul and Body, as that of Men & Brutes" (p. 49).

And then: ". . . herein alone, I conceive, does the Spirit or Soul of an *Angel* (for I take the boldness to call that *Soul,* whatever it is, that has power of vitally actuating the *Matter*) differ from the *Soul* of a *Man,* in that an *Angel* may vitally actuate an *Aerial* or *Aethereal* Body, but cannot be born into this world in a *Terrestrial* one" (p. 52). In all the activities that More hypothecates of the spirit world he includes both angels and souls of the dead as existing in vitalized bodies of tenuous matter.

This contention that all finite spirits actuate "vehicles" of some kind of matter More thought extreme enough to need apology in his Preface. He has, he grants, "offended against the authority of the Schooles" — though he can think of nothing else to oppose his opinion. The Schools themselves, however, "trespass against a more antient authority . . . the Pythagoreans, Platonists, Jewish Doctors, and Fathers of the Church, who all hold that even the purest Angels have corporeal Vehicles." In claiming that all non-human spirits are "purely immaterial" the Scholastics have made a "very hideous Chasme or gaping breach in the order of things," and have laid the ground for all kinds of heretical thought. Thus the Psychopannychites "support their opinion of the *Sleep of the Soule*" after death with the scholastic doctrine that the soul is then "utterly rescinded from all that is corporeal"; and indeed if the Scholastics are right, thinks More, then certainly "it is impossible that she should know any thing *ad extra,* if she can so much as dream."

An important use which More makes of his theory of the "vehicle," but one which he does not mention in his Preface, is to support his own unorthodox opinion that the soul pre-exists. In Book II he explains first how human souls in life vitalize the body, and when his explanation has led to an acknowledgment that animal souls pre-exist he boldly produces his arguments that souls of men also were created before birth (p. 238 ff.). The last difficulty about it that More feels he has to meet is the question of what draws the soul to imprison itself in the earthly body. He answers with a dissertation on the three kinds of vehicle: the ethereal, in which the soul that once enters will stay forever; the aerial, in which a soul may remain for ages; and the terrestrial, "the shortest of all" (p. 262). The soul seeks these vehicles because of a "vital congruity" between its "Plastick part" and the particular kind of matter that it is especially suited to control. The attraction is not, of course, in any "gross Mechanical waye" (p. 263) but rather is analogous to that which music may have for a man. Then, notably changing his analogy, More says: "Where the carcass is, there will the Eagles be gathered"; the soul's "*Plastick* power being reached and toucht by such an invisible reek, (as Birds of prey are, that smell out their food at a distance) she may be fatally carried, all Perceptions ceasing in her, to that Matter that is so fit a receptacle for her to exercise her efformative power upon" (p. 266). Since all souls, whether of men or angels, have some plastic faculty, all will necessarily seek some sort of matter.

In fact, says More in a Hobbesian vein, the universe is "so thick set with *Matter*" that any finite spirit must always be in some body, "for to be where no *Body* or *Matter* is, is to be out of the World" (pp. 268-269).

Later More touches on the grounds we have to think that "the lower sort" of "*Genii* or Angels" are "vitally united to Vehicles of Aire." Their "ignorance in Nature," he says, seems manifestly to betray it. "For it had been an easy thing and more for their credit, to have informed their followers better in the Mysteries of Nature; but that themselves were ignorant of these things, which they could not but know, if they were not thus bound to their *Aiery* bodies. For then they were not engaged to move with the whole course of the Aire, but keeping themselves steddy, as being disunited from all Matter, they might in a moment have perceived both the *diurnal* and the *annual motion* of the *Earth*, and so have saved the Credit of their followers, by communicating this theory to them; the want of the knowledge whereof spoiles their repute with them that understand the Systeme of the world better then themselves . . ." (p. 331).

Compared with ethereal vehicles, then, the airy are not very serviceable, for the parts of the air, indeed, are "so stubborn and so stiff" that under compression they do not lose their shapes but spring back like steel when the pressure is relieved, as may be seen in experiments with wind-guns. The ethereal matter is much more manageable since its particles are of "smooth sphaericall Figures" that enable it to be "so exceeding liquid that it will without any violence comply to any thing." Besides, says More, we know that God's goodness "may be justly thought to have privileged" the occupants of ethereal vehicles, which are reserved for "perfectly-obedient Souls . . ." (p. 336).

The condition of souls in even aerial vehicles is exceedingly free compared with that of those in terrestrial ones: ". . . those *Genii* of the Aire . . . may by the power of their minds accomodate

themselves with more pure and impolluted Matter, and such as
will more easily conspire with the noblest and divinest functions
of their Spirit" (pp. 300-301). The plastic power of such Genii
over matter "*Michael Psellus* sets down, from the singular knowledge and experience of *Marcus* the Eremite, in these matters; who
describes the nature of these Δαίμονες as being throughout Spirit
and Air, whence they hear and see and feel in every part of the
Body" (p. 301).

In a later discussion of the vehicle, More digresses to give a
perfectly serious answer to the objection "which Lucretius has
started of old" that the region of the lower air "being so obnoxious
to Windes and tempests, the Souls will not be able to keep their
Vehicles of Air about them. . . ." We "may be easily delivered of
this solicitude," says More, since "that *Winds* are nothing else but
Watery particles at their greatest agitation, Cartesius has very
handsomely demonstrated in his *Meteors:* Which particles doe not
so much drive the Aire before them, as pass through it. . . . One
part of the Aire . . . is not driven from another. . . . This therefore being the nature of the Winde, the Aire is not torn apieces
thereby. But the *Vehicles* of the *Genii* . . . are muchwhat of the
very nature of the Aire; whence it is plainly impossible that the
Winde should have any other force on them, then what it has on
the rest of that Element . . ." (pp. 361-362). Thus easily and with
no least sense of incongruity does More mingle such diverse authorities as Descartes, Lucretius, and Psellus, and to them then
adds his own rationalizations. The *Genii,* he says, could run before
the wind if they needed to or take shelter as we do — the more
easily because "prognostick of storms" is "more perceptible to
them then to any terrestrial animal. . . . And yet they need not
be so cautious to keep out of danger, they having a power to
grapple with the greatest of it, which is their *Statick* faculty; which
arises from the power of directing the motion of the particles of
their Vehicles" (pp. 362-363). By this power, established says More
in Axiom 31, angels can easily force their way against the strongest
winds. The vehicle is unharmed, furthermore, by rain, hail, snow,
or the thunder stone, "For they pass as they doe through other
parts of the Aire, which close again immediately, and leave neither
wound nor scarre behinde them" (p. 364).

In Book III More explains the daemonic senses in tedious detail, and satisfies himself that daemons see and hear as we do,
though more generously and acutely as befits their superior vehicles. They have a sense of touch, too, he says, and, to speak his

mind freely, perhaps even smell and taste, or something analogous
to them. "Which if we should admit, we are within modest bounds
as yet in comparison of others; as Cardan, who affirms downright
that the Aerial *Genii* are nourished, and that some of them get
into the Bodies of Animals to batten themselves there in their
Blood and Spirits. Which is also averred by *Marcus* . . . in *Psellus,*
who tells us that the purer sort of the *Genii* are nourished by
drawing in the Aire, as our [animal] spirits are in the Nerves and
Arteries; and that other *Genii,* of a courser kinde, suck in mois-
ture, not with the Mouth as we doe, but as a Sponge does water"
(p. 370).

More gives no direct assent to these gross notions; he seems
unwilling to mar his picture of the heavens by acknowledging its
inhabitants thus outstandingly inhuman. He had said in his
Antidote Against Atheism that angels have no settled shape but
what they choose to give themselves [13] and he stood to it in the
Immortality of the Soul; yet he decided there, too, that ". . . the
Genii . . . whatever their shape be in private, appear in a more
operose and articulate form when they are to converse with one
another. For they can change their Figure in a manner as they
please, by Axiome 34." They choose, of course, the human form —
"at least the better sort of them" do (pp. 382-383).

In this form the angels may perhaps eat and drink, though
More must confess, he says, that "there is no small difficulty . . .
whence the good or bad *Genii* may have their food; though it be
easy enough to conceive that they may feed and refresh their
Vehicles" (p. 422), for if a genius works his body hard "it lessens
in some measure and therefore admits of a recruite: which must
be either by formal repast, or by drawing in the crude Aire onely,
which haply may be enough; but it being so like itself alwaies, the
pleasure will be more flat." So he decides that angels "may have
their times of Refection, for pleasure at least, if not necessity . . ."
(p. 423). In the upper atmosphere where the good daemons dwell,
the Spirit of Nature may silently send forth whole Gardens and
Orchards of most delectable fruits and flowers, of an aequilibrious
ponderosity to the parts of the Aire they grow in . . . so that the
inhabitants "if they will recreate their palats, may tast of such
Fruits, as whose natural juice will vie with their noblest Extrac-
tions and Quintessences," including a heavenly grape, a cherry,
and a nectarine (pp. 424-425). This food "received into the bodies
of these purer *Daemons,* and diffusing it self through their Vehicles, may cause such grateful motions analogical to our taste, and

excite such a more then ordinary quickness in their mindes, and benign cheerfulness, that it may far transcend the most delicate Refection that the greatest epicures could ever invent upon Earth; and that without all satiety and burdensomeness, it filling them with nothing but Divine Love, Joy, and Devotion" (pp. 426-427).

Unlike Fludd, however, More never anywhere subscribes to the view that angels might receive nourishment from earthly food.

The bodies that served angels thus for perception and the pleasures of the table varied in "the Splendor and Beauty of personal shape," which angels assumed "according to the degrees of *Vertue* and moral *Affections.*" Even earthly bodies, which are not very "yielding to the powers of the Mind," may alter in visage "according as persons are better or worse inclined," and the same thing is true "in far greater measure, in the other state," where the "outward form is wholly framed from the inward Imperium of our Minde: which by how much more pure it self is, it wil exhibit the more irreprehensible pulcritude in the outward feature and fashion of the Body" (pp. 410-411). Even "the worst kind" of genii — by which More seems to mean fallen angels — "are likewise for the most part in Humane form, though disfigured with ugly circumstances: but . . . they figure themselves also in Bestial appearances; it being easy for them to transform their Vehicle into what shape they please. . . ." They often appear as animals to human beings "that entertain them and sometimes to them that would willingly shun them" (pp. 407-408).

In their human shapes the genii might give "much content to one another in mutual Conferences concerning the nature of things, whether *Moral, Natural,* or *Metaphysical*" (p. 416), and, More says, might even indulge the "Amorous propension" (p. 418); for though "there be neither Lust, nor difference of Sex amongst them (whence the kindest commotions of minde will never be anything else but an exercise of *Intellectual love,* whose Object is *Vertue and Beauty*) yet it is not improbable but that there are some general strictures of discrimination of this beauty into *Masculine* and *Feminine*. . . . Which dress . . . is easily fitted to them by the power of their Will and Imagination. . . ." How competent that power must be we can judge by the fact that the mere fancy of an earthly mother may determine the development of the foetus (pp. 413-414).

The genii, then, in the appearance of men and women "sing and play, and dance together, reaping the lawful pleasures of the very *Animal life,* in a far higher degree then we are capable of

in this World. For everything here does as it were taste of the
cask, and has some courseness and foulness with it. The sweet
motions of the [animal] Spirits in the passion of *Love* can very
hardly be commanded from too near bordering upon the shameful sense of *Lust;* the Fabrick of the terrestrial Body almost neces-
sitating them to that deviation. . . . But in that other state, where
the Fancy consults with that first Exemplar of Beauty, *Intellectual
Love* and *Vertue,* the Body is wholly obedient to the imagination
of the Minde, and will to every Punctilio yield to the impresses
of that inward pattern; nothing there can be found amiss, every
touch and stroak of motion and Beauty being conveyed from so
judicious a power through so delicate and depurate a Medium.
Therefore they cannot but enravish one anothers Souls, while
they are mutual Spectators of the perfect pulcritude of one anothers persons, and comely carriage . . ." (pp. 420-421).

More was here on ground that Christian angelologists very
rarely trod. Opinion was virtually unanimous that as angels did
not propagate, so they performed nothing among themselves that
could be called an amorous activity. Thomists and Puritans are
one in the explanation that as angels are without seed, so they are
without concupiscence. Thus Andrew Willet, who wavers between
a patristic and a Thomistic notion of the angelic nature, says that
even if we grant that angels have a kind of body, yet they certainly
have no seed and so would embrace each other futilely, which,
he implies, we would make ourselves ridiculous to consider. In
heaven is no marriage or giving in marriage.[14]

More, recognizing the chance that someone might impute
coarseness to his conception, apologized for it in advance. Nothing
in his descriptions of the "Aerial and Aethereal Elysiums," he
says in his Preface, but "might become the most refined spirit in
the World." Love of God and neighbors is the greatest happiness
in the next life as in this; among the angels not even the "External
incitements thereto" are "rightly to be deemed Sensual, but Intellectual . . . and therefore whatever our *Elysiums* seem to the rash
and injudicious, they are really no other thing than pure Paradises
of intellectual pleasure; divine Love and blameless Friendship
being the only delight of these places." More's anthropomorphic
angelical life obviously did not include all the pleasures of human
life, whatever near equivalents he may seem to suggest.

Since angels have bodies that are subject to pleasures and pains
and to wear and renewal, have they, then, to expect the common
fate of such bodies, the arrest of death? In a sense, yes, More grants

of some of them. They may die upward out of the airy into the ethereal, where they will dwell forever (p. 522). But no such thing as total separation from bodily instrument awaits any created soul. The world may burn as the Stoics say, and give great pain and uneasiness to all aerial daemons, or the sun may eventually go out, as astronomers prophesy, and leave them in fearful darkness; but always some matter will exist to make a fact the soul's life in time and space. As for the ethereal genii, they are beyond all cataclysms of nature, for their matter is so refined that they "can turn themselves into a pure actual Light when they please" (p. 543), and their "prevision and sagacity" is such that "the least blast of misfortune shall never be able to blow upon them, nor the least evil imaginable overtake them" (p. 546).

So More concludes this "small glance at the Mysteries of Providence, whose fetches are so large, and Circuits so immense, that they may very well seem utterly incomprehensible to the *Incredulous* and *Idiots*. . . ."

III

In various of his other works More seems occasionally to contradict some things that he says or implies of angels in *The Immortality of the Soul;* but he never wavers from his central contentions: first, that angels are purely spiritual "souls," extended, indiscerpible, and penetrable; and second, that they vitalize aerial and ethereal bodies. In these things More had many and strong followers; but he also had opponents — both "unbelievers" of the pattern of Reginald Scot, and traditionalists who were annoyed with him for so boldly redesigning a branch of theology that might well have been thought finished before his time.

Of the unbelievers the principal one to meet More head on was John Webster in his perversely tortuous attack on the theory of witchcraft. Webster's overall argument is often so conditioned, oblique, and involved, that to know exactly where he himself stands or what application he intends of a particular point is difficult; but it does seem plain enough that on the nature of angels Webster was an unavowed Hobbesian and that his direct attack on More was chiefly an attempt to convict More of sharing at bottom the opinion of Webster and Hobbes that angels were material beings. Webster claims first that by attributing extension to angels More really acknowledges their materiality, and then that by attributing vehicles to them he has simply repeated his acknowledgment in a more conventional form.[15] Webster "makes it all one," as More's defender, Benjamin Camfield, says, "to prove that angels are corporeal and that they have Bodies or Vehicles joyned to them; whereas there is an apparent difference between these two. . . ." [16] The specific properties of penetrability and indiscerpibility which More uses to distinguish spirit from matter, Webster shrugs off with the remark that More has not proved but simply asserted them, and has done it in the face of the damaging fact that the great Van Helmont supposed some matter to be penetrable (p. 199).

To make his own case that angels are material, Webster appeals to the ancient distinction that all created beings must be body compared with God, though compared with men some may be called spirit (p. 208). He takes no notice of all the zealous contenders for angels as spirit who had both confirmed and vastly qualified this truism, but infers from it that all "created substances" are bodily. Borrowing from Hobbes, he says that even the particles that carry vision to the eye are corporeal and the images we see in mirrors, though they have far more of the nature of what we call "spirit" than "many things else that have been vainly supposed to be Spirits" (p. 204). If angels were simply and absolutely spiritual and incorporeal, then they would be of the same essential Identity with God; they must, therefore, as the learned Dr. Fludd says, be Alterity, a compound of an active part and a passive, of an *internum* and an *externum*. More himself, Webster gibes, has granted that angels are compound beings (p. 207).

In paralleling More's doctrine to his own as expressed by Fludd, Webster was evidently just playing with words as part of his effort to quote More against himself. However such twists may make the views of More and Webster superficially resemble each other, they are actually far separated by differences of aim and of the consequences the authors draw from them. A revealing example of this difference in a seeming agreement appears in their opinions of the tempter in Genesis. Moses, says Webster, did not mean that Satan was *in* the serpent, but by the word *serpent* metaphorically signified Satan (p. 144). With what seems exactly the same reading, More had explained in his *Conjectura Cabbalistica* that the tempter was not a possessed serpent, as most interpreters had it, but that by *serpent* we are to understand "that it was an evil spirit, not a natural serpent . . . that brought much mischief upon mankind." Why, he asks, "should the Serpent be cursed for the Devils sake?" To "talk thus of the Serpent and the Devil at once" is to

confound the literal interpretation of the Bible with the philosophical.[17] Certainly More and Webster have here the same conclusion, but in the ultimate uses they turn it to and in their
reasons and their demonological detail they are miles apart.
Webster's reason for insisting on the metaphorical understanding
of *serpent* was the same one Reginald Scot had for the same insistence: he wanted to wipe out this classic example of daemonic
possession. More's reason, on the other hand, was that the interpretation suited his characteristic doctrine that the fall of angels
and the fall of man were both essentially the decline of pre-
existing souls into inferior vehicles. More conceives the entire
temptation to have gone on in the ethereal realm and Eve to have
existed only as the feminine or appetitive principle in Adam.
Webster, on the other hand, thinks of the orthodox literal garden,
with man and woman assailed by Satan's spiritual promptings.

According to More and his allies in urging pre-existence, the
fall of angels rooted in nothing more than an over-balancing inclination to the pleasures of the vehicle. The sin, More seems to
say, was not in rising against God from pride or envy, but in the
angels' "wholly betaking themselves to the ANIMAL LIFE without rule or measure." The vehicle itself is the ground of the fall,
for "it is out of the conjunction of these two Principles, *Spirit* and
Vehicle, that there ever could be brought in any inward *Temptation, Distraction,* or *Confusion* in any of the Orders of the Genii
or Angels." The pollution of the vehicle More calls the "rebellion" of the angels; it *changed their pure Aethereal Bodies into
more Feculent and Terrestrial,* (understanding *Terrestrial* in as
large a sense as *Cartesius* does, which will take in the whole Atmosphere). They have forfeited therefore these more resplendent mansions for this obscure and caliginous *Air* they wander in. . . ." [18]

The fall of Adam, More thought, was the same sort of thing.
A tarnished genius called Satan, aroused the feminine (that is,
appetitive) part of the ethereal Adam so that its satisfaction seemed
to him more compelling than contemplation of the divine. The
foul connections created by such errant taste drew this pre-existent
soul into the flesh.[19]

Webster could have consented to none of this; he explicitly
rejects More's notion that the angel is simply a discarnate soul,
the soul an incarnate angel. We can tell nothing of the angel, he
says, by what we may know of the soul. The human soul "had a
peculiar kind of Creation" unlike that of any other creature. "It
is safer to believe the nature of the Soul to be according to the

Analogy of Faith, and the concurrent opinion of the learned, than to sift such deep questions by our weak understanding" (p. 202).

In taking this position Webster rather overstated traditional pneumatology, which did incline to find a close resemblance between soul and angel; but certainly most of "the concurrent opinion of the learned" was strongly against pre-existence of the soul and was very uneasy, therefore, with More's doctrine of the vehicle. One influential person who became impatient with More's whole theory of angels at the same time that he approved More's aims against atheists, Sadducees, and mechanists, was the inexhaustible Richard Baxter, a man who wrote at least as voluminously as More did, and who turned often and with apparent relish to questions of spirits. Baxter had his own works defending the soul's immortality, and in one of them, arguing against Gassendi's mechanist ideas on the principles of individuation among created spirits, he professes to find that More's cherished definition of spirit as indivisible and penetrable is a positive handicap. After a long and involved account of various theories of the angelic nature he concludes with characteristic Puritan modesty that since the essential nature of angels is *"lubricous* and *uncertain,* and beyond the reach of man's understanding" we ought to confine our definition of them to what we know of their operations and not try for a clear idea of their substance.[20]

Later in the same work Baxter lists among objections sometimes brought against immortality that "The Platonists and some Platonick Divines, have so many dreams and fopperies about the soul's future state, in aerial and ethereal vehicles, and their durations, as maketh that doctrine the more to be suspected." To this obvious deprecation of More's ideas Baxter then largely consents, though of course he finds no ground in it to give up immortality. He lists nine reasons the Platonists give for believing in vehicles; then: "I name their reasons, that you may be charitable in your censures; but the truth is they talk of unrevealed or uncertain things, which do but trouble the heads of Christians to no purpose . . ." (p. 575). He rejects, among other doctrines, "their conceit of the soul's pre-existence. . . . We think not that God punisheth men for sin in another world, while he totally obliterateth the memory of the other world and of their sin" (p. 577).

In these strictures against Platonistic ideas Baxter does not directly name More; but in 1682 they fell into open conflict after More published in *Sadducismus Triumphatus* a somewhat condescending answer to a letter which Baxter had written at More's request expressing his views on More's theory of spirits. Evidently More either did not receive or did not heed such a warning as Worthington had once given a friend about Baxter: "[He] is not prone to commend what is done by others. . . . If you write to Mr. Baxter, you must write warily. . . . It may beget another letter in print perhaps." [21] More's answer did indeed beget another letter from Baxter, this time a hundred pages in print, and to this More, as likely as any man to break into print, returned another sixty-odd pages. By this time the controversy was involved almost past following and somewhat embittered, but it is pleasant to see that ten years later in his last book the aged Baxter could speak kindly if non-committally of "Dr. *More's* Opinion that all Spirits are the Souls of Some Bodies." [22]

In his published answer to More, Baxter begins by saying that he had no idea his little letter "should occasion you to benefit the world with more of your information." He wishes that More had spared him the title "Psychopyrist," because though he believes indeed that the essence of all created spirits is fire, he means a supernatural fire. [23] He then starts out, with repeated digressions against More, to justify his doctrine, which in outline is that of Ambrose and Lawrence and many another Protestant who wanted to accept neither the Scholastics on angels as pure spirits nor the Platonists on them as dichotomous, and who thought he found a third possibility in the writings of some Fathers. His stand, Baxter says, is analogous to that of a Dr. Glisson who "supposeth all Matter to be animated without composition"; what the Doctor supposes of matter "I say only of Spirits" (p. 6). They are *"Ignis eminenter,"* "not a Compounding part, but the form of a simple substance . . ." (p. 13). Their superior fire is an active principle, the thing perhaps that William Gilbert calls the *anima Telluris* (p. 38). More has advised Baxter to study Descartes' ideas on light; but if More himself had read Telesius, Campanella, the Stoics, and others he would know more than Descartes did, for a man half Descartes' age should be able to understand that light is not the same thing as motion. "I therefore return your counsel, study more thoroughly the nature of Aethereal Fire" (pp. 57-59). More is not necessarily correct, notes Baxter, that ether (that is, Fire) is material; he ought to be at least as uncertain about it as Baxter is, for he seems to make his *Spirit of the World* what Baxter calls Fire (p. 66). More has condemned Baxter's Fire and that of the Fathers and "old Philosophers" as mere metaphor, but he himself admits that "the vehicles of Angels are *Igneous* or *aethereal*" and he certainly does not intend metaphor (p. 72). If we come right down to it, the word *spiritus* itself is metaphor in a sense (p. 78).

As for More's own notions of spiritual substance, Baxter doubts whether all More's talk against materiality is not just "to hide the name of your own opinion, for that which others call materiality" (p. 52). More says that spirits have extension and "spissitude," that is, "more substance in less compass," and this sounds to Baxter more like corporeity than anything he could possibly signify by Fire. Does every created spirit, as More claims, "actuate some matter or other"? Well, says Baxter, philosophers have much freedom, of course, but "I must tell you that I have long taken it for a matter of very great use to distinguish unknown things from known, and to bridle my understanding from presuming to enquire into unrevealed things." And it is unrevealed that all spirits actuate matter (p. 4). By making out all spirits thus to have vehicles, More seems to Baxter to reduce God to the status of *anima mundi* (p. 48). It is evident, too, from this that More, like Glanville, is for pre-existence of souls (p. 59), a sorry error, Baxter implies.

More's anonymous riposte to Baxter meets every charge, as Baxter had met every lordly correction that More originally put upon him, and complains of Baxter's discourtesy in prolonging the controversy after he had been responsible for starting it. The whole thing came, said More, of Baxter's slighting in some of his works the doctrines of *"Penetrability* and *Indiscerpibility,"* which "for their certain Truth and usefulness the Doctor thought fit to communicate to the World." [24] The trouble with Baxter is that out of his ignorance of the atomic philosophy he has mistaken fire itself, "a *congeries* of agitated particles," for spirit, whereas it is only an instrument of spirits. Baxter's averseness from pre-existence, too, and from believing in the motion of the earth handicaps him (p. 243).

And so these great didactics fought round and round each other's claims, and broke off at last in weariness without any sign of settlement while the whole question died so thoroughly that twenty years later when John Beaumont struck one of the last blows for angels he had no word of opposition in his four hundred pages for any angelologist whatever, except unbelievers like Van Dale and Bekker, because he tried to show nothing at all of angels but that they existed and sometimes appeared to men.[25] In their complex dispute neither More nor Baxter did much service to spirituality in religion or even to the bare belief in apparitions. Particularly, it would seem, More's whole great effort in pneumatology probably confused more believers than it convinced unbelievers. The sceptic who read More could feel comfortably that he had now seen the best face that could be put on angelology and that it did not by any means suit the requirements that science had established as grounds for conviction. Of orthodox believers, many, certainly, must like Baxter have felt impatient at the way that More had altered their old defenses.

IV

A "numerous company of Authors," says Webster, have written of spirits and apparitions, "yet they have for the most part but borrowed from one another. . . . So that thereby there hath been no right progress made truly to discover the theory or ground of these dark and abstruse matters, nor no precise care taken to instance in matters of fact, that have been warrantably and sufficiently attested . . ." (Preface). This criticism puts an accurate finger, certainly, on some of the flaws of angelology; yet when Webster himself comes to write of angels he uses both the methods and the data of members of this same "numerous company" and does it without noticeably improving either. He and More (who was in some ways farther emancipated from the "numerous company" than Webster) taken together are a strong indication that in the seventeenth century, at any rate, very little "right progress . . . truly to discover the theory or ground of these dark and abstruse matters" was possible. Angelological speculation was in a sense like paleontological speculation in the early nineteenth century: whereas the paleontologist was given some anatomy of his beasts but not their functions, the angelologist was given, he thought, some operations of angels but not their nature. What use did the Permian dimetrodon make of the magnificent sail that stood along his spine? Obviously, supposed at least one theorist, he sailed with it, like a skiff or an iceboat. Ridiculous inference, says modern authority. What kind of creature, asked the angelologist, could speak inaudibly to a friend of Jean Bodin and then appear to him as a round, shining light and afterwards as a fair boy? Obviously a being of fire, Baxter would have said. Rather one whose vehicle was fire, corrected More. An immaterial being with power to shape whatever matter he needed, thought Scholastics and perhaps Bodin himself, yielding to them.[26] Most probably God made it special bodies of nothing, bodies which

returned to nothing after use, says Lawrence. No, surely a permanent body, objects Webster, for it is "horrid" to think that God
would waste bodies he created (p. 215). Ridiculous all, says modern authority; ridiculous as much in the data as in the inferences.
And certainly Bodin's tale is less fixed ground to rest on than the
dimetrodon's petrified skeleton.

Bodin's story may be unreliable, the seventeenth century might
concede, as coming from an earlier age and from a man who even
in the judgment of Henry More was addicted to ascribing things
to spirits when he need not.[27] For a firmer testimony than Bodin's,
Boyle and Glanville and More himself tried to collect facts with
that "precise care" which Webster stipulated. They could do no
better than an invisible drum-beating and a bodiless voice that
seemed connected with a flinging about of kitchen utensils. Still,
plainly a being that beats a drum resembles a man, and more
plainly yet one that speaks French resembles a man. This resemblance may convince whoever will be convinced that from
man's nature we may conjecture something of the angel's. Just so,
of course, from man's use of the sail we infer the dimetrodon's.

What of the angels who ate with Abraham, then? No one doubts
that story, since the Bible gives it, and it certainly shows angel
like man. Yes, agrees Fludd, obviously it shows that angels have
body and take food like man. On the contrary, says Salkeld, it
shows they have no body and take no food, for like Raphael with
Tobias they only seemed to eat. In heaven, though, they may eat
and so have body, notes Glanville; the bread of angels may be
more than metaphor. On the other hand, shrugs Hobbes, almost
all that the Bible says of angels may be metaphor; and Webster
and Scot urge angelologists to rest wholly on the Bible and believe
innocuously in angels that are entirely without temporal mani-
festation. Let angels be as remote as the dimetrodon.

The Bible certainly, agrees Boyle, is our true source on angels,
and we can gather from it wonderful things, such as the reason
of the early creation of angels: ". . . man was not created till the
close of the sixth day (the resident's arrival being obligingly
suspended till the palace was ready to entertain him) yet, that
none of God's works might want intelligent spectators and admirers, the angels were created the first day." [28] Comenius agrees
that God made the angels for spectators of the rest of his work
and says that of course angels would have been created first of
things because of the natural order that calls for the highest first.[29]
As from the dimetrodon's sail we infer a service for it to have per-

formed, so from a service which angels might have performed we infer them to perform it, and having them in that service, infer their peculiar fitness for it. But if from the dimetrodon's sail we can conclude that he sailed, why does not the sailfish sail? If God made creatures in the order of their worth, angels first, then why man last?

Still, angels seemed indispensable to top the scale of nature; they gave a geographical balance to the order of creatures, since without them grand areas of the universe must have been supposed uninhabited. The microscope, says Glanville, of the Royal Society, shows every minute region thickly peopled by its peculiar animals; surely then, "the upper stories are furnished with inhabitants." [30] Because the dimetrodon had a sail, God must have made the winds to fill it.

Piety, of course, called forth such reasoning. Perhaps it was impatience as much with such piety as with such reasoning that put angels out of the intellectual fashion before anyone really knew enough about the "upper stories" to be sure what inhabitants they might be furnished with. "It is simply not civil language in these days," says Beal in a letter to Boyle, to refer sickness to devils or cures to angels, though the experience of physicians leads Beal to ascribe many cures to divine intervention.[31] In the seventeenth century angels were better suited eventually by the confined piety of the Puritan and the diffuse piety of the occultist than by any kind of rational piety — Webster's or Boyle's or More's or even Aquinas's. No Christian "that ever I yet heard of," prefaces Ambrose stoutly, doubts angels' ministrations, for the Bible gives them. This strong clinging to the rock of Scripture was still at least formally unassailable in the seventeenth century. We must, of course, Ambrose adds, be neither fervid nor curious about angels, and in this he is divided from Fludd, who also rests on the Bible. Fludd says he is come to prove — by which he means to proclaim, to reveal — that "all sympatheticall and antipatheticall effects do proceed from the secret and occult actions of the ministering spirits of this world." Genesis records a mighty difference among angels: the separation of Lucifer's rebels from the faithful by the interposition of the firmament. The "very Angells of heaven, (which is their externall)" are subject to passions, "as well sympatheticall as antipatheticall," and so, concludes Fludd, are able to produce both kinds of accidents in the spirits of elementary creatures.[32] This is as arbitrary as Ambrose's sturdy generalization and as much less coherent as it is more sweeping. But evidently, as appears in Webster's taste for Fludd, it could appeal amazingly to a congenial mind and might find such a mind in circles where we should least expect it.

The fact is, of course, that angelology was an extremely flexible study, so that unexpected alliances and hostilities are always turning up. This is particularly true in the seventeenth century, when most angelological heresy was no mortal error, and when much that was new had come to the front in thought and had disordered without quite displacing what was old. Philosophers were patching the cosmos together anew; all the seams were showing, and anyone could, within wide limits, re-stitch the pattern to suit his own needs and views, especially in angelology, which was as little hampered by hard fact as any kind of thought then current. Individual angelologists, true, might be uncompromising in following out a chain of reasoning, as More and Baxter show. But the very rigidity of such individuals in their differences, and the number and diversity of authorities show that the study itself was certainly viscous if not fluid.

A person who found himself in the mid-seventeenth century wanting to say something of angels, not in a systematic way but in a way to appeal imaginatively to many sorts of thinkers without seriously affronting any, and at the same time wanting to keep inviolate his own views, could find enough overlap of thought and enough ambiguity of expression to be easily safe most of the time. Most important to him would be a devout use of the Bible; then for detail that the Bible did not cover, he had his choice of dozens of authorities for whatever kind of show he wanted to make and need not care too much whether they were compatible in their whole doctrines. The voicing of any angelological heresies he felt he had to give room to, he might cover with complaint against someone else's credulity or incredulity and with a show of learned confidence that here after all was nothing new or startling.

Just so, John Milton wrote of angels in *Paradise Lost*.

Chapter VI

Milton's Problems with Angels

When John Milton was about twenty years old he recorded in an academic exercise his only surviving direct comment on angelology. Speaking of the delights of knowledge, he listed some subjects of man's study: "the law of the heavens, . . . the changing winds, all the vapors and gases which the earth and sea belch forth, . . . the secret powers of plants and metals, . . . the most exact structure and surgery of the human body, . . .and finally the god-like power and force of mind. . . ." And then to these, in the climactic position that the times often gave it in such lists — climactic, yet with a flavor, too, of afterthought — he added angelology: "whether any knowledge comes to us about those beings which are called Lares, Genii, and Demons?" [1]

By his use of the terms *Lares, Genii,* and *Demons* Milton probably shows that he spoke of the secular or Platonistic angelology, and most noticeably he does not commit himself to its soundness — not even in this rhetorical exercise done at what was perhaps the peak of his admiration for Platonism. He acknowledges by implication the great place and importance of information about daemons *if* we can get any. It becomes an educated man, he seems to say, to have heard of these beings and to have weighed the question of their science. But Milton will not claim sure authority for such a science.

Years later at the height of his powers, Milton wrote of angels as a theologian in his systematic treatise of Christian divinity. He had here no room for doubt that the Bible gives us some knowledge of angels, and he treats of their creation, history, and characteristics with a firm hand so far as he conceives the Bible to take him. Then he stops short with a text often in the mouths of Protestant angelologists about "intruding into those things which he hath not seen, vainly puffed up with his fleshly mind." [2] This text all sorts of angelologists had quoted, even those who pressed hardest toward the unseen things; but in Milton, as in Calvin and Zanchy and Peter Martyr and their English counterparts, it signifies a true unwillingness to go beyond Scripture. Plainly Milton in his maturity was almost as uncertain of theological speculation on angels as in his youth he had been of philosophical. The general principle about the vanity of inquiry into hidden things that he stated in his Commonplace book and put into Raphael's mouth against Adam's too curious questions (*Paradise Lost,* VII, 109 ff.) undoubtedly was a part of Milton's attitude towards angelology.[3]

Milton probably never had at any time in his life even a seed of the wide-eyed receptivity to spirit belief that distinguished John Pordage and perhaps hardly more of the prolix practicality about it of Henry More or the willing digressiveness of Richard Baxter. Just possibly his everyday belief in angels amounted largely to the sort of formal acknowledgment that Selden and Harvey and even Hobbes were not beyond; or more likely it was the reverent insistence of Boyle on the plain word of revelation and the rational-minded readiness of Worthington. But whatever kind of belief Milton had for every day, the work he planned called for him to write of angels, and as he did it he may very well have felt, like Mede and Lawrence and Ambrose, that though a man might say far too much of them, yet he might say too little as well. In the *Christian Doctrine* and *Paradise Lost* he treated of angels as their turn came without any scanting or any deprecation and with some attention to the hoary study of them. More than once, too, he gave a sign that like Robert Fludd he found angels serviceable and appropriate in his grand picture of the world and believed in them as they fit that place, whatever he may have thought of contemporary apparition.

The record of Milton's acquaintance with angelologists of his own century and of the preceding one is scanty. Milton does certainly seem to have known Burton's *Anatomy of Melancholy,* with its tumbled digest of demonology, and he speaks of some of the work of Comenius, though not of the cosmological treatise that contained a considerable chapter on angels. He went through a bitter controversy with Bishop Hall, but long before the Bishop published his *Invisible World Discovered.* He knew Henry Lawrence very favorably and taught his son. He mentions John Dee as a mathematician and traveler, and speaks often of King James and several times of William Perkins, a Cambridge authority on witchcraft. He mentions once apiece Cajetan and Bellarmine, who had a good deal to say on angels, and also Delrio and Maldonat, who wrote each a well-known treatise on them. He speaks several times of Zanchy, chief of Calvinist angelologists, and of Peter

Martyr and of the prominent legalists and witchmongers, Jean
Bodin and Thomas Erastus. He is known to have owned a copy
of Bodin's manuscript *Heptaplomeres,* which is full of inconclusive talk about spirits.[4] He mentions Ludwig Lavater, whose *Of
Ghosts and Spirits* has been used to help interpret *Hamlet,* and
Lavater's father-in-law Henry Bullinger, whose long sermon on
angels had been translated into English in 1577 and several times
reprinted. He refers once in passing to the *De Subtilitate* of
Jerome Cardan, which contains a book on angels and one on
devils. This is about the sum of Milton's sure acquaintance with
the more prominent angelologists of the sixteenth and seventeenth
centuries, and he does not anywhere touch upon the angelology
of a single one of them. In fact, Milton nowhere refers to any
angelologist as such, and nowhere names at all More, Glanville,
Fludd, Ambrose, Baxter, Scot, Pordage, Salkeld, Agrippa, Paracelsus, Trithemius, Wier, Remy, Le Loyer, Casaubon, and many
other men prominent in angelology.

But, of course, Milton surely knew of many men that he does
not mention, and more books. He does not mention Joseph Mede,
for instance, yet Mede was perhaps the best liked and best endowed fellow of Christ's College during Milton's time there. He
does not mention Henry More, yet More was a student at Cambridge with Milton, and according to tradition, at least, they
knew each other. Afterwards More's works were too many and
too prominent for Milton to have been oblivious of them. True,
More, Glanville, Baxter, and Casaubon were active angelologists
in years when Milton was blind and presumably not reading as
widely as once. Yet in the very period of More's greatest angelological output we know that Milton was busily acquiring books.

This was the period, too, of the occultist translations in England, and though Milton would hardly be indebted to them, he
could not have been ignorant of Paracelsus and Agrippa. No
doubt he disapproved of both pretty comprehensively, but he
must have read them. An anonymous translator says of Agrippa
in 1670 that "if the reader pretend to traffic at all in the Common-
wealth of learning" he can be no stranger to Agrippa.[5] The same
thing was even more true of Paracelsus. It was true in a degree
too, of course, of Fludd, and probably of other contemporary
angelologists.

Whether Milton knew the writings of these men or not, he certainly knew those of most patristic and many scholastic angelologists — Tertullian, Clement of Alexandria, Origen, Augustine,

Aquinas, and Scotus — and he knew the Neo-Platonists Proclus and Porphyry, Plutarch and Apuleius, and "thrice-great Hermes," all of whom he mentions.

No one would claim, certainly, from a survey of what we know of Milton's intellectual interests as seen in the record of his reading that angelology was prominent in the life of his mind. He had no ideas or impulses about it pressing enough to send him out into the stream of its controversies in the aggressive spirit in which, for instance, he swam against the current on the question of divorce. The stubborn fact remains, nevertheless, that Milton did write much of angels and in doing it showed that neither his learning nor his interests were unsuited to some of the ideas and attitudes of his time on them. A far better evidence of this than his passing mention of angelologists is the appearance in *Paradise Lost* and other works of patristic, scholastic, Platonistic, and Reforming ideas on angels. Usually the proximate source of these ideas is beyond our tracing; Milton might have drawn from Aquinas, for instance, the idea that angels know intuitively, or from the writers who had used Aquinas before him, or from the sources that Aquinas himself used among the Fathers and Neo-Platonists.[6] We have no way to tell, and a nineteenth-century bibliographer who said that Milton certainly availed himself of Salkeld's *Treatise of Angels,* and another that he actually helped Lawrence to write his work on angels were vaporing. The only evidence for either assertion is the considerable number of ideas the two works have in common with *Paradise Lost;* since these same ideas are common to dozens of angelologists they do not easily link any one to Milton. But they do link angelology itself to Milton.

To only one angelologist does Milton show a verbal resemblance strict enough to indicate a direct levy. Two passages of *Paradise Lost* parallel two in Michael Psellus's *Dialogue of Daemons* not only in idea but in the grouping and order of ideas and even in some of the language. The ideas are those which Agrippa had cited dispersed and with changed order from Psellus on the daemonic substance as simple, sexless, alterable, fluid, and sensitive throughout; in *Paradise Lost* I. 423-431 and VI. 327-392 they are as pure an angelological transplantation as a poem can contain. They are angelology in the same way that the famous inconclusive discussion of the Ptolemaic and Copernican systems between Raphael and Adam is astronomy — that is, such a versified show of "science" as will serve the turns of the story and save the poet from an imputation of ignorance on the matters he talks of.[7]

In *Paradise Lost* it is very hard to know where the boundaries come of what may be thus called its angelology. Not everything Milton says about angels connects with the "science," for some of it certainly is invented to suit his tale or to give him a striking image. For instance, Milton shows us Satan disguised as a "stripling cherub," speaking and spoken to as though he were young in heaven's ways and would develop as his adolescence passed. If Milton had any kind of warrant for this, it is certainly from art, not from angelology, whose authorities often complain of the artist's liberty in showing ageless angels as children or young men.[8] Theologians virtually all agree that angels are not one younger than another and that they do not age. The ascription of youth suited Milton's story, but it is not angelology. Similarly Uriel's ride down the sunbeam is not angelology, nor the tears such as angels weep that well into Satan's eyes. Milton is not giving us angelology either when he says that angels' natural flight is upward or when he says that no falsehood can endure touch of celestial temper. Addison points out that the perfume of Raphael's wings is Milton's invention. All these items and others like them are predominantly literary and so outside angelological "science." They are not out of key with the angelology Milton has, but they are not themselves traceable to the speculation of angelologists and are not speculation on Milton's part.

But when Milton has Satan say that hell is always with him, even when he is locally in the Garden, or when the "stripling Cherub" pays "honour due" to his superior, Uriel, as "is wont in Heav'n" (III. 737), then Milton is giving his reader widely acknowledged fact about angels, which the great angelologists had worked out in all its paradoxical details. Whoever does not understand that in these and similar items Milton has bound angelology into his poem is misled about both Milton's invention and his debts and about the understanding that his contemporaries might have of his work.[9]

Some of Milton's debts on angels are, to be sure, no more angelological in a strict sense than are his inventions. The Bible, on which he relied for every detail that it could supply, is rather a ground for angelology than angelology itself, and the classical myth-makers are not truly daemonologists, though the seventeenth century freely referred to them for authority on daemons. When Milton puts an angel in the sun and the Cherubim at the gates of the lost Paradise, he is certainly following the Apocalypse and

Genesis, and when he has the warring angels pelt one another with hills and the rebels fall for nine days he has unmistakably borrowed from Hesiod imaginative items of titanic conflict and disaster, a purely literary debt distinct in kind from his debt to speculative Psellus for facts about the angelic nature. A notable difference exists between men who stimulated Milton's imagination, like Hesiod, and daemonological authority, like Psellus.

What Milton takes from such sources as the Bible and Hesiod may, nevertheless, have angelological overtones. Milton is tinting the Bible with generally received theological speculation when, for instance, he construes as angels those Cherubim who expelled Adam and Eve at the eastern gate of Paradise,[10] and in giving the name *Uriel* to the angel in the sun he is suggesting to us some much-questioned occultist lore about angels assigned to the heavenly bodies. When Milton calls the devils "Giant Angels" (VII. 605) he is levying not only upon classical myth, but upon writers to whom such phrases as Henry More's "rebellious titans" to signify devils was an angelological commonplace. Milton's expression "Giant angels" suggests, too, the giants of the Old Testament, whom demonologists identified with devils: ". . . giants are called with divels after a common name Enakim," says Agrippa, "because they did not partake of the image of God. . . ."[11] Much of Milton's levy, then, on the classics and the Bible brings him by associations of which he must have been conscious to the fringes, at least, of angelology.

Besides these associative hints of the "science" and the opportunistic use that he makes of Psellus, Milton had some items of angelology in *Paradise Lost* that were a generally acknowledged part of Christian doctrine. Thus he touches on the time of the angels' creation, the preservation of the elect in their purity, the Seven before the Throne of God, Michael as the head of angels, and the nature of the sons of God who coupled with the daughters of men. All of these matters Milton considered seriously in his *Christian Doctrine* and undoubtedly he meant them seriously in *Paradise Lost*. Although in most of them he stood with a minority of theologians of his time, the very explicitness of his stand shows that he considered the cogitations of theologians on these things to be a worthy elaboration of the Bible and that he put forward his own thoughts in the same spirit. He could hardly have handled these questions rooted in divine revelation as casually in *Paradise Lost* as he used mere natural speculation.

Finally, in two very bold passages Milton sinks himself most deeply into angelology by disagreeing on two points with nearly all its authorities and doing it not for literary purposes, as in the episode of the "stripling Cherub," but as part of a serious speculation of his own. Angels, he says and has Raphael say and explain at length, can receive and digest earthly food, and they can make love with each other in a way analogous to sexual intercourse. Milton enters here into questions debated among angelologists and almost unanimously decided against his view. That he is as explicit and explanatory as he is, can mean only that he finds some serious interest in the questions and has a serious answer to make to them. The passages on the eating and the love-making are angelology more pure than the borrowings from Psellus, with which Milton has shored his narrative, for they are Milton's own theories for the sake of which he has risked his narrative. Lucretius is not more surely a philosophical poet than Milton here is an angelological one.

These two passages together with those from Psellus and a few others that run to eight or ten lines each are what may be called the *concentrated angelology* in *Paradise Lost* as distinct from the *diffuse angelology,* which comprises many brief and scattered items. By the freest count the two sorts together probably do not make up a thousand lines. Yet because of the prominent place angels have in Milton's poem the proper understanding and toleration of these lines that tie them to the "science" is of some critical importance.

II

Milton had three general problems with his angels: first, how to keep them largely suited to the staid Protestant interpretation of the Bible in spite of the fact that he needed more details than such interpretation provided; second, what "authentic" speculation, his own or borrowed, beyond the strict warrant of the Bible he might use to fill out his scheme of them; third — and this, of course, was the basic problem of literary manipulation and invention — how to treat graphically these essentially unpicturable beings without abandoning or discrediting either the doctrine or the speculation on them. All of these problems, which his times and his materials virtually forced on him, Milton perhaps aggravated by building up his independent-minded passages on angels' eating and love-making to accent his strongly held notions on matter.

So far as most readers since 1700 are concerned, Milton might have spared his labor on the first two problems. Few care now, certainly, whether his angels suit Protestant doctrine or not, and none whether his further items are authentic angelology. But many critics, without even noticing that Milton faced these two problems, have complained about his handling of the third.

A minor complaint against the angels is, for instance, that in spite of their special powers, they are disappointingly ineffective as agents in the action. The guards of Eden are unable to secure their charges, or the warriors in heaven to damage their foes. The elect angels shrink from the burden of the Atonement, and Raphael's warning to Adam achieves nothing. Raphael and his scouts patrol the mouth of hell during the days of Creation, but are admittedly functionless there, only a gesture of state. Even Satan is unimpressive in his deeds as compared with his words and could do nothing at all without the permission of the very throne he was opposing.[12]

The fact certainly is that the activities of the angels do not seem as dramatic as Milton might perhaps have wished them to; but, as most of the critics seem to admit, he could do very little about it. The angels as deathless beings under God were given un-equivocally by Christian theology generally and by Milton's own stubborn belief, and the idea of God as ruler and overseer of all creaturely actions is inescapable in any story grounded as thor-oughly as Milton's had to be in Christian theology. Even if Milton had found it doctrinally possible to stretch his levy on Psellus to include the Greek's ambiguously-given article that demons are mortal, he would have been poorly served by it, for although a demonic death or so might have spiced the battle in heaven, still the fact that angel could slay angel would have meant that the blisses of heaven and pains of hell were terminable and so would have thrown out of gear Milton's whole purpose to tell of God's eternal grace and wrath. As for the theological paradox that the good angels must serve God though he is beyond service and the evil oppose him though he is beyond opposition, it was funda-mental to the Christian scheme of justifying God's ways: the creature is utterly dependent upon the Creator for his powers, though morally independent in his choices. Milton could not have dispensed with this paradox however desirable it might have been dramatically to make Satan more of a match for God.

Probably, however, to Milton's contemporaries the theology that bound the activities of the angels did not cramp the dramatic power of *Paradise Lost* nearly so much as it does to us. Worked into a story where God must show as a kind of dictator, this theology reduces the angels in the eyes of the modern reader and alienates that reader from the story's God. But the seventeenth-century reader was accustomed to feel the creature flattered by his very creatureliness. Perhaps this reader was more conscious than we of the "fact" behind Milton's story: however much God may seem a temporal ruler in our talk of him, he is yet in fact the infinite ruler. Hardly a single treatise on angels for a thousand years but had explained that the good angels were unnecessary to God, though appurtenant to his glory, and that the evil were active by his sufferance, though against his commands. What, asks Lawrence, can we say that angels do? Nothing, in any absolute sense, is his answer. Yet the angels were prodigiously impressive beings to him. Why does God permit works of Satan? asks Ambrose. Because, is his stern reply, God wills evil in the world, though he does not command it.[13] This dire statement of God's will is somewhat stronger medicine than we can normally swallow; but the idea does not estrange Ambrose, for he understands in it not a tale of tyranny and caprice, but man's poor way of stating the permission God gives to evil, in which he does not participate and by which he is unstained.

To the modern reader, with no sense of a war still going on in the earth between angels and devils, no historical conviction of Satan's mighty counterattack in the Garden, and no custom of looking at events as God's providence over his creation, the activities of Milton's angels are likely to seem ornately pointless, noticed out of all proportion to their results. But the seventeenth-century reader was sure that angels fought genuinely every minute for his soul, that all his pains and doubts rose from Satan's success in Eden, and that God appointed the least action of the least sparrow. He would not perhaps find the angels diminished by Milton's conventional statement of God's surveillance and would have been shocked by any intimation in the story that angels were necessary to God or could act or even exist without his sustenance. For this reader perhaps, the effect of the work would have suffered more from a tactful scanting of the facts of angelic creatureliness than it did suffer from angelic "ineffectiveness."

Whether or not this is so, the critics of *Paradise Lost* have been willing to be comparatively generous about the ineffectiveness, and have concentrated against what Milton gives (too freely, most think) on the "bodily" nature of his angels. In Dr. Johnson's track,[14] the critics note that spirit in itself supplies no images, that

Milton's ambiguously spirtual angels supply some images apparently inconsistent with his stated scheme of angels, and that Milton has made that scheme rather obtrusive. The whole angelic action, these critics feel, and particularly the war in heaven, is deeply marred by an unresolved contradiction between attributes explicitly ascribed to the angels and other attributes demonstrated in their activities. In fact, says Mr. A. J. A. Waldock, the most recent to follow Johnson's general line, Milton becomes so obviously self-contradictory in his account of the angels that in one place, at least, he is "treating us very nearly as morons." As for his general view of angels, the defects in it are so serious and his determination to draw our attention to every one of them is so marked that he deserves our mockery.[15]

This seems rather a confined reading of *Paradise Lost*. Undoubtedly Dr. Johnson and those who follow him are right in a way on some of the specific items they list, and we have to admit, too, something of his general contention that Milton "perplexed his poetry with his philosophy" (p. 82). But even if we meet the charges against him squarely on the ground chosen by his accusers, we need not grant that he anywhere treats us as morons, or that he deserves our mockery.

The first thing to do in considering Milton's handling of his angels is to distinguish the wholly literary pictorialization that was unavoidable if Milton was to present angels directly, from a special pictorialization that follows upon his "philosophy" — a "philosophy" that is not what Dr. Johnson thought it. When Satan expands and contracts himself and changes his shape, and when his "discontinuous wound" closes like water behind Michael's blade, it is according to the "philosophy" which Milton has chosen to follow, a Platonistic-Protestant angelology that ascribed ethereal body to angels. But when Satan walks on the burning marle or lies on the burning lake extended many a rood or does any other ordinary action according to the rules of extension, time, and place, Milton has conveyed nothing about special angelic metaphysics, but has simply represented the angel to us in the only way that the limitations of language allow — in what Dr. Johnson notes as "images of matter" (p. 91). The minimum of this necessary representation is plain if we consider how much of the angelic action Milton could have given under his plan to make a play of *Paradise Lost*. In drama the shape, dimensions, and motions of such angels as appear on the stage speak for themselves, and few or no specifically angelical wonders such as Satan's

dilation against Gabriel are possible. The question of how anthropomorphic the dramatist ought to make his angels hardly
arises; the narrow range that the stage allows to direct presentation settles the question. Angels are *presented* outwardly like
men; they may, without contradiction, be *thought* of as spirits.
Similarly in *Paradise Lost* when Satan and the other angels have
size and shape and when they perform man-like actions, Milton
is simply telling his story in the only way a story can be told, and
the reader still may suppose that so far as the "philosophy" is
concerned his angels are abstract intelligences. The well-under-
stood convention of the stage on this matter shows that such
anomalous adaptations in *Paradise Lost* do not prejudice any
"philosophy" Milton may join to them. The "image" and the
"philosophy" may co-exist peacefully.

When, therefore, Dr. Johnson cites Satan's walking on the marle
and his sinking in chaos and Uriel's descent on the sunbeam (p.
82) he has pointed to no real ascription of body to the angels, for
these things express no metaphysics for the world of *Paradise Lost,*
but just Milton's inventions to convey a picture. Uriel's gliding
on sunbeams signifies not a special feat angels can do, but Milton's
literary device to get Uriel to earth and off again in a noteworthy
manner and to make vivid the decline of the sun and the coming
of night.

But when Johnson wonders how Satan, complete with spear and
shield, "animates the toad" and how the demonic host is at large
though without number in Pandaemonium (p. 81), he is ques-
tioning images that go beyond mere literary device and necessity
and are identical with Milton's metaphysics of angels. Milton had
facilities in his epic, as he would not have had in his drama, for
any superhuman performance he thought proper to angels. They
change shape and color, they expand and contract, their substance
divides and reunites under blows. These Psellian powers Milton
explains to us, and we see the angels exert them. Whatever images
of such exertion Milton forms for us convey his "philosophy" directly. If these images are grossly and unmistakably inconsistent
with each other and with Milton's "philosophy," then certainly
his picture of the angels is maladroit to say the least.

In the battle in heaven angels of both sides are hampered by
their armor. Why did they not contract themselves and slip out
of it? And why was the armor itself uncontractible in heaven
whereas the whole demonic host apparently contracted it to enter
Pandaemonium? And how, knowing that angelic substance yields

like air or water, can Moloch threaten to bind Gabriel and drag
him at his chariot wheels? Milton seems convicted of inconsistencies in the use of his scheme.

But these inconsistencies are not nearly so clear-cut as at first
glance they seem. Though Milton did have trouble making his
Psellian theory fit his story at all points, the particulars usually
designated as irreconcilable are not necessarily so. If we take at
face value the detail both of Milton's explanations and of the
critic's objections and try to make for Milton the further explanations which, without abandoning his system, he might have made
for himself if he had cared to give still more lines to such prosy
stuff, we find that hardly a single inconsistency remains. Although
we hear Moloch's boast against Gabriel, we do not see it accom-
plished; perhaps it is just battlefield hyperbole. Did the devils
contract their equipment to enter Pandaemonium? Perhaps they
stacked arms before entering; Milton does not say. May we be
sure from what Milton gives on the angelic power of contraction
that the angels could flow instantaneously out of or into their
armor? He does mention that they could have evaded cannon
balls by "quick contraction or remove" and that Satan at Ithuriel's
touch expanded like a train of powder ignited. But these things
do not, perhaps, give Dr. Johnson the right to suppose that
angels could perform with quite such dispatch the possibly complex job of disarming. Dr. Johnson thought that Satan took his
spear and shield with him into the toad; but Milton does not say
that he did. In fact, Milton does not speak of Satan *in* a toad, but
only of Satan squat *like* a toad. These vapid explanations are no
more literal-minded than the objections they meet and only one
step more conjectural; perhaps they are permissible if the objections are.

But we have surely to be a little shamefaced about the whole
paltry speculation. A poem on the scale of *Paradise Lost* justly
claims a certain magnanimity of its readers, a willingness to shrug
at trifling inconsistencies of circumstance. As Mr. T. S. Eliot says,
we ought not "to expect a kind of consistency which the world
to which Milton has introduced us does not require." [16] Even
though Dr. Johnson and those who follow him be acknowledged
accurate in their observations, they have not been generous
enough in allowing for them. When we consider, says Professor
Bush, that Milton could use for his characters "only supernatural
beings and two scarcely normal human beings," then the "wonder
is not that Milton did not overcome all his problems but that he

triumphantly overcame so many of them." [17] Milton's difficulties
and his successes alike with his angels are so vastly greater than his
failures that even if Dr. Johnson were right, to stress his observations would be petty.

Mr. Waldock feels, however, that Milton has literally begged
for just such stress by the stress he himself puts on the nature of
angelic substance, that by going to the length of circumstantial
explanation, Milton has justified the circumstantial interrogation
the critics put him to (pp. 108-111). If Mr. Waldock is right in
this, then whether or not the critics have convicted Milton of
inconsistencies, he has genuinely compromised the dignity of his
great work. If the angelological involvements of the battle in
heaven and the detail of the passages on angels' eating and love-
making are sheer obduracy on Milton's part, just his gratuitous
determination to meet every "awkward question" head on, then
he has certainly invited the critics' heckling, and win or lose, the
squabble justly reduces him. If on the other hand, Milton had
in his own time better reasons for insisting on his "philosophy"
than easily appear now, and if the "philosophy" had itself more
intrinsic dignity than we normally see in it, then the worst we
can impeach him for is having written here to the taste of a time
in this radically unlike our own.

What reasons, then, did Milton have for his "concentrated"
angelology? Tasso and Spenser could write long narrative poems
occasionally using angels in the action without any nodules of
theory on the angelic substance, so why not Milton? As one critic
says, Spenser perhaps would hardly have been aware of the problem posed by angels' peculiar substance.[18] Certainly he does not
hamper his narrative with much explanation of angels. Tasso,
who thought himself intimately involved with an angel in real
life, stops for no more than a stanza or so of *Jerusalem Delivered*
to say in the scholastic vein how Gabriel "roll'd the air around
his viewless essence," and how Satan "a painted cloud . . . to the
figure of a man compress'd. . . ."[19] What demand of his subject
or his public, then, led Milton to freight his story with angelological exposition?

A brief and obvious answer is that unlike Tasso and Spenser,
Milton was telling a story that required angels not merely as
"machinery" but as characters. He wrote about angels because his
subject was angels, or so largely so that to suppose that he could
have treated it without some detail on them would be like supposing that Thomas Heywood could have written his *Hierarchy*

of the Blessed Angels without detail on them. Throughout thousands of lines angels are the only figures on Milton's scene. He had to make them known with a certain intimacy and at the same time to invest them with the wonder proper in literature to supernatural beings. He could do neither one without some statement on their nature.

In such statement, however, *Paradise Lost* exceeds not only *Jerusalem Delivered,* the *Faerie Queen,* and Vida's *Christiad,* but most of those hexameral poems with which it shares main parts of its story. The hexameral dramatists such as Andreini, Grotius, Vondel, and Dryden, give their space on angels largely to the history of them, not the "Philosophy." Such "philosophy" as they have room and means for they direct mostly to the angelic morals and politics, not to the metaphysics. The dramatic form is, of course, very likely the major reason for this; in it the question of the metaphysics of angels need not arise; Dryden converting *Paradise Lost* to drama had very different problems of presentation from Milton's. But another reason, perhaps, is that the dramatists did not undertake to tell in detail both wings of the story of the fall, that in heaven and that in the Garden. Milton did tell both, and the fact that he had to show extensively the same angels both in the celestial or infernal scene and in the mundane raised a question of their nature that was not acute for Grotius and for Vondel: has the angel one "proper shape" for both the temporal world and the eternal, or is he to man's eyes "only seemingly the angel," accident, not substance? This central question of angelic metaphysics most of the hexameral poets could gloss over because their stories did not require them to present angels with vividness and prominence and genuine standing in both worlds, and because most of them were Catholics and hence committed to the Thomistic scheme that angels were quite different to the eye from what they were to the understanding. Milton, however, had to tell equally of both worlds, and of heaven through angel speaking to man. This made inevitable some overt notice of the difficulties of communicating heavenly events to earthly understanding and elicited Milton's up-to-date suggestion that earth is perhaps much like heaven (V. 574-576). Milton chose, as a good Protestant might, to unify his vast stage by making the Satan whom Gabriel confronted in the Garden metaphysically present just as he was to his followers in hell, and the Raphael who talked intimately with Adam not "seemingly the angel" but really so, and Michael essentially himself, in the Garden as well as in Heaven, though when he appears to Adam he takes the shape of an unwinged man, just as Satan speaking to Uriel "casts to change his proper shape" (III. 634).

This particular integrity in *Paradise Lost* is not very noticeable to moderns, but when Henry More and others were arguing much Milton's solution of this same metaphysical problem in their effort to make spirits plausible to the newly rationalistic age, Milton may have seemed to many to have achieved a very desirable consistency and clarity.

Sixteenth and seventeenth-century hexameral poets who lay out the nature of angels with as much detail as Milton or with more are the didactics Du Bartas, Heywood, and Samuel Pordage. Milton's performance can hardly be compared with theirs as a literary job, because his closely consecutive narrative has little kinship of style with their succession of disconnected stories set like stones in the mass of a predominant exposition. But unquestionably, as one authority says, Milton did share by choice something of the "scientific and Protestant didacticism of Sylvester's huge translation." [20] He felt an obligation to edify the reader not only as Tasso and Spenser did with the general moral lesson of his tale but by a convincing "scientific" background.[21] To fulfill this obligation adequately Milton had to establish himself as a writer informed about angels and able in the discussion of them. Such validation was particularly necessary because whatever early confidence in his angelology Milton could gain from his reader was going to have to carry the burden of his radicalism on angelic eating and love-making. Partly to the end, therefore, of showing his competence as well as of serving his narrative, Milton borrows from Psellus his widely-considered ideas about the angelic substance as expandable, pan-organic, and the rest of it. After thus using Psellus to validate himself in Book I as a competent authority, he could hardly afford to repudiate his borrowings for the battle in heaven, as Mr. Waldock thinks would have been tactful. The Psellian material is not, however, a part of his angelology which Milton genuinely cared about.

Certainly he did care about the angelic eating and love-making, for they grow out of his idea of the continuity of nature. Milton included them in *Paradise Lost* because he believed solidly in this larger idea which they helped to make graphic. As Professor Tillyard says in discussing Raphael's explanation of his eating, "about the world-order Milton speaks with the serenity of strong and abiding conviction." [22] His words on the place of angels in the world-order carry the dignity of his conviction; he is not insisting on the eating and love-making from sheer obduracy. An indication of this is that he did not, as Mr. Waldock asserts, drag to light every "latent embarrassment" (p. 108) in angelology. Milton ignores entirely, for instance, such prominent and complex questions as how angels may be said to be in place and whether they are dichotomous.[23] His purpose to justify God's ways by showing the pattern of God's creation did not require an opinion on these questions, and he did not burden his story with one. He burdened it so little, in fact, with angelology in comparison with what he might have done, that a contemporary reader who tried Pordage's *Mundorum Explicatio* on its publication in 1662 and then *Paradise Lost* five years later might have thought that Milton had but sketched his theories and had stayed most austerely free of gratuitous angelology.

Mr. Waldock, however, feels that even if we grant Milton's earnestness, we have not helped him, because "his view of angels . . . was rather nonsensical" and if he believed in it that makes it only *"more . . .* reprehensible," since as a "literary craftsman" Milton ought to have demonstrated that "his ideas, when worked out in detail, could make at least some show of coherence and common sense" (p. 108). It comes down to a question, then, of what kind of angelology can be coherent and commonsensical for an epic.

If Mr. Waldock is saying that to the modern reader all angelology that is not pure symbolism is likely to seem nonsense so that our judgment will usually go against Milton on angels almost automatically, he is noting a direct aesthetic fact, which is certainly respectable as such. But what he seems to say in the end is that Milton's "view of angels" is more "nonsensical" than angelology need be. "Seventeenth-century science," he decides, "can do better than this" (p. 109). He is, then, explaining the fact of our spontaneous modern distaste by a very unlikely opinion: that we know too much angelology to be taken in by Milton's spurious brand of it.

The fact is that seventeenth-century angelological "science" when transferred to narrative poetry could not do a bit "better than this." The faults we think our common sense finds in Milton's account of the angels come not from special deficiencies in the angelology he used but, first, from the fact that all angelology instantly impresses our commonsense as deficient, and second, from the fact that no angelology was put together with literary adaptation in mind. Mr. Waldock seems dissatisfied with Milton's answers to the "puzzles of digestion, elimination, 'sex' " (p. 108); but surely the only mortal failure in them of the angelological "coherence and common sense" which he marks as the touchstone of excellence is consequent on his own shadowy pre-conceptions about angels. As for the difficulties on armor and the angelic substance, they arise from the fact that no angelologist reflects in any way very helpful to a narrative poet on such things as heavenly arms and armor. So far as his "science" took him, Milton showed his angels coherently enough. When he had to spring from its principles into the unavoidable particulars of the angelic fight, meeting such questions as whether celestial armor was contractible, he had no longer "authentic" angelological explanation to offer. But he did have a stiff necessity still to protect the "authentic" scheme he had already set up. Surely he would have done worse to loiter over the details of his improvisations on the armor than to leave us in the shadow of the questions Dr. Johnson raised. Milton asks here simply acceptance of his authority as a story-teller, and counts on the reader's every-day serious acquiescence in the generalities of angelology to make his swiftly-sketched "philosophy" plausible and to lend it dignity.

Comparatively few readers of *Paradise Lost* since Milton's own century have either known or respected angelology enough to give such acquiescence; consequently many readers have found the "philosophy" unsympathetic. Their spontaneous failure of sympathy is certainly one of the facts about *Paradise Lost* which no amount of antiquarian spade-work can change, and if a critic wants to say that *Paradise Lost* is the poorer for us because its ideas on angels are now dead, he is pointing to a pertinent fact. But to say that Milton by awkwardness or stubbornness blocked the accommodation of these dead ideas to our commonsense is to slight much of the intellectual history of the critically evolutionary seventeenth century and of the centuries since.

With the material he had available in angelology Milton made a splendidly integrated and consistent job of the angelological structure he undertook to raise. Most of the cracks we see in it have been opened by time and the native flaws in his materials. Not even a partisan of Milton and of angelology could contend that Milton has made the angelological lines of *Paradise Lost* into his greatest poetry; the work does not gain from the facts that most of its characters are angels and that their shifts between eternal and temporal surroundings compel detailed attention to their nature. But if we allow for Milton's special problems and the interests and tastes of his time, we can see that Milton has not bungled his angels.

III

Direct evidence on what the seventeenth century thought of Milton's angels is slight. Most of those in the century who commented on *Paradise Lost* came after the time that angelology was generally respected, so that if Milton wrote Psellian material into his poem partly to gain standing with persons who would recognize and respect it (Henry More, for instance, and Sir Kenelm Digby) then he did so upon a swiftly declining market. Milton was, as has been often noticed, a poet of the early and middle century, a poet of the Renaissance, publishing at the beginning of an entirely different era. His pains to present an "authentic" angelology such as would have appealed to the Renaissance were, perhaps, largely lost in the Neo-Classical swing of taste.

At least two men, however, of Milton's century did comment on the angelology of *Paradise Lost* from the point of view of the angelologist. The first of these was Richard Bovet, who in 1684 sustained Henry More's campaign for spirits with a collection of "well-attested stories of witches and apparitions," which he named *Pandaemonium* out of *Paradise Lost*. Bovet mentions Milton only once, but then with entire approval. In discussing the idolatry of the first ages after the Flood he says that a list of the gods of the heathen "is excellently drawn up by the Pen of the Learned and Profound Mr. John Milton in his Paradice lost." [24] Bovet must have found angelologically acceptable, too, Milton's paraphrase from Psellus, for though he gives no specific credit to either Milton or Psellus, he is plainly indebted to them both when he describes the nature of spirits: "Their essences being soft, subtil, and uncompounded, not manacled with textures of flesh, nor encumbered with solid Bones and Joints; they can dilate or condense themselves into what forms they please, and appear in semblances bright, or obscure, to execute their Airy purposes . . ." (p. 14). Bovet was evidently willing to treat *Paradise Lost* in the most literal way as what some modern scholars have suggested Milton might have designed it to be in part: a blow at materialism, which Milton struck alongside More and Glanville and Ross and the others who asserted the reality of spirit against Hobbes.[25] Bovet seems to have been a man of small parts and little learning, even in angelology, so that his attention to Milton's angelology and his approval of it probably is not much to lean on in estimating the design Milton had for it and the reception his century gave it. Still, Bovet is an undeniable example of a reader interested in angelology and receiving *Paradise Lost* as a treatment of it.

The second man to write of Milton from the point of view of the angelologist was the aged Samuel Morland, who in 1695 gave a page or so to pointing out that the detail of the battle in heaven might be all very well for a versifier or a speculator, but would never do for a literal and godly statement about angels. It contains, Sir Samuel thinks, a deplorable excess of literary invention mixed with its levy on the Bible. His displeasure with the battle is plainly that of a man who has been offered a statement that turns out to be unreliable. He wanted from *Paradise Lost* in angelology what was doctrinally sound and no more; in his view, as in Mr. Waldock's, Milton over-reached himself. But to Sir Samuel, Milton's excess was that of an angelologist who asserted more than he could know to be so rather than of a literary man who used more angelology than his work could well absorb.

Proclaiming his own inability to compose "some short Discourse concerning '*Blessed* and *Apostate Spirits*,'" Sir Samuel disparages Milton to his reader, who, he says,

would be very little satisfied with my Endeavours, in case I should, in imitation of a late very learned Author, try to squeeze a plausible Description of *Lost Paradise* out of *St. John's* Vision in the isle of *Patmos,* and fancy to myself a formal and pitcht Battle, upon a vast and wide Plain, in the North part of Heaven, fought between two mighty Hosts of Blessed and Revolted Spirits, conducted and led up by mighty Arch-Angels (for their Generals) riding in Brazen Chariots, drawn by foaming Steeds and clad with *Adamantine* Coats, one of which was, by a massy Sword, cut down to the wast, and stained with Angelic blood: Where the one of these Armies dug up the Terrain of Heaven, and with the Materials they there found, made Powder, Bullets and great Guns (it is a pity that Bombs were not in use when he wrote that Treatise) and with them did great execution upon their Enemies, who in revenge tore up great Mountains by the Roots, and hurl'd them at their Heads, with a great number of other Romantic Stories, which is to jest with God's word, and much fitter for Poets and Painters, who when they are got to the top of their Parnassus, frame to themselves Idea's [*sic*] of what Chimera's or Goblins they please.[26]

Sir Samuel's remarks have been taken as aimed, like Dr. Johnson's, at the materiality of the battle.[27] Actually, however, Morland is disturbed that the imaginative success of Milton's scene may pass it with some for doctrine, not, like Johnson, that discrepancies between Milton's imagination and his "philosophy" may have spoiled them both. He goes on to make clear that his objection

to Milton's angelology is not its materiality but its circumstantial-
ity, a thing in which Plato, Aristotle, Seneca, and the School-men
with "their vain Distinctions and splitting of Hairs, with their
lame Definitions, and Explanations of *Obscuram per Obscurius*"
(p. 14), also offend. Sir Samuel declines to depend on even "the
Ancient, Pious, and Learned Fathers," for most of them were
"somewhat tender in delivering their Opinions about the Doctrine of Spirits, but wisely waived the positive Determination of
Questions, Relating to the *Invisible World,* and those deep Mysteries of *Incorporeal Beings,* as not to be fathom'd by the Line
and Plummer of Human Understanding." Sir Samuel will content himself "with what Light I can get from the Holy Scriptures . . ." (p. 15). His complaint against *Paradise Lost,* then, is
not that it has too much angelology to be a good poem, but that
it contains angelology that is too imaginative and speculative to
be good doctrine. Sir Samuel's exclusive trust in Scripture for
knowledge of angels is undoubtedly paralleled in Milton himself
except that Milton made allowances for poetry, whereas Morland
seems to notice no difference between *Paradise Lost* and a sermon.

As Bovet is a clear specimen of a seventeenth-century reader
interested in spirit lore and pleased to find it competently handled
in *Paradise Lost,* so Morland is an equally clear specimen of one
who is both interested in spirit lore and suspicious of it, and who
is quick to proclaim it overdone in *Paradise Lost.* These two
readers help to show what kind of contemporary problem Milton
was up against in his writing of angels.

Most of the rest of seventeenth-century comment on Milton's
angels is pretty strictly from the literary point of view — and it is
a point of view become distinct from the theological and philosophical. In the 1580's Puttenham could mark as one of the glories
of Greek poetry that it had gradually come "to know and consider
of the substances separate and abstract, which we call the diuine
intelligences or good Angels (Daemones). . . ." [28] He seems to
assume that the acquisition and dissemination of such knowledge
was part of poetry's aim. But for John Dryden the question about
angels was not so much what the poet could know and disseminate
on them, as whether he could manage them in accord with the
function which sound criticism assigned to supernatural beings in
poetry. Angels, it is true, seemed to Dryden the best kind of machinery, since nearly everybody believed in them; but *Paradise
Lost's* gracious plenty of angels was not an advantage to it in his
eyes but a handicap, for they could be machines only, and there

were too many of them in proportion to the human characters.[29]
To Neo-classical critics the problem of the authenticity of angels
in literature, of their soundness as doctrine or "science," is strictly
in the background. Whereas Morland disliked the battle in heaven
because to him it was angelology that professed more knowledge
than man had, Charles Gildon liked it because to him it was poetry
that achieved a striking picture: ". . . never was scene so lively
shown, as that of his *Pandaemonium* in the first Book. Once more,
and you are no less astonisht at his Description, than he makes the
Angels, to be at the Report of their Adversaries Thundering
Fire-works."

Gildon's admiration for *Paradise Lost* included, certainly, not
only its literary force but its truths; thus he is gratified that it
shows "an *Angel* discovering himself not a little *Man's Superiour*
by Creation, in *Place* and *Power* more, but in *Knowledge* most of
all. . . ." [30] The fact that angels were exalted and truly existent
beings gave them perhaps a special aptness in his eyes for poetic
use, and poetry a special obligation to display them grandly. But
Gildon's controlling interest in the angels of *Paradise Lost* was in
what was done with them to adorn the epic.

John Dennis, criticizing in 1696 the machines of an imitator of
Milton as described in such pictorial detail that they lost all force
of the supernatural, granted that Milton himself had been sensa-
tionally successful with "the Rebellion and Fall of these Evil
Angels, and their dismal Condition upon their Fall, and their
Consult for the recovery of their native Mansions, and their
Original Glory. But then we are to consider, that these Angels,
according to the System of *Milton:* which an English Poet who
treats of these Matters after him, is certainly oblig'd to follow,
were very different just upon their Fall, from what they are
believ'd to be at present. . . . That this was *Milton's* Hypothesis,
is apparent from Several Passages. . . ." [31] Plainly Dennis, like
Gildon and Dryden, took angels seriously enough both in literature and in doctrine to be swayed in his critical principles by
broad aspects of angelology. But plainly too, his interest is, like
theirs, in literary values first. He troubles with angelology only
as it bears upon literary effect.

Dennis and Gildon and Dryden unquestionably admired Milton's handling of his angels in general, and if they find the "concentrated" angelology a weakness they do not say so. But the very
fact that they can discuss Milton's angels without mention of the
most characteristic passages about them is, perhaps, indicative that

criticism was already a little out of touch with Milton's design. In the spirit of the eighteenth century Dennis, Gildon, and Dryden ignore all "technical" angelology; they neglect the Psellian passages and those on angelic eating and love-making because for their time to criticize them was the job of a theologian or a philosopher, not that of a man of letters, whose interest was now becoming defined as primarily in literary values. They touch angelology at all only as it bears upon literary effect, and in its technical aspects never.

A semi-literary man who does have a little to say at the end of the century on Milton's concentrated angelology is Patrick Hume, the learned first annotator of *Paradise Lost*. In his notes "wherein the Texts of Sacred Writ . . . are quoted; the parallel places and imitations of the most excellent Homer and Virgil, cited and composed; all the obscure parts rendered in phrases more familiar. . . ." [32] Hume handles Milton's angelological passages as they touch Scripture or as it seems to him that they are of the "obscure parts." He refers to angelologists very rarely and with evident distaste. But he had to give some attention to the Psellian material and to the feeding and loving of the angels if he was to carry out the promise of the title-page.

Of the lines on angels' ability to condense and dilate, assume either sex, and so on (I. 423-430), Hume gives a verse paraphrase, intended certainly for the instruction of the simpler of his readers, since it does no more than reduce Milton's already plain words to others of one and two syllables. Then he notes fastidiously in Latin that of course some notion of the succubus and that sort of demon can be got from these words, but that he rejects it as alien to the purity of our poet. It seemed to him, we gather, a barbarous medievalism. Evidently he took no trouble with the differences between the scholastic conception of the succubus and the less well-defined Platonistic notion that Psellus presents. Hume does give general notice to the conventional idea of angelic substance when he remarks on Milton's phrase "incorporeal Spirits" (I. 789) that angels are "not cloathed or clogg'd with gross Earthly Bodies, for Incorporeal is declarative of their Nature." Similarly he acknowledges in considering Eve's demonic dream that we cannot doubt the devil's ability to distemper the humors. These and his several other such comments were entirely in line with reticent Protestant angelology.

Hume takes no exception, either critical or angelological, to the passage on Raphael's eating (V. 404-443). He sees it as a well-enough aimed blow at the Scholastics, and he justifies Milton out of the Bible, which, he says, affirms literally that angels eat. He acknowledges the inquiry a little too subtle for man's capacities, but does not seem to feel it a blot on the poem. The related question of the loves of the angels (VIII. 615-629), however, he thinks "curious" in the extreme. Christ settled that matter clearly in Mark 12.25: "When they shall rise from the dead, they neither marry nor are given in marriage, But are as the Angels which are in Heaven." Milton, Hume implies, has most unbecomingly ventured to give a different sentence.

Plainly Hume is pious about angels but indifferent or hostile to angelology. He thinks highly of Milton's poem, and not the less because it contains angels seriously portrayed. But he has no appreciation for any particularly angelological pains Milton may have taken with his work. The same is true for most others who commented on *Paradise Lost* in Milton's century. Evidently the death of some of the ideas *Paradise Lost* is said to be a monument to began to take place almost as soon as Milton got them on paper. However unfortunate this may be for his continued appeal, it ought not, perhaps, to be brought up against his reputation for poetic workmanship.

Chapter VII

Milton's Doctrine of Angels

THE BEST PLACE to look for what Milton really believed in theology is, presumably, his *De Doctrina Christiana,* the private and tersely confident scrutiny and determination of "the several points of my religious belief by the most careful perusal and meditation of the Holy Scriptures themselves." [1] He designed it to be his guide to salvation and executed it, he says "with all possible fidelity, seeing that I could have no wish to practise any imposition on myself in such a matter" (Pref., p. 7). He did not, of course, believe it all alike, and indeed says in his Preface that he worked at his task of applying "the rule of Scripture" until he was satisfied that he "had discovered, with regard to religion, what was matter of belief and what only matter of opinion" (Pref., p. 9). Much of the *Christian Doctrine* is Milton's opinion, largely in form of disdainful comment against conventional dogmatisms whose proclaimers he thinks to have been rashly confident in questions to which no sure answer is possible; he appends his "more probable" answers. Another large part is conventional notice of conventional matters which he seems to suppose generally and sensibly agreed on. Now and then, however, the fervency and fixity of his belief compels him not only to launch spirited assaults on the "mistakes of those who are reckoned for orthodox and their incautious handling of Scripture" (Pref., p. 15), but also to counter them dogmatically with positive views of his own. Presumably not only these assertive passages but the whole of the *Christian Doctrine* expresses the conclusions of Milton's gravest reflection. If, therefore, a theological idea in *Paradise Lost* is twin to one in the *Christian Doctrine,* it would seem likely to retain in the poem some doctrinal status.

This does not mean that parts of *Paradise Lost* are simply versification of the treatise. Rather, as one critic says, it means that some of the things Milton seriously believed in theology lent themselves to his poetry.[2] The fact that they could be thus accommodated, however, surely cannot deprive them in the poetry of

123

their standing for Milton as things theologically true. However
serious he may have been about his invented Abdiel, he surely
did not intend him in *Paradise Lost* to be on quite the same footing as the biblical Michael, and did not expect the reader to take
him so. Milton did not hesitate to invent Abdiel for the poem,
and to invent or borrow whatever else he needed. Still the serious
core of his angelology in *Paradise Lost* must be what he found in
the Bible or inferred from it, and the plainest sign of much of this
core material is correspondence with the *Christian Doctrine*. As
the critic says, Milton's beliefs cannot be deduced from his poetry;[3]
but on the other hand what he believed for the *Christian Doctrine*
he believed also when he duplicated it for *Paradise Lost*.

Now, the special sections on angels in the *Christian Doctrine*
have no hint whatever of the heresies on angelic eating and love-
making that seem so aggressively put in *Paradise Lost,* nor of the
highly serviceable Psellian borrowings on the angelic substance as
sexless, contractible, and the rest of it. Evidently Milton did not
think that these details on the angelic nature could be directly
drawn from the Bible or were speculation necessary to be saved.
They were angelology too doubtful and too personal to him to
be suitable to the profound reserve and conviction of the *Christian
Doctrine*. The Psellian material in *Paradise Lost* is just literary
opportunism, and that on the eating and love-making is a deduction from Milton's ideas on the nature of matter — or perhaps,
more properly, an illustration of those ideas.

Paradise Lost does have, nevertheless, a good many points in
common with the *Christian Doctrine*. Some of these are flat-
footedly heterodox; more are orthodox enough. On all Milton is
forthright, though he is not uncompromisingly positive on all. In
both the treatise and the epic Milton says that angels are spirits
and sons of God, that they see God dimly and are around his
throne praising him, that seven particularly are before the throne,
that the good angels are in a kind of order, which persists among
the fallen, that the fallen can do nothing without God's permission, and that the elect are impassible, although they do not look
into the secrets of God, so that in *Paradise Lost* God must instruct
even Michael before he can know the future. In these things
Milton is one with most Christian angelologists, whether Protestant or Catholic. To an orthodox and instructed reader of *Paradise Lost* they would, doubtless, be reassuring evidence that Milton
was piously informed about angels — as, indeed, he was.

Doctrine to Milton, too, were some opinions dissenting from

those which most of his readers probably held. In both *Paradise Lost* and the *Christian Doctrine* Milton asserts against much Protestant opinion that by the name *Michael* the Bible signifies not Christ but the first of angels, and against a majority of all denominations that the angels were created long before the world. These things could but come as a mild shock to the perhaps considerable proportion of his readers who thought with Andrew Willet, for instance, that to suppose Michael a prince of angels was one of the marks of a papist, or with George Hakewill that it was "most strange . . . that so many, specially of the Greeke Fathers, held that the Angels were created long before the visible world. . . ." [4] Against almost everybody, too, Milton thought that hell was a local place outside the universe, and that elect angels stand by their own strength, not by a compulsive grace. To one instructed by Salkeld or equally by Lawrence, these ideas would have seemed revivals of long-exposed error. Milton himself evidently had some concern that he might lose ground with the readers of *Paradise Lost* by such unorthodox angelology, for in the Argument to Book I he takes the trouble to explain that "in the opinion of many ancient Fathers" the "Angels were long before this visible Creation," and that Hell is "describ'd here, *not in the Centre* (for Heaven and Earth may be suppos'd as yet not made, certainly not yet accurst) *but in a place of utter darkness, fitliest called* Chaos. . . ." The modern reader, untroubled about the rights and wrongs of angelology, may suspect, in spite of the appearance of these items in the *Christian Doctrine,* that Milton clung to them more for literary convenience than from religious conviction.[5] But the fact is that though in *Paradise Lost* Milton does stretch the *Christian Doctrine* a little, (as in the use he makes of the name *Beelzebub* for that of a companion of Satan instead of as an alternate name for Satan)[6] he does not actually contradict in *Paradise Lost* a single doctrine on the angels that he gives in the treatise. The *Christian Doctrine* seems the touchstone by which to judge what in *Paradise Lost* Milton meant with the last seriousness. If, then, he made an occasional orthodox eyebrow rise with his angelology he usually did it over something on which he probably thought any real compromise impermissible.

Milton was able to reassure conservative readers of *Paradise Lost* not only by those orthodox items which the poem shared with the *Christian Doctrine,* but also by many others, which he left out of the *Christian Doctrine.* They expressed views which, perhaps, he could not fetch directly from the Bible, yet which had

wide acceptance among pious angelologists: devils can suffer physical pain and are in a sense always in hell; they were the deities
of heathendom; God created men to repopulate heaven after the
fall of angels; Satan tempted Eve from the mouth of the possessed
snake; angels, good or evil, know the world by intuition rather
than by discourse, and can control the humors in men's bodies to
produce dreams and visions. These things, though not in the
Bible, were generally-received inferences of the most respected
theologians, and Milton could use them with security that they
would be understood and accepted.

II

Some of the questions on which Milton was orthodox in *Paradise Lost* had ramifications that his story compelled him to notice
with attention to details of angelology. Sometimes he speaks out
on these details plainly and decisively; more often he enters into
them reluctantly and ambiguously or treats them with a lordly
unconcern. When he wrote of how Satan inspired Eve's corrupt-
ing dream (IV. 801-809), Milton had to touch on the intimate
means an angel has to get at the human mind: "Assaying by his
Devilish art to reach The Organs of her Fancie . . ." or to "taint
Th' animal Spirits that from pure blood arise. . . ." The general
idea that angels touched the mind of a man by managing its
bodily instruments was standard among pious angelologists who
cared little for the details.[7] In recounting how Satan addressed
Eve from the snake's body Milton touches, too, on the means of
devilish speech, a thing little debated among the pious, though
they insisted on the fact of angelic speech.[8] It is, he says indiffer-
ently, either "with Serpent Tongue Organic, or impulse of vocal
Air. . . ." In these passages, which express no choice between
alternatives, Milton seems to indicate both his acquaintance with
angelological detail and his Puritan indifference to it.

But sometimes he had to fix on one of two theories; thus he
takes the orthodox reading of Genesis that Satan possessed the serpent, not the unorthodox reading that by "serpent" Genesis meant
Satan. Milton could not have done otherwise, for he had to tell
the Genesis story graphically; he could have left Satan himself out
of it almost as soon as he could have left out the snake. He had
to choose, too, between the demonology which said that possession
meant a slimy local entry of the dark angel into the carcass of his
victim, and that which said that it meant simply a chaste applica-

tion of the demonic power to the springs of the victim's physical action. For reasons that were perhaps largely literary, since they do not appear in the *Christian Doctrine,* Milton has Satan his "essence to incarnate and imbrute"; "in at his Mouth / The Divel enter'd . . ." (IX. 187-188). Nothing in *Paradise Lost* is more explicit than this "foul descent," which was certainly part of Milton's technique for degrading Satan and which accords with a school of demonology more literal-minded in its doctrine of possession than anything the Church of England, for instance, was willing to countenance.[10]

Along with the orthodox opinion that the temptation was the work of Satan in the serpent, Milton accepts the orthodox opinion that the curse against the tempter included the helplessly participating brute. The Genesis story lays the curse on the serpent, and unless Milton had been able, like More and Scot, to suppose that by *serpent* Genesis always meant Satan (see above, pp. 60, 91), he was compelled to admit the snake cursed. Scot and More had pointed out the trouble this admission made, however, in justifying God's ways toward snakes, and Milton perhaps felt the force of such contention, or at any rate the danger that in *Paradise Lost* he would show God in an unsympathetic light. Though he seems in one passage to meet the question of the snake's punishment squarely enough with a Genesis-like statement of it and the orthodox justifications, yet the whole impression from all that he says about the curse on Satan and his instrument may leave the reader doubtful whether Milton sympathized with the curse on the brute or has even asserted very firmly that the curse belongs to the brute. Certainly Milton says no more than he has to of the snake's punishment, and his justification of it is a bare and abstract statement unembellished with any of the harsh-sounding analogies frequent in the commentaries, such as one which Salkeld relishes that God cursed the snake in hatred of Satan as a person who dislikes a musician may spitefully break his instrument.[11]

Milton seems to suggest the guiltlessness of the beast in telling how Satan seized him sleeping, and perhaps to state it outright when Christ prepares to judge the offenders. Christ says that Satan is absent, "Convict by flight," and then: "Conviction to the Serpent none belongs." (*Paradise Lost* X. 84). "Serpent" here may mean Satan, and "Conviction" may mean, as the usual gloss is, "formal proof of guilt." If, however, "Serpent" means the brute, the simplest reading would seem to be that conviction does not belong to him because the deed did not.

When, however, Christ had heard Eve plead "The Serpent me beguil'd and I did eat," he

> . . . proceeded on th' accurs'd
> Serpent though brute, unable to transfer
> The Guilt on him who made him instrument
> Of mischief, and polluted from the end
> Of his Creation; justly then accurst,
> As vitiated in Nature . . .
>
> (X. 164-169)

This seems definite enough, and it was orthodox. In Milton's time the medieval conviction that the animal creation was wholly for man's sake was still in great force, so that the snake "polluted from the end Of his Creation" seemed quite naturally cast out.[12]

Yet Milton's statement is curiously ambiguous. Who was "unable to transfer The Guilt" onto Satan? The brute is so unable, it would seem — or is it Christ, who, finding Eve's arraignment aimed at "The Serpent," could not openly correct it to apply to Satan? At any rate, the passage goes on to explain that Adam's and Eve's understanding of the curse as only upon the brute was a consequence of their being as yet uninstructed:

> . . . more to know
> Concern'd not Man (since he no further knew)
> Nor alter'd his offence; yet God at last
> To Satan first in sin his doom appli'd,
> Though in mysterious terms, judg'd as then best:
> And on the Serpent thus his curse let fall.
>
> (X. 169-174)

The curse itself Milton then paraphrases from Genesis, and like Genesis he marks no distinction of what the commentators usually conceived to be its two parts: that which condemned the beast-serpent to crawl and eat dust and that which condemned the devil-serpent to exchange bruises with the seed of Eve.[13] That Milton had this division in mind appears, though, when Satan reports to hell:

> True is, mee also he hath judg'd, or rather
> Mee not, but the brute Serpent in whose shape
> Man I deceiv'd: that which to me belongs,
> Is enmity, which he will put between
> Mee and Mankind; I am to bruise his heel;
> His seed, when is not set, shall bruise my head.
>
> (X. 494-499)

Immediately, though Satan finds that the first part also of the curse belongs to him: "down he fell, / A monstrous Serpent on

his Belly prone . . . punisht in the shape he sinn'd / According
to his doom . . ." (X. 513-517). Evidently the whole "doom" which
Christ pronounced "in mysterious terms" was aimed at Satan.

This cannot mean, of course, that Milton allowed the brute
exempt, for after the fall it went "with indented wave, Prone on
the ground," (IX. 496-497) and no doubt ate dust as the doom
had it. The brute suffered, then, beyond the general disability
common to all nature after the fall; but Milton did refrain from
aggravating his stern problem of justifying God's ways by stress
on the special pains decreed to the helpless snake, who had slept
"Fearless unfear'd" (IX. 187) when Satan seized him.

An orthodox stand which Milton could take more gracefully
than that about the serpent but on which he has been much mis-
understood, concerned the ancient question of the sons of God
who, according to Genesis 6, visited the daughters of men and
begot giants. The Book of Enoch had explained the fall of angels
out of this episode, understanding "sons of God" to designate
good angels seduced by fleshly pleasures. Many ante-Nicene Fathers subscribed to this interpretation, but St. Augustine made
authoritative the less spectacular view that these sons of God were
the merely human descendants of Seth, and Augustine's reading
was authoritative in the seventeenth century among both Protestants and Catholics.[14] It was so firmly established, in fact, that
George Hakewill, citing examples of great men's errors, could list
the older opinion with confident astonishment that holy Fathers
had countenanced such superstition,[15] and Milton, discrediting
Justin Martyr for purposes of his contentions against episcopacy,
could point with contempt at Justin's support of it.[16] In Paradise
Lost when Michael shows Adam a vision of the daughters of men
seducing the sons of God, the event both as Adam sees it and as
Michael explains it conforms to the Augustinian reading of Genesis. The seduced were not angels but the godly progeny of Seth,
"whose lives / Religious titl'd them the Sons of God" (XI. 623),
and whose offspring were "Giants of mighty Bone . . ." (XI. 642).
Earlier in Paradise Lost, too, when the naked Eve serves Raphael
at table Milton says

> . . . if ever, then
> Then had the Sons of God excuse to have bin
> Enamour'd at that sight; but in those hearts
> Love unlibidinous reign'd. . . .   (V. 446-449)

Plainly Milton rejects in Paradise Lost the ancient view that good
angels were corrupted by the beauty of women.

A prominent modern editor, however, supposes that in these lines on Eve and Raphael "Milton interpreted the 'sons of God' as the fallen angels" and that he does the same in *Paradise Regained*, II, 179.[17] If this is so, then Milton's stand in Book XI of *Paradise Lost* expresses a conviction which he held most lightly, since he so easily subverted it in *Paradise Regained* for poetic purposes.

But the passage in *Paradise Lost* on Eve and Raphael does not in fact say a word about evil angels as the sons of God, but merely that the sons of God (obviously here Raphael and his fellow elect angels) were never ensnared by women, because the love they knew was unlibidinous. This in itself entirely suits the orthodox interpretation of Genesis 6 — and the line in *Paradise Regained*, properly interpreted, suits it too. In *Paradise Regained* the line occurs when the powers of hell have gathered to find a stratagem against Christ; the first suggestion is Belial's to put women in his eye. Satan replies scornfully that Belial speaks out of his own weakness:

> Before the flood thou with thy lusty crew
> False titl'd sons of God, roaming the earth
> Cast wanton eyes on the daughters of men,
> And coupl'd with them, and begot a race.
>   (II. 178-181)

This speech does not say that the sons of God in Genesis 6 were fallen angels, but rather as plainly as Milton can put it that the fallen angels who trafficked with women are miscalled sons of God; they are "False titl'd Sons of God" and so are not referred to in Genesis 6 at all. The passage is no contradiction of Milton's orthodox interpretation in *Paradise Lost* XI, but rather asserts that the work of angels with women, though it took place, is wrongly connected with the verse in Genesis. When Milton has Satan say that Belial is "False titled" a son of God, he means that Belial is not a son of God and should not be confused with sons of God, though like those sons of God who were Seth's, he did couple with daughters of men.

Who, then, is guilty of this false titling? Evidently Belial himself and his associates, to acquire credit for their lusts and their progeny or to lead men to faulty exegesis. Or perhaps the false titlers are the exegetes themselves who went so far astray as to think that Genesis described Belial's activities. Either way, Milton does not alter his stand that the sons of God in Genesis 6 are Seth's. Satan's words in *Paradise Regained* are simply an intima-

tion of how, in Satan's view and in Milton's, the unorthodox interpretation arose. With his deliberate qualification "False titl'd"
Milton did his best to clear himself of just the accusation of inconsistency which commentators have made against him and to
prevent just the confusion into which they have fallen. Aware of
so much that was heterodox in his angelology, Milton might have
been discouraged to think that one of his plainest and most consistent adherences to orthodoxy could be misread as it has been.

III

On the three principal angelological controversies between
Protestants and Catholics (those on worship of angels, the personal guardian, and the Dionysian orders) Milton does not have
to commit himself very deeply in *Paradise Lost,* and he seems willing to let them go without joining the arguments directly,
although his personal views were probably Protestant. In the
Christian Doctrine he is bluntly anti-Catholic on the question of
worship, for instance, saying flatly that "papists err . . . in worship
paid to angels," and then again attacking the "subterfuges by
which the Papists defend the worship of saints and angels . . ."
(II. v. 145). In *Paradise Lost,* however, he says nothing explicit,
though Adam twice reverences angels, "as to superior Nature,
bowing low." Such reverence Protestants acknowledged proper,
but carefully distinguished from the lesser worship which Catholics approved to angels under the name of *doulia.* (See above
pp. 12, 49.) In his account of Adam's courtesies to Raphael and
Michael, Milton does not insist on the distinction, does not take
the opportunity, as he took some others, to digress against Cath-
olicism.

We have no way to tell surely whether the merely tacit service
in *Paradise Lost* to this Protestant opinion represents any studied
restraint on Milton's part, any decision to refrain his partisan
views for the sake of peace with all his audience on so tender and,
for the poem, unimportant a question. But the fact is, nevertheless, that on the other two questions also he takes no partisan stand
in *Paradise Lost,* although on these too he was almost certainly
of the usual Protestant opinion. In the track of Calvin, Zanchy,
Peter Martyr, Lawrence, Ambrose, and most other Protestant
angelologists admired in England by the godly, he notes in the
Christian Doctrine that the ministry of angels is "especially to
believers," and he quotes the text on which these Protestants
always rest: "are they not all ministering spirits, sent forth to

minister for them who shall be heirs of salvation?" (I. ix, 101).
Like these Protestants, too, Milton acknowledges no particular
assignment of angels, except those to attend religious assemblies
and those to preside over nations. He probably agreed with Calvin,
who said ". . . whether to euerie of the faithfull be a seuerall
Angell assigned for their defence, I dare not certainely affirme. . . .
For if this do not content a man, that all degrees of the armie of
heauen do watch for his safetie, I do not see what he can be the
better, if he understand that there is one Angell peculiarly appointed to keepe him." [18] In *Comus* the Elder Brother is secure
in his faith that "A thousand liveried Angels lacky" his chaste
sister (1. 450), and Milton seems careful to show in the opening
speech of the attendant Spirit that it is not permanent or single
in its assignment to the Lady but descends for the special occasion.

It is true, as Mr. C. S. Lewis points out in arguing for a Platonistic element in the angelology of *Paradise Lost,* that the attendant Spirit is significantly called *Daemon* in the Cambridge
Manuscript.[19] Undoubtedly Milton remembered the Platonists on
guardians. But it is equally significant that he did not retain
Daemon in the published version. He seems to have surrendered
whatever extra grace might be thought to go with the pagan term
in order to keep the Protestant idea uninfected.

It is true, too, that Milton used the Catholic idea of guardians
in a Latin Epigram to Leonora Baroni: "An angel each man —
such be your belief, ye peoples — / has as his lot, a winged angel
from the heavenly ranks," [20] but no more can be made of it than
a fanciful compliment to Leonora's voice. In *Paradise Lost* Milton
twice makes comparisons that involve Jacob's "Guardians bright"
(III, 512, XI, 215), but not in such a way as to indicate that he
thought this assignment of angels to be routine for Jacob or for
the rest of mankind. Most pointedly Milton does not mention in
Paradise Lost the angel Raziel, whom Cabalistic tradition named
as Adam's,[21] and he does give Adam two different angels sent to
him for two different jobs. On the whole, then, his poetry duplicates the reserve of the *Christian Doctrine* on the guardian, though
without any open flouting of other opinion.

This is the pattern, too, of what Milton has to say in *Paradise
Lost* on the angelic orders. He is not exact about them nor combative and uses a terminology that is familiar and traditionally
appealing to all, yet is offensive to no one, and is serviceable to
the turns of his story. If he goes perhaps a little beyond what he
gives in the *Christian Doctrine,* one has to look hard to see it.

In the *Christian Doctrine* Milton is not voluminous, certainly, on the orders. In his first section on angels he says simply that they "are distinguished from one another by offices and degrees" (I. ix, 111). Among his proof texts are those on which Dionysius and most other constructors of angelic hierarchy had chiefly relied — Colossians 1.16, Ephesians 1.21, 3.10, and 6.12, Genesis 3.24, Isaiah 6.2 — and they supply the names *Seraphim, Cherubim, Thrones, Dominions, Virtues, Powers, Principalities,* and *Angels.*[22] All of these but *Seraphim* and *Cherubim* are from the New Testament. Nowhere in the proof texts or in the *Christian Doctrine* or in any of Milton's prose is the least statement on the proper arrangement of these "orders," and conspicuously missing from among them is *Archangels,* the order which Dionysius put next to the end between Principalities and Angels in the above list. Milton himself never mentions Archangels anywhere outside of *Paradise Lost* except once to quote I Thessalonians 4.16.

In *Paradise Lost,* of course, Milton uses the word *Archangel* repeatedly, and commentators have assumed that he meant it to designate an order.[23] The fact is, however, that he probably uses it to distinguish "offices," not "degrees." In every appearance in *Paradise Lost* it may best be taken as a title of high command or special mission. If this was Milton's intention, it was in accord with the express judgment of most pious Protestant writers. The function of Archangels, says Joseph Mede, is "to be Rulers and Princes of the whole Angelical host. . . ."[24] Gervase Babington thinks that the name "signifieth a deputation to some high and difficult worke . . ."[25] and Heinrich Bullinger says that angels are called archangels, when they are "sent in message in God's greatest matters. . . ."[26] Such is the opinion also of Gumbledon, Zanchy, Peter Martyr, and many other Protestant exegetes who are most dubious of Dionysius' assertion that *Archangel* is one among nine graded terms for angelic orders.

In *Paradise Lost* Milton names only Satan, Uriel, Raphael, and Michael as archangels.[27] The three good angels of the list all have special worldly missions — Uriel to be regent of the sun, and the others to convey God's messages to Adam — but plainly they have a rank in heaven as archangels aside from these missions. Michael, at least, is "The great Arch-Angel" (VI. 257) during the battle in heaven, and Satan before his fall was "of the first, / If not the first Arch-Angel" (V. 660) in heaven. In these uses the term seems to show personal rank, not simply membership in an order. The only passage in *Paradise Lost* that might be read to signify an archangelic order is that which tells the effects of Satan's artillery on Michael's followers: ". . . down they fell By thousands, Angel on Arch-Angel rowl'd . . ." (VI. 594). But even here the meaning of "Arch-Angel" may perfectly well be simply "superior angel."

On the other hand, Milton never expressly denies the archangelic order, and the other eight terms that Dionysius used for orders Milton seems to use for them too. He mentions Nisroch as "of Principalities the prime" (VI. 447), and Zophiel as "of Cherubim the swiftest wing" (VI. 535). God puts "Thrones, Princedoms, Powers, Dominions" (III. 320) under Christ, and "Cherub and Seraph, Potentates and Thrones / And Vertues" (VII. 196-197) are about him when he goes to creation. Satan addresses "Thrones, Dominations, Princedoms, Vertues, Powers" (X. 460). Raphael speaks of "Standards and Gonfalons" that "for the distinction serve / Of Hierarchies, of Orders, and Degrees" (V. 590-591), and he seems to indicate the Dionysian division into three hierarchies of three with the phrase "Seraphim and Potentates and Thrones / In their triple degrees" (V. 749-750). Milton speaks of "Scepter'd Angels" to whom God gave power "to rule, / Each in his Hierarchie, the Orders bright" (I. 737), and he even hints that his top two ranks are as Dionysius gives them: "The great Seraphic Lords and Cherubim" (I. 794) sit in hell's council uncontracted while the lesser devils swarm reduced in the outer courts.

All of these things suggest the Dionysian scheme, but notoriously Milton uses the terms of rank so fluidly that no one has been able to organize his use into a consistent pattern. Although he mentions Beelzebub, Gabriel, Zephon, Ithuriel, Zophiel, and Uzziel only as Cherubim, Abdiel only as Seraph, and Nisroc only as Principality, he names Raphael once as Seraph (V. 277) and again as Virtue (V. 371), and to the rest of the great spirits — Satan, Gabriel, Uriel, Michael — he applies only the general term *angel* or the special title *Archangel*. Adam speculating on Michael's rank names only Potentates and Thrones (XI. 231-232). God bids Michael to choose "from among the Cherubim" a force to dispossess Adam and Eve (XI. 100), and it is Cherubim that finally do the job with the "brandisht Sword of God before them" (XII. 628); but once Milton refers to Michael's band as *Powers* (XI. 221). The term here has not necessarily a hierarchical signification, perhaps, any more than Michael's later reference to them just as *Guards* (XII. 590). Satan's first call to his followers is "Princes, Potentates, Warriors . . ." (I. 315). Gabriel as leader of the angelic guard is simply "Chief" (IV. 550, 864), though his detail is "the Cherubim" (IV. 778). Obviously Milton sometimes uses the hierarchical terms virtually without hierarchical meaning, since he can mix them easily with such variations as *Chief, Guard, Warriors, Armies, Sanctities, Ardors*.[28] When he seems closest to Dionysius he is yet careful not to join him. Thus when he names three orders "In their triple degrees," he selects not the commanding orders of each hierarchy (Seraphim, Dominations, Principalities) but a mixture, "Seraphim, and Potentates and Thrones" (V. 749-750). The meter governs in such enumerations, of course, except that Milton never lets it produce a plainly Dionysian array.

Both Milton's flirting with the Dionysian orders and his evasions are entirely in the Protestant tradition. Babington, Willet, Perkins, Hall, Mede, Bullinger, Ainsworth, Zanchy, Peter Martyr, and dozens of others admit that the diversity of names in the Bible argues divers orders; but all of them reject Dionysius and his detailed distinction of exactly nine degrees in three hierarchies. Andrew Willet argues that if we were to accept Dionysius, Michael could not be the ranking angel of heaven, for he would have to be a Seraph, whereas Scripture calls him only Archangel.[29] And so in *Paradise Lost* he is Archangel and ranking angel, but never Seraph. Salkeld opposes Dionysius' claim that angels of the top three ranks only attend the Throne of God and are never sent to men, by pointing to the Seraph who brought the lighted coal for the lips of Isaiah. Dionysius had been explicit that this Seraph was not of the superior order, though in a sense properly called by its name, but *Paradise Lost* has no indication of appeal to this rationalization on how an angel could be a Seraph yet not be one. Milton's Seraph, Raphael, is unmistakably from before the throne of God.

Some scholars have argued that in using the terms of rank very generally and in naming individual angels under more than one order Milton was availing himself of Dionysius' principle that an angel might properly be attributed to any rank lower than his own and that all angelic appellations were common in so far as all angels had a fellowship in the likeness of God and in the reception of light from him.[30] But plainly the authority Milton depended on was nearer to him in both time and temper than Dionysius was. No one can show, says Mede, voicing the view general among Protestants, that "some of these names concur not, as Angels to be a common name to all the rest. . . ."[31] Salkeld and Zanchy and many others agree that the term *angel* is general (it

is so used almost invariably in *Paradise Lost*) and that the others
overlap in ways we cannot distinguish.[32]

In one or two things Milton did go a little further toward
Dionysius than the stricter Protestant angelologists might approve.
Zanchy and Babington and John Deacon and his collaborator,
John Walker, do not, for instance, allow *Seraphim* and *Cherubim*
as of orders at all, and Willet thinks that to extend these terms to
apply to fallen angels is actual blasphemy, since the Bible uses
them only of heavenly beings.[33] The fact that Milton did not follow the strictest Protestant usage and that unlike the partisan
Catholic, Vondel, he nowhere interrupted his story with exposition on the orders, perhaps indicates a conciliatory attitude on his
part, or at least a wish to use the Dionysian tradition for poetic
purposes without assenting to the Dionysian doctrine. His achieve-
ment with the hierarchical terms in *Paradise Lost* is a sort of general allusiveness that does not seriously exceed what Protestants
would accept nor yet fall wholly short of what Catholics claimed.
The notable thing about his handling of the terms of angelic rank
is not a Puritan bluntness, the flat dismissal of a controversial
tradition, nor yet any detailed justification from the tradition,
but an adroit use of its terms without undue recognition of
authority in it.

IV

In thus making great use of the terms of angelic rank without
committing himself explicitly to any school of thought about them
Milton was following a discreet literary method of indefiniteness
which many commentators think he would have been well advised
to follow also on the terms of angelic substance, and which some
have thought that he did actually follow, at least to the extent of
leaving us uncertain in *Paradise Lost* whether he conceived of
angelic substance as purely spiritual in the Thomistic sense or as
some sort of tenuous body. He does speak repeatedly of the angels
as *pure spirits, intelligential substances,* and the like, and Raphael
tells Adam that he can describe the war in heaven only by likening
"spiritual to corporal forms" (V. 573) — a stipulation sometimes
taken to express Milton's whole solution of the problem of nar-
rating the doings of angels. Milton conceived those beings, the
theory is, as in themselves abstract; but, like Raphael, he put them
into metaphor. Against this view, however, is the fact that Milton
does not seem to speak metaphorically when he describes, for instance, the devils contracting themselves to enter Pandaemonium

(I. 777-792), or to conceive the angels as abstract beings when he has Raphael assimilate human food and appear to Adam and Eve in his proper person, not "in mist" (V. 435). Another interpretation, then, is that either deliberately to meet the varying stresses of his long poem or by oversight Milton split his conception of angelic substance between the Thomistic and the Platonistic.[34]

The fact seems to be, though, that Milton did not thus contradict himself, but that he adhered throughout *Paradise Lost* to a rather literal view of the angels as bodily creatures who could be truly present in time and space to man's senses. Henry More states the general choices that the times gave Milton: "Concerning angels, some affirm them to be *fiery* or *airy* Bodies; some pure spirits; some Spirits in airy or fiery bodies. . . ." [35] The first class here is of such Protestant angelologists as Zanchy and Baxter, developing some Patristic ideas; the second is of the scholastic-minded; the third is of "Platonists" like More himself, who depended heavily on the idea of angelic dichotomy to explain how angels could be spirits and still could act in the physical world. Whether or not Milton conceived his angels dichotomous is hard to say; that he did think them either to be "in airy or fiery bodies" or "to be *fiery* or *airy* Bodies" seems reasonably evident.

The fact that Milton often calls his angels *spirits* and has Adam address Raphael as "pure Intelligence" (VIII. 180) does not in itself signify a Thomistic conception of angelic substance.[36] The phrase "pure Intelligence" may, of course, mean unspotted mind as well as unmixed mind, and in the vocabulary of seventeenth-century angelology to call a being *spirit* or *intelligence* did not necessarily signify that it was in every sense free of matter. Dozens of demonologists who assert matter proper to angels call them spirits though incorporeal, or bodily though immaterial. Thus Michael Psellus says that angels have an "immaterial" body, and Fludd that the bodies of devils are of a "spiritual substance." [37] More fights tooth and nail for angels as "pure spirits," "immaterial substance," yet inflexibly ascribes them bodies.[38] Zanchy, who scorned the scholastic notion of the angelic substance and provisionally decided against it, could still say without inconsistency that almost everyone knows angels to be incorporeal substances of a spiritual nature and free from all matter.[39] Archbishop Ussher says that they are "incorporeal" though "they have their spiritual matter," and Baxter that though we call spirits "immaterial" still they have a spiritual "matter." [40]

Obviously distinctions are necessary to explain such usage, and

in fact many and intricate distinctions went with the whole controversy on angelic substance. The simplest and most generally-
received were first, that matter as tenuous as an angel's may be
called spiritual, and second, that an angel, like a man, is unmixed
spirit if we speak of his "soul" only, but compound of body and
spirit if we speak of his total being. In asserting an angel to be
an "Intelligence" and "free from all gross and putrefying mass of
body" Cornelius Agrippa does not intend to deny his distillate
and undecaying rarefaction of body.[41] Henry More goes further
when he says that to suppose no created spirit incorporeal in any
sense save that of rarefaction is erroneous; the "vehicle" is rarefied, but the "soul" of the angel is unmixed spirit.[42] In the light
of such accounts of angels even Milton's phrase "incorporeal
Spirits" may be taken to mean simply "immortal beings free from
gross matter." The Bible teaches us, Milton says in the *Christian
Doctrine*, what a spirit is, or rather what he is not; he has not
flesh and bones (I. ii.41). Plainly the angels of *Paradise Lost* are
without flesh and bones; but this is not to say that they are simple
forms, as the Thomists have it.

Nor does Raphael's necessity of "lik'ning spiritual to corporal
forms" to make heaven's war intelligible to Adam imply the
Thomistic view of angels. For Raphael does not mean that he
will speak in bodily terms of that which has no body, but that he
will reduce to terms of a body known to Adam the activities of
a kind of body normally above reach of human sense and so out
of Adam's experience.[43] At least, Raphael may well be thought to
mean this; the reading is not the only one possible if the passage
is taken alone, but it is easily satisfactory in itself, and it agrees
with what Raphael has already explicitly said of angelic substance
in his discussion of the scale of nature.

Milton does, in fact, expressly repudiate the Thomistic idea of
angelic substance, along with its related idea of angelic apparition
as by means of an "assumed" body. When Raphael eats with
Adam it is not "seemingly / The Angel, nor in mist, the common
gloss / Of Theologians" (V. 434-435), but Raphael himself present in his own person, eating with "real hunger" and able to
"trans-substantiate." The phrase "in mist," which Milton ascribes
with a shrug to "Theologians," would seem surely to mean "in
assumed body made of vapors," a body which the angel could
manage to the point of putting it through the motions of eating,
though without nourishment either to him or to it.[44] Scholastics
say almost with one voice that angels' assumed bodies were usually

made of clouds or "mist," that they merely represented the angel (were "seemingly the Angel"), and that they could not assimilate earthly food. These opinions were so commonplace and so commonly linked together that Milton could reject them all with a touch. In rejecting them he seems to reject also the idea that angelic substance cannot manifest itself directly to human sense.

Milton's own notion of the angelic substance is certainly neither so clear nor so philosophically serviceable as St. Thomas's. The angelology that seceded from scholasticism was, as one critic of Milton says, "insusceptible of precise statement," and Milton's not least.[45] Most angelologists would have thought Milton's statement on how Raphael could "corporeal to incorporeal turn" full of difficulties and his accompanying passage on the scale of nature no better at the point where it bridged without death the gap between man's substance and angel's.

> O *Adam*, one Almightie is, from whom
> All things proceed, and up to him return,
> If not deprav'd from good, created all
> Such to perfection, one first matter all,
> Indu'd with various forms, various degrees
> Of substance, and in things that live, of life;
> But more refin'd, more spirituous, and pure,
> As neerer to him plac't or neerer tending
> Each in their several active Sphears assigned,
> Till body up to spirit work, in bounds
> Proportiond to each kind. So from the root
> Springs lighter the green stalk, from thence the leaves
> More aerie, last the bright consummate floure
> Spirits odorous breathes: flours and thir fruit
> Mans nourishment, by gradual scale sublim'd
> To vital Spirits aspire, to animal,
> To intellectual, give both life and sense,
> Fansie and understanding, whence the Soule
> Reason receives, and reason is her being,
> Discursive, or Intuitive; discourse
> Is oftest yours, the latter most is ours,
> Differing but in degree, of kind the same.
> Wonder not then, what God for you saw good
> If I refuse not, but convert, as you,
> To proper substance; time may come when men
> With Angels may participate, and find
> No inconvenient Diet, nor too light Fare;
> And from these corporal nutriments perhaps
> Your bodies may at last turn all to Spirit,
> Improv'd by tract of time, and wingd ascend
> Ethereal, as wee, or may at choice
> Here or in Heav'nly Paradises dwell;

> If ye be found obedient, and retain
> Unalterably firm his love entire
> Whose progenie you are.
>
> (V. 469-503)

Milton's fondest admirers may admit that even if Milton had written this passage out at length in prose it would probably have seemed still uncertain in meaning by comparison with the work of Aquinas.

A few things are plain, nevertheless, about its philosophical and theological connections, even as it stands in verse, and the first is that though in intention non-scholastic or anti-scholastic, yet in that reluctant way common in Protestant angelology it depends largely on the scholastic scheme and method [46] and has a specific point or so in common with Scholasticism. For instance, Milton, like Lawrence and other Protestants, agrees with Aquinas that the angelic intellect is intuitive (V. 488-489). This scholastic vestige in *Paradise Lost* does not, however, signify, as one scholar has supposed, that Milton's conception of the angelic substance was scholastic.[47] Peter Martyr had made the point in angelology: ". . . the schoole diuines haue decreed, that . . . bicause those heauenlie minds haue no need of images or of senses . . . it should be superfluous for them to haue bodies." But Peter was unconvinced, and so were Lawrence, Zanchy, and others; they can ascribe both body and intuition to angels.[48] Plainly Milton too ascribes both in Raphael's speech, and his view taken as a whole in against Scholasticism.

A second thing that is clear in the scale-of-nature passage is that Milton shares with pious Protestant angelologists certain general ideas which they had adapted from both patristic and scholastic writings. One of these is the widely handled and mis-handled idea that the corporeality — or alternatively, the spirituality — of angels was a fact, but a relative one: ". . . in comparison of God," says Isaac Ambrose, "they are bodies, but in comparison of us they are pure and mighty spirits." The Scholastics took this to suit their own doctrine of angelic substance, but Protestants turned it to mean that angels were in a way corporeal. And so Raphael seems to say that all creatures are of prime matter. Whether they have it in a gross form or a rare depends on whether they are far from God or near to him, but all are material:

> . . . one first matter all
> Indu'd with various forms, various degrees
> Of substance, and in things that live, of life;

> But more refin'd, more spiritous, and pure,
> As neerer to him plac't or neerer tending. . . .
>   (V. 472-476)

Milton's spirits are thus some form of the "one first matter," and plainly the most "refin'd . . . spiritous . . . and pure" form of it, an "Ethereal" form to which the bodies of Adam and Eve may eventually turn if they persist in obedience.

This does not mean that Adam and Eve will become separated forms or that the angels are so. The angels of *Paradise Lost* are what the age called *ether* or the *empyrean* or *heavenly fire;* Milton repeatedly refers to them as "Ethereal substance" (VI. 330), "Empyreal substance" (I. 118), "Empyreal forme" (VI. 433), and to heaven as of "Ethereal mould" (II. 139). He means, like Platonistic philosophers and Protestan theologians, some quintessential matter.[49] This opinion that the angels were of the same substance as the highest or empyreal heaven with which they were created was a common one among Protestants, who wanted to reject or at least to question both Platonists on angels as dichotomous and Scholastics on them as pure forms, yet felt the need for some sort of answer on angelic substance. Ambrose, Lawrence, Baxter, Zanchy, Deacon, and Walker, and many others sketch the notion of celestial fire as angels' proper substance. Thus Henry Vane says that the creation of the angels "is described by the light which God made on the first day," by which the Bible signifies "The heavenliness of their frame and constitution. . . ." They are "separate in their beings from all sensual life, in the form of invisible spirits, whereof the material heavens in their creation are the first shadow . . . as man in his bodily state was made *dust of the ground,* so the *Angels were made a flame* of fire, in their natural constitution." [50]

Such vague inference from Scripture was no equal substitute for Scholasticism's magnificently thought-out articles on angelic substance, but its very indefiniteness was a merit in the Bible-bound opinion of Protestants. Both Ambrose and Lawrence specifically eschew positive and detailed opinions on substance, and in this they resemble many earlier Protestants: Zanchy, who proclaimed both Scholastics and Platonists probably wrong and the Fathers probably right, yet would himself give no formal thesis on the subject; Heinrich Bullinger, who says that "what the nature of angels is, it cannot be thoroughly declared of any man"; and Peter Martyr, who rejects many opinions on substance without quite stating what he himself thinks.[51] All of them cite the modesty of St. Augustine and St. Bernard, who held that the Bible made plain the existence and the ministry of angels but not their nature.[52] The doctrine that angels were celestial fire was what godly Protestants used, then, as the utmost they might be reasonably confident of; Psalm 104 said that God made his "angels spirits and his ministers a flame of fire."

In the *Christian Doctrine* Milton does not go beyond this characteristic Protestant conclusion; angels are "spirits," he says, and "of ethereal nature," citing Psalm 104 and its echo in Hebrews 1.7 among his proof texts. Evidently the same reserved opinion is the backbone of what he offers in *Paradise Lost* as serious doctrine on angelic substance. To it he attaches the serviceable Psellian notions, and upon it he builds his little heresies about angels' eating human food and making love with each other. As joined with them, his Protestant view that angels are heavenly fire is undeniably anti-scholastic. But even without them, *Paradise Lost* would show no more indecision on angelic substance than do a dozen Protestant divines who doubt the scholastics on it, and hesitate only to be dogmatic and detailed in their counter-theories.

Most of Milton's serious angelology, then, has affiliations with that common in Protestant theology, seen at its closest to Milton geographically, at least, in the work of Lawrence and Ambrose and the other Puritan angelologists. *Paradise Lost* shows explicitly their emphasized doctrine on angels' ability to control the human fancy, their doctrine about the sons of God and the daughters of men, about Satan in the serpent and the curse on them both. These are not peculiar, certainly, to Puritans or to Protestants, but still belong to them too. More significantly, Milton preserves in spite of the demands of his story most of the sceptical attitude of the Puritans about the angelic orders and the individual guardian, and he certainly does not diverge in the action of *Paradise Lost* from the Puritan view that angels were not to be worshipped. Finally, his idea in *Paradise Lost* of the angelic substance seems to suit the Puritan compromise on the angel as in some sense bodily, though of a body almost spirit. In addition to these explicit agreements with Puritan doctrine Milton seems also to have in *Paradise Lost* the Puritan indifference to speculation more detailed than piety calls for; he does not care exactly how angels control the fancy, or what the orders are, or what precisely the substance — once it is conceded to be inferior to God's, superior to ours, hence immortal, invisible, and swift, yet in some senses bodily, best described as like that of the highest heaven.

Milton expresses some ideas on the angels that contradict the Puritans in content and some that seem, on the surface at least, to contradict the whole spirit of their pious Protestant reserve. But what he shares with the Puritans in both content and mood is probably the dominant part of his angelology.

Chapter VIII

Milton's Casual Borrowing on Angels

☞ THE CONVENTIONAL RESERVE that Milton shows in *Paradise Lost* about the exact nature of angelic matter and about the angelic orders reflects, no doubt, his true alliance with Protestant theologians, his devout unwillingness to exceed what the Bible gave on such mysteries. He could not, however, limit himself in the poem on all phases of angelology to what was matter of faith. His project of describing the war in heaven and angelic visits to man compelled him to give at least some superficial account of the system of operation of angelic substance, and for such account the Bible was too sketchy a guide. His conviction that the angels were in some way material and that matter was good pointed him clearly to Platonistic theories of operation, and for Platonistic theories generally he had had in his youth, at least, some taste. Milton needed also in his grand scheme more names of angels, particularly of good angels, than the Bible provided; he had his choice of thousands in some Cabalistic sources which Puritans usually did not much study. He does not, certainly, offer *Zophiel* and *Abdiel* and the other obscure angels' names as of equal authority with *Michael* and *Gabriel* and the rest of those which he takes from Scripture for *Paradise Lost* and mentions, too, in the *Christian Doctrine;* but neither did he necessarily coin the obscure names, as many scholars have supposed that he did, for they existed ready to his hand.

The attitude that a godly contemporary of Milton's might take toward levy upon platonistic sources in angelology appears in Meric Casaubon's introduction in 1659 to Dr. Dee's journal of his traffic with spirits. Casaubon's interest in the publication was to show by it that spirits existed and worked in the world; for the sake of this demonstration he had to allow at least the general soundness in Dee's work of a sort of speculation that seemed to the godly always dangerous and presumptuous, however convincing. The "ancient Platonick Phylosophers of the latter times," Casaubon says, "understood much more than most Christians" of the lore of spirits. Not that he holds meagerness in angelology to be discreditable to Christians, for Casaubon himself thinks "no study is more vain and foolish," and once he had satisfied himself in some matters of faith, he would not go three steps "to know as much as the profoundest Platonick or Phylosopher yet or Magician of them all ever knew." But just the same, the Platonics do understand spirits best, since they have studied them most, and what they assert of them agrees with our experience of such beings.[1]

Whether Milton thought that what he borrowed for *Paradise Lost* from Platonists, ancient or contemporary, agreed with current experience of spirits he left no way to tell. But he evidently found that it fitted into the requirements of his story and did not necessarily contradict the general pattern of belief that he constructed for himself from the Bible. His most definite levy is the two passages he takes from Psellus. The first comes early in the poem and prepares the way for most of the special feats which the angels perform.

> For Spirits when they please
> Can either Sex assume, or both; so soft
> And uncompounded is their Essence pure,
> Not ti'd or manacl'd with joynt or limb,
> Nor founded on the brittle strength of bones,
> Like cumbrous flesh; but in what shape they choose
> Dilated or condens't, bright or obscure,
> Can execute their aerie purposes,
> And works of love or enmity fulfill.
>
> (I. 423-431)

The parallel passage in Psellus:

No daemon is either male or female by its own nature. Sex belongs to compounds; but the bodies of daemons are truly simple, ductible, and flexible, very easy and apt to all configurations. Just as we suppose that clouds show the figures now of men, now of bears, now dragons, and other things, so the bodies of daemons; but with this difference: whereas clouds assume various figures when agitated by external winds, daemons do it by their own plan just as they wish. They vary the forms of their own bodies, and sometimes contract into a smaller mass and again extend themselves in a longer, as we see happen in the earthworm, only they do it in a better substance more easily ductible. This diversity occurs not only in magnitude but even in figures and colors; they vary multiform. Indeed the body of a daemon is designed by nature for each of two courses, for insofar as it is easily yielding by nature it is transformed into various sorts of figures and insofar as it is of air it assumes diverse figures and colors. The air, however, is colored extrinsically, whereas the body of the daemon takes various sorts of color from the intimate action of the phantasy, just as when we are very angry the cheeks pale, when we are embarrassed they blush.[2]

Both Milton and Psellus join five ideas in identical order: (1) demons can "assume" either sex or both [3] (2) by virtue of their uncompounded substance, which (3) lets them take what shape they like, (4) expand and contract themselves, (5) make themselves bright or dark.[4]

As Addison and others after him have pointed out, the notification in Book I that demons can condense and dilate themselves enables the reader to see the marvelous as probable when the contracted multitude makes itself at ease in Pandaemonium (I. 775-795), and when Satan expands himself against the angelic guard in Paradise (II. 985-990).[5] The phrase on demons' power to be bright or obscure similarly supplies a rationalization for the guard's turning fiery red as it bends its horns in toward Satan (IV. 977-978) and for Raphael's blush (which Walter Raleigh thought a shocking specimen of Milton's invention)[6] when Adam asks about angelic love (VIII. 618-619).

When Milton and Psellus say that the substance of spirits is sexless because "uncompounded" they do not mean, of course, that it is form without matter, but simply that it is not differentiated into members. That this is the sense of it in *Paradise Lost* appears in the second passage for which Milton levies on Psellus. Milton explains that angels, though material enough to bleed, are without organs: "All heart they live, all Head, all Eye, all Eare, All Intellect, all Sense . . ." (VI. 350-351). During the battle in heaven when Michael struck Satan down "The griding sword with discontinuous wound / Pass'd through him, but th' Ethereal substance clos'd / Not long divisible . . ." (VI. 329-331). Then while Satan bled a "Nectareous humour," his party rescued him and carried him to his chariot "Gnashing for anguish and despite and shame. . . ."

> Yet soon he heal'd; for Spirits that live throughout
> Vital in every part, not as frail man
> In Entrailes, Heart or Head, Liver or Reines
> Cannot but by annihilating die:
> Nor in their liquid texture mortal wound
> Receive, no more than can the fluid Aire:
> All Heart they live, all Head, all Eye, all Eare,
> All Intellect, all Sense, and as they please
> They limb themselves and colour, shape, or size
> Assume as likes them best, condense or rare.
>   (VI. 344-352)

Milton has here three ideas which Psellus also connects closely: the demon's pain when his substance is cut, his quick and thorough healing, and his "panorganic" substance. Ficino's translation of Psellus closes thus:

That which feels is not the nerve itself but the spirit in it. . . . Certainly the compound body never suffers in itself, but only when it participates with the spirit; indeed when it is deprived of the spirit it is also deprived of feeling. Thus the body of the demon is through its whole self naturally sensual in accordance with its individual parts and without medium sees, hears, touches, suffers. It suffers with contact and division like a solid body, but there is this difference: that solid bodies when they have been divided are restored either rarely or not at all; but the body of the demon when it is cut soon is recreated in itself again and coalesces like water and air. . . . Yet meanwhile it suffers while divided, for which cause it fears the edge of the sword. . . .[7]

Certainly what Milton takes from Psellus does not retain in *Paradise Lost* the tone of the original, for though it is a considerable and characteristic part of Psellus' demonology it is not joined in *Paradise Lost* with the other items that in Psellus give an impression of highly grotesque and unanthropomorphic creatures. According to Psellus an angel's proper shape is spherical and a demon's oblong; a demon has seed, though no members or sex, and spawns animalculae; he leaves excrement behind him and, if he is burned, cinders; he speaks to men by slipping directly into their minds and he absorbs a humorous nourishment like a sponge.[8] Milton keeps clear of these grotesqueries to draw his picture of the angels as heroically manlike. Furthermore whereas Psellus' chief emphasis is on the physical being of demons (the lowest of them hideous parasites living in slime, the highest wavering shapes in malignant thin fire) Milton has instead the biblical emphasis on angels as moral beings, enemies or messengers of God.

Even when directly using Psellus' ideas on transformation and recreation of demonic substance Milton distorts Psellus, for he ignores the fact that Psellus is talking about demons chiefly as they are in relation to man. Milton for his part uses the ideas rather in describing the relation of spirit to spirit. In the Psellian passage in Book I, Milton notably does not speak of the bodies of demons, which to most readers might have meant "assumed" bodies, but of their "essence pure," and he has them change their size and shape to each other in the infernal world, whereas Psellus in his parallel passage is talking of apparitions to men in the temporal world. The sword that girds through Satan in Book VI is a celestial weapon from the armory of God; the sword Psellus speaks of as frightening to demons is the earthly steel.

Plainly Milton has no interest in being faithful to Psellus, but is just picking some handy scraps out of his work. He might have found Fludd just as usable: "What should hinder spirits, by contraction of this their external substances, to appeare when they please visibly, and organically to talke with a person, as the tempting spirit did to Christ: and againe by an immediate dilatation of the same external aery spirit, to become inuisible, no otherwise than a smoake by dilatation vanisheth. . . ." [9] "Millions of spiritual creatures walk the earth / Unseen" (IV. 677) by Adam and Eve, but the spiritual creatures named Raphael and Michael show themselves at will, the one in his proper shape, the other as a stern man. When angel was visible to angel in heaven or hell the substance was the same proper substance that Adam and Eve saw, though the shape and the degree of rarefaction might be different. Well, then, when Satan swelled against the angelic guard (IV. 985-988), did he grow less visible to them? And if not, how but by such "dilatation" did he make himself invisible to his devils in Pandaemonium when he returned there to take his throne unseen (X. 445)? Perhaps the most reasonable answer is that though Milton wanted a show of "science," he was not really trying to write angelology throughout.

II

Milton's general idea that beings of varying rank and goodness represent stages in a cosmological succession of bodies from gross to rare, bodies alterable as the beings that possess them tend toward God or away, has its parallels, of course, among Platonistic philosophers as among Protestant theologians. Robert Fludd diagrams the stages by which God's light enters the world and by which the soul regresses through increasingly tenuous substance to perfection. Above the earth and its water and the three regions of air come fire and the heavenly bodies, the moon lowest, and then the Primum mobile and finally under God the nine orders of the angels. Fludd asserts that ethereal fire is more subtile than any element and the empyrean more subtile yet. In explaining this succession of things he says: "So is a Starre of Heauen called *Densior pars sui orbis*, that is, *The inuisible aethereall spirit or thin body of heauen, thickened into the visible body of a Starre.* So also may fire be condensed into ayre, and ayre into water, and water into earth. And againe, that earth may be rarefied into water, and water into ayre, and ayre into fire, for such is the natural rotation of the elements." [10] And thus Raphael explains to Adam that the air feeds the heavenly bodies,

> . . . those Fires
> Ethereal, and as lowest first the Moon,
> Whence in her visage round those spots, unpurg'd
> Vapours not yet into her substance turnd.
>
> (V. 417-420)

The moon herself exhales nourishment to higher orbs. The chain of such contribution accounts, in Raphael's showing, for the phenomenon of a heavenly being eating Adam's food and for the prospect that Adam himself if he remain sinless "with angels may participate" (V. 494).

The angel, Fludd goes on, is of the spiritual substance of that higher world from which the stars are concreted and so "of a thinner or thicker consistence, according unto the dignity of the Angel." [11] This, of course, is an ancient notion, and Fludd cites it in a respected form from Augustine: ". . . the grosse, malignant and darke spirits . . . by their fall, haue indued the grosser ayre . . . and therefore is Satan called by the Apostle, *The Prince of the ayre*." [12] Just so Milton says that Satan and his followers, once "Spirits of purest light," have "gross by sinning grown" (VI. 660-661), so that when the mountains hurled by the loyal angels crush their armor into their substance they are short of their former agility in contraction and can "wind / Out of such prison" only after pain and trouble. This is, of course, a commonplace of Christian demonology which Fludd works out in a detail that Augustine and the Protestant theologians and Milton cared nothing about. Still, Milton is generally in line with Fludd when he has Satan say in *Paradise Regained* that his angels, once "Aethereal Thrones," have become "Powers of Fire, Air, Water, and Earth" (II. 121-124), and when he shows us the darkening and degeneration of Satan's substance as well as of his character.

When Platonistic thinkers speak of angels as ethereal or empyreal in substance they usually intend not the proper essence, as most Protestant theologians seem to, but some "vehicle" joined to the essence. Against Baxter, for instance, Henry More asserts flatly that ether is *body* and in angels is the substance of the vehicle only.[13] Baxter answers by iterating his uncertainty about the nature of ether and, though he does not deny the vehicle, pointedly notes that it is a thing entirely untouched on by Scripture.[14]

In *Paradise Lost* the question of this dichotomy of essence and vehicle in angels simply does not come up, and though some scholars have supposed that Milton must have thought angels dichotomous [15] the indications seem to be that he never considered

it seriously, but like Baxter and Lawrence and other godly Protestants preferred simply to let the problem go unattempted. Certainly he could hardly have subscribed to More's doctrine that
the angel is a spirit equivalent to the human soul except that it
informs an ethereal or aerial body instead of a terrestrial one. True,
nothing explicitly said about angels in either *Paradise Lost* or the
Christian Doctrine prevents this interpretation, but Milton's whole
conception of the human soul taken with the parallel he evidently
intends in *Paradise Lost* between soul and angel would seem to
be against it. Since Milton and More disagreed extremely about
the soul, the probability is that they disagreed also on the angel.
More's cherished conviction of pre-existence supports his contention that man dies into an angel-like condition, putting off a terrestrial vehicle and putting on an aerial, and it is supported by
that contention; but it is totally incompatible with Milton's
equally cherished conviction that "the whole man is soul" and is
born and dies as one. More himself makes the point that Psychopannychites deny vehicles.[16]

A very different notion of the angelic dichotomy from More's,
and perhaps better suited to Milton's views, was Robert Fludd's.
Fludd's notion that the angel was composed of an "internal" and
an "external" did not seem to mean that these parts were separable; to Fludd the angel had no identity but as an existing combination of internal and external, whereas for More an angel's
identity, like a man's, rested wholly in its "soul." Fludd's idea
would seem to suit the nebulous opinion of Protestant theologians
that angels were unitary beings of rarefied body. And so Milton,
who thought man also to be a unitary being, saying "the whole
man is soul, and the soul man," may have thought the whole angel
to be one, a creature parallel to man in a higher, more subtile
being of the same kind, only analytically divisible, as in man the
spirit may be distinguished in thought from the body considered
as a "mere senseless stock."

But though Fludd does seem to say that the angel is a whole
and single being, yet he seems to say also that it is so by a real
union of substances that exist in themselves: the external is a kind
of prime matter, and the internal, the breath of God, is of God's
essence. Milton, on the other hand, expressly denies that the life
God breathed into man is of his essence. Milton may have thought,
then, like Fludd, that the angel had an internal inspired by God
and an external of some kind of matter — ether or the empyrean —
but he could hardly have thought, like Fludd, that the internal

was the superior and virtuous part of the combination, for to Milton "Matter, like the form and nature of the angels itself, proceeded incorruptible from God." Perhaps Milton thought the angel's internal, like the spirit of man, merely "an inspiration of some divine virtue fitted for the exercise of life and reason. . . ." [17] Whereas Fludd's way of thinking makes for emphasis on angelic dichotomy, Milton's all but amounts to a denial of it.

III

However lightly Milton may have taken his debt to Platonistic philosophy on the angelic nature, he probably took more lightly yet any debt he may have had to the allied system of the Cabala for angelic names. Although he shares many names with Agrippa and Fludd and a few with Cabalists more obscure, he shows not a jot of their interest in the names for their own sake or in the special powers supposed to go with them. He could hardly have felt the remotest sympathy with such a lurid conjuring book as the *Sepher Raziel,* where one of his names has its only known appearance before *Paradise Lost,* or with the even more disreputable *Key of Solomon* or with the *Heptameron* falsely attributed to Peter of Abano. Whether Milton casually borrowed from such works or merely shared with them by a chance crossing of the currents that eddied angels' names through all sorts of Renaissance writing, he surely could have had nothing but scorn for the manuals of magic, and probably he was no friend to Agrippa and Fludd, however much some of his material may have paralleled theirs.[18]

Still, the fact remains that of the thirty-odd angels' names in *Paradise Lost,* considerably more than half, including some of the obscure ones, appear in Agrippa's work and again in Fludd's. Virtually all the rest show up in one or another occult writing. For his principal angelic actors, of course, Milton used names that are in the Bible, names in which he believed: *Michael, Raphael, Gabriel, Satan* or *Lucifer, Beelzebub,* and the like. For the rest he picked euphonious names, most of them Semitic, with reasonably appropriate significations, and he preferred, surely, that they too be in the Bible: *Adramalec, Ashtoreth, Chemos, Nisroch, Asmodai.* In all, twenty-one of his thirty-odd names are in the Bible, counting the apocryphal books, as of angels or (the same thing) of pagan gods. This duplication of Scripture did not in itself, however, separate Milton from the occultists, for the Bible was their primary source as well as his; the names that Milton

shares with the Bible are among those that he shares too with
Agrippa's *Occult Philosophy*. Such names in *Paradise Lost* had,
then, not only scriptural warrant but also associations with various
esoteric systems. When Milton speaks of the seven angels who
stand before God, he appeals not only to Revelation 8.2, which
does not name the angels, but to innumerable commentaries and
expansions upon it, many of them occult, that do name them.
When he lists the four chief angels — Michael, Gabriel, Raphael,
Uriel — he has not only availed himself of the four principal
names of good angels that the canonical and apocryphal books
provide, but has of necessity touched the vast Jewish tradition
that binds these four together as the major angels correspondent
to the elements, the directions, the seasons, and to various nations
and days and months and other things invisibly swayed by God's
messengers. When Milton goes further, then, and uses additional
names entirely outside the Bible's meager provision, he has slid
over very easily into sole companionship with the occultists, without subscribing at all to their purposes. As Masson says, Milton
does seem to have "helped himself" to the obscure names quite
casually "from mere tradition." [19] He used them in his poetry for
what values the tradition could add to it. Nothing suggests that
he was seriously bound to the tradition by intellectual taste or
conviction.

The occultists wanted far more names than any literal reading
of the Bible afforded or any ordinarily pious angelology required.
They put into use, therefore, various devices for expanding the
short list of names about which the Bible seemed explicit. One
such device was an anagrammatic deducing of the names of angels
who were anonymous in the Bible from the words describing their
activities, and another was simply transferring to angels the names
of men and places in the Bible. Of these devices Milton seems
definitely to use the second — or rather to avail himself of the
results angelologists before him had got from it. *Abdiel, Ariel,
Arioc, Uzziel,* and *Zephon* among Milton's more obscure names
all appear in the Bible only as of men or of places, not of angels,
and illustrate Agrippa's observation that "he that is inquisitive"
may find out the names of good or evil spirits from the names of
notable men or the places where such men were. Thus *"Uriel
from Uriah,* the prophet," *Chemos* from "the Idol of Moab," and
Adramalec from "the Idol of the Assyrians." [20]

Of the obscure names which Milton uses, *Ariel* gives the clearest
example of the tangle of associations that might surround such a

name in the literature of angelology. Milton mentions it only once, along with *Arioc* and *Ramiel*, as of a fierce evil spirit beaten by Abdiel in the first day's fighting in heaven (VI. 371). It means "Lion of God," and is in the Bible only as the name of a man, an altar, and a city. What warrant, then, did Milton have for it as an angel's name and what warrant for giving it to a fierce and evil spirit after Shakespeare had showed Ariel as a frail and merely mischievous one?

Jewish and pseudo-Jewish demonological writings name the angel Ariel quite early. One Milton scholar finds him in the pseudepigraphical *Book of Enoch* of the first or second century before Christ and also in the Coptic *Pistis Sophia,* which names him as in charge of punishments in the underworld.[21] In the *Testament of Solomon,* dating from somewhere between the second and the fifth centuries after Christ, Arael is an angel who controls demons.[22] In some material of approximately the same date professing to be The Wisdom of the Chaldaeans, Ariel is an angel who assists Raphael in the cure of disease.[23]

From such conceptions of him as a good spirit, or at least a dignified one, doubtless developed the usage picked up by Christian students of the Cabala like Agrippa, Fludd, and Athanasius Kircher, who give the name *Ariel* to the spirit of earth.[24] The name turns up, too, as that of the spirit of earth on the pentacle of the sun in the *Key of Solomon,* an unsavory specimen of the "practical" or conjuring Cabala.[25] Directly out of the Cabalistic books comes a curiosity-feeding use which Thomas Heywood makes of the name and others like it in his *Hierarchie of the Blessed Angels,* where rehearsing avidly the opinions of the "Rabbins" and "Cabalists" he rattles off half a dozen occult classifications of angels plus the appropriate names, including "Earths great Lord, *Ariel.*" But he adds very piously that

> . . . other names than are to us exprest
> In sacred Scriptures, none ought to deuise,
> Since from such Curiosities arise.

The names the Rabbins give, he avers, are simply fancies built on etymologies; thus the name *Tharsus* was originally attributed to the angel of water simply because it means water (in what language he does not stop to say) and similarly *Ariel* to earth because it means earth.[26]

No doubt Milton shared Heywood's professed scruple about the Cabalistic manufacture of angels' names, but the fact that he used

some that seem Cabalistic perhaps indicates that he found a literary value in them and could square his religious principles with
availing himself of it. He does not make Heywood's blunt appeal
to curiosity; nevertheless, in having Abdiel overthrow Ariel and
Arioc and Ramiel Milton is appealing indirectly to the time's
association of those devils with wizardry and superstition. In the
battle in heaven, he reminds us thus indirectly, the spirits who
later inspired and answered godless invocation were apostate and
defeated.

Milton had, however, further and more accurate warrant for his
use of *Ariel* than its various appearances in books of magic and
demonology. Aquila and Symmachus in their very early translations of the Old Testament took the name *Ariel* to signify the
pagan city of Arina, which worshipped the idol Ariel (otherwise
Mars), and Eusebius of Caesarea notes their view in his *Onomasticon*.[27] From some such source, no doubt, Agrippa explains that
though "*Ariel* is the name of an angel . . . sometimes also it is
the name of an evil demon, and of a City which is thence called
Ariopolis, where the Idol was worshipped."[28] Milton's Ariel, then,
fierce in the fighting in heaven, was, like many of his fellows in
Paradise Lost, a heathen god, and like many he got his name from
a biblical place. His fierceness in battle is that of the god of war.

In *Of Reformation* Milton speaks scornfully of the Old Testament translations of Aquila and Symmachus,[29] and he quite probably knew the opinion of St. Jerome, who translating Eusebius
on Ariel, says that he himself thinks the Bible uses *Ariel* to signify
simply Jerusalem or the Temple.[30] His view was well-established
among exegetes long before Milton's day or Agrippa's. Agrippa,
of course, after the fashion of Cabalists, both Jewish and Christian, was casting back to an old, discredited reading of the Bible
for the sake of the latitude it gave him. Milton was surely doing
the same thing, though for a poet's reasons, not a theosophist's.

The rest of Milton's obscure names of angels seem to have associations very like those of *Ariel,* though not so much is known
about them.[31] *Arioc, Abdiel, Uzziel,* and *Zephon* are all in the
Bible as names of men or places, and in various religious or occult
writings as of angels. *Abdiel* and *Uzziel* are both in the *Sepher
Raziel,* for instance, and *Uzziel* in several other mystical and Cabalistic works.[32] Arioc, known to demonologists as the spirit of revenge, is named by a German humanist in a mid-sixteenth-century
discourse on spirits that was turned into English by Thomas Nashe
in *Pierce Penniless* and more formally by Robert Turner in one

of his numerous occult translations of the 1650's.[33] *Zephon,* according to John Selden, was the name of a heathen idol or Baal, worshipped at the city of Baal-Zephon.[34] Why Milton applied the name to an elect angel does not appear, but Agrippa says ". . . as divers men have many times the same name, so also spirits of divers offices and natures may be noted or marked by one name . . . so the same names . . . may be applied sometimes to the order of a good Demon, sometimes to a bad." [35] Perhaps Milton knew somewhere in the literature of angelology of a Zephon that was a good angel. Or perhaps he did not — and cared very little.

Two of Milton's names, *Ithuriel* and *Zophiel,* do not appear in the Bible at all. *Ithuriel* scarcely appears, either, in the literature of angelology, unless we take some liberties in transliteration. The closest known duplication of the name as *Paradise Lost* gives it is on a pentacle in the notorious *Key of Solomon,* an occurrence that can merely indicate that the name though obscure in the literature of angels did exist there.[36] *Zophiel* is almost as dark to us. In the *Sepher Raziel* either of two different Hebrew names may express Milton's use, which, showing Zophiel as a scout for Michael's army, seems to fit his name to the Hebrew meaning "Spy of God." [37] *Zophiel* appears, too, in the Roman alphabet in Fludd's *Mosaical Philosophy,* but apparently as a faulty transliteration of a Hebrew name whose meaning has no link with the function which Milton gave to the angel.[38] Agrippa and others have some much-tangled variants — *Iophiel, Zaphiel, Zaphkiel* — in which mis-prints trip over mis-translations and mis-transliterations so freely as to make it nonsense to search among them for the name Milton uses.[39]

And, in fact, it sometimes seems nonsense to refer Milton at all to the occultists, men whom he never mentions or even hints at and quite possibly despised. Yet he did share their material, and occasionally his use of a detail is so close to theirs that some sort of debt seems very likely. Thus when Milton gives the name *Azazel* to a "Cherub tall" who claimed the bearing of hell's standard "as his right" (I. 534), he would seem to be following a Cabalistic item on the organization of the devils that appears many times in Fludd's works. We read in the Cabalists, says Fludd, that as there are four commanders in the army of God, namely Michael, Raphael, Gabriel, and Uriel, so in the army of Satan are four standard-bearers ("signiferi"), Samael, Azazel, Azael, and Mahazael.[40] Milton could have run across this in other places besides Fludd's work — Reuchlin had it and Archangelus of Borgo Nuovo, and before them the Jewish Zoharist, Menahan ben Ben-

jamin Recanati [41] — so that Milton's explicit naming of Azazel as
standard-bearer certainly does not connect him directly to Fludd.
Still, Milton does give Azazel the standard as the Cabalists do. He
understood perfectly well, of course, that, as Selden and Samuel
Bochart had pointed out, *Samael,* which the Cabalists yoked with
Azazel, was simply a variant for *Satan,* and he probably sneered
with Selden at "Jewish astrologers" who thought it to belong to
a separate devil.[42] Similarly Milton must have known that the
name *Azazel* was in the Bible merely the word for the scape-goat
(Leviticus 16.8). He could have had no real deference for the
Cabalists' conversion of *Samael* and *Azazel* to their elaborate uses.
The very form of Milton's levy on the Cabalist idea — arbitrary
selection of one name out of four and the ignoring of the notion
of a parallel between the armies of heaven and of hell — suggests
how little he cared for Cabalism as a system. Yet the facts remain
that he does certainly take *Azazel* as a demon's name out of Jewish
occult tradition, and that his explicit assignment to Azazel of hell's
standard appears in that tradition. However little respect Milton
may have had for the Cabala, he unquestionably calls up Cabalistic
associations in *Paradise Lost* and probably not by mere chance.

IV

In much the same casual yet association-packed way that he used
proper names of angels Milton used also some terms that various
angelologists had picked out of the Bible and had made more or
less common as of angelic orders: Warriors, Gods, Messengers,
Wheels, Sons of God, Tempter, Accuser. Milton uses most of these
vaguely hierarchic terms in a vaguely hierarchic way, mingling
them occasionally with the far more familiar terms of Dionysius.
The Bible is Milton's sufficient source and authority for all; it was
the source, too, of the occultists, who used these terms with a
special application probably well known to Milton and certainly
known to many of his readers.

When Milton calls Satan *Accuser* and *Tempter* (IV. 10) and
when by intimation, at least, he lets us know that the devils are
Aerial Powers and *False Gods,* he has touched directly a much-
repeated classifications of evil spirits into nine orders designated
by these and similar terms.[43] Milton does not, however, anywhere
say that these terms designate orders or so use them as to connect
them in any systematic way with the names of the great devils that
went along with them in the hierarchic scheme. In the evil hierarchy Beelzebub is chief of the first order, the False Gods; Belial of

the third, the Vessels of Wrath; Asmodeus of the fourth, the Re-
vengers of Evil; Astaroth of the eighth, the Accusers; and Mammon of the ninth, the Tempters. In this system, Satan, upon whom
Milton concentrates all, is prince of the fifth order, the Deluders,
"who," says Agrippa, "seduce people by their miracles, as the serpent seduced *Eve*." Milton, however, called Satan from Ephesians
2.2[44] "Prince of the Aire" (X. 185; XII. 454), so keeping company
with a host of pious commentators and diverging from the classification of devils, which made Aerial Powers the sixth order, with
Meresin as its chief. Plainly the correspondence between *Paradise
Lost* and this ancient circumstantial superstition is peripheral and
perhaps accidental. But plainly, too, it helps give a shading to
Milton's language of which, whether he wanted it or not, he must
have been conscious.

The Jewish orders of good angels — orders which Agrippa and
Fludd and other occultists respectfully match with the Dionysian
and which the Puritans often sneer at — took their names all from
the Old Testament and they were such names as Christian writers
too might take from there and use without any intention of signifying orders. *Malachim* was, of course, simply Hebrew for *Messengers,* and *Bene Elohim* (Sons of God) was applicable to man
as well as to angels generally. *Ophanim* (Wheels) certainly seemed
in Ezekiel to signify heavenly beings, but not necessarily an order
of them. Milton refers frequently to angels as Sons of God and
as winged Messengers, but never in any way that requires us to
understand orders; he seems merely to have borrowed the biblical
terms as synonyms for *angels.* He does use *Wheels,* however, to
signify heavenly beings in a way that hints strongly at hierarchy,
for as one scholar has noticed, Milton always associates Wheels
with Cherubim,[45] the second order in the Dionysian scheme as
Wheels was in the Cabalistic. When Christ rides out to realize in
Creation his "Great Idea" (VII. 557), Milton seems to identify
the Cherubim on whose wings the Son is uplifted (VII. 218) with
the "fervid Wheeles" (VII. 224) that pause when they have conveyed him into Chaos. Cherubim and Wheels, it would seem,
compose as one Christ's "Celestial Equipage" (VII. 203). This
vehicle most commentators think the same as the chariot from
which Christ had overthrown the rebels, and they find Milton's
major source in Ezekiel, where also Wheels compose the chariot
of deity along with *Hayyoth* (Living Creatures) later spoken of
in the singular as *Kerub*.[46]

In using Ezekiel Milton was bound to duplicate to some extent the Cabalistic angelologists, who, of course, had drawn plentifully from the same source. Milton's similarities to the angelologists have some special significance, perhaps, in the fact that like them and unlike Ezekiel he connects Cherubim and Wheels to the work of creation. This connection appears in Agrippa, for instance, who, explicitly identifying Wheels with Cherubim, says that through them works the second name of God, which signifies "divinity full of Ideas," or the creative force. The name, Agrippa says, is "attributed to the Son and hath his influence by the order of Cherubims, or that the Hebrews call *Orphanim,* that is, forms or wheels. . . ." It works in the starry heavens, where God "fabricateth so many figures as he hath *Ideas* in himself, and distinguisheth the very Chaos of the creatures. . . ." [47] Milton shares with Agrippa, then, the linking of Cherubim and Ophanim in the work of creation done by the Son according to the *"Ideas* in himself," or, as Milton puts it, his "Great Idea." The Cabalistic exposition, it ought to be said, is less of the original creation, though that seems included, than of the continuing sustenance of the world, and it posits the intermediary work of angels in creation to a degree that could hardly have been agreeable to Milton or to any other Christian intent on monotheism. Neither Agrippa nor the Jewish Cabalists on whom he relies seems probable as a near source for Milton. Still, the general notion of the Wheels as an order of angels does glimmer faintly in the great unexplicit complex of his picture of creation.

V

The final unavoidable connection Milton has with occult sources in the work of filling out his picture of angels is in the missions he assigns angels. Jewish lore long before Milton had given Adam his tutelary spirit and the planets their rulers and demons their powers in nature.[48] On these things as on others, the Bible had supplied hints to them as well as to Milton, and their expansions of such hints were surely known to many who came to read Milton's more restrained expansions of them, and known to Milton too, so that he was to some degree entangled with them whether he wanted it or not. His problem with them, as with many bits of angelology not grateful to Protestant ears, was to keep clear of what might seem a plain conformity to them and clear at the same time of any argumentative or dogmatic repudiation of them, which would have interrupted his story and also deprived it of the imaginative appeal that cabalistic mysteries had for many seventeenth-century readers. Milton's practice, then, is to allot some of the same functions to angels that the Cabalists did, but, if he names the angels, to use different ones from the Cabalists, and if not, to speak a little vaguely. Whereas Raziel, an angel unmentioned by the Bible, is Adam's instructor according to Reuchlin, Fludd, and many others,[49] Milton gives Adam instead two different instructors, each with a biblical name. Milton assigns an angel to the sun, as do the Cabalists; but instead of Michael or Raphael, whom they give, he names Uriel, whom they do not even list among the angels of the planets at all.[50] If, as one great scholar has argued, Milton makes Gabriel angel of the east,[51] he does it against all that the Christian Cabalists, such as Agrippa and Fludd, helped by the more restricted writers who complained of them but repeated their notions, had made widespread about the matching of angels and directions.[52] Milton's only real connection with the Cabalists in these matters is that he seems to suggest an occult scheme without affirming any particular one. He leaves by indirection an impression of interesting and faintly illicit lore, though the foreground of what he has to say is distinctly biblical. Uriel in the sun, we gather, is the angel St. John saw there (III. 623). Yet he may be also some such mystical ruler of that orb as Fludd and Agrippa ascribe to it.[53]

That angels ruled the planets and had other ordinary power in nature much as the occultists laid it out, Milton seems to hint when he describes the changes God ordered after man's fall. The heavenly choir sang the praises of God while he

> . . . calling forth by name
> His mightie Angels gave them several charge,
> As sorted best with present things. The Sun
> Had first his precept so to move, so shine,
> As might affect the Earth with cold and heat
> Scarce tollerable, and from the North to call
> Decrepit Winter, from the South to bring
> Solstitial summers heat. To the blanc Moone
> Her office they prescrib'd, to the other five
> Thir planetarie motions and aspects
> In *Sextile*, *Square*, and *Trine*, and *Opposite*,
> Of noxious efficacie, and when to joyne
> In Synod unbenigne, and taught the fixt
> Thir influence malignant when to showre.
> Which of them rising with the Sun, or falling,
> Should prove tempestuous: to the Winds they set
> Thir corners, when with bluster to confound
> Sea, Aire, and Shoar, the Thunder when to rowle

With terror through the dark Aereal Hall.
                                    (X. 649-667)

Milton says that God calls forth his angels by name, but Milton
does not name any of them. He does name, apparently as receiving
God's commands, the sun, the moon, the "other five" planets, the
fixed stars, and the four winds. Are we to suppose that instead of
the angel Milton lists each time the thing it rules? or that he
speaks here of these natural bodies and forces as *angels,* a thing
Puritan angelologists sometimes asserted might be done? Or are
we to think, as seems to fit the sense a little better, that the celestial
bodies and the winds got their orders at secondhand from their
controlling angels? The passage leaves no way to tell surely. It is
of an evident and evidently intentional ambiguity.

Fludd in his theories of meteors and of the weather and of
disease ascribes great power to the angels of the four winds, both
the good and the evil, and to the angels of the planets even wider
power through the astrological influences which, as channels of
God's will, they direct upon earth. Fludd has these notions from
Agrippa and the Jewish Cabalists and in variant form from the
Neo-Platonics and Neo-Pythagoreans. Many conventionally pious
angelologists, Protestant and Catholic, pick them up and retail
them with varying expressions of disapproval. Milton certainly
was familiar with them, and as certainly he duplicates parts of
them in the equivocal passage on God's orders to "His mightie
Angels." Early commentators on *Paradise Lost* [54] complained of
his not only duplicating here the ignorant theories of astrology,
but countenancing them. The closely related theories of angelology Milton did not quite countenance, though any who cared
to think that he did might read his lines to suit.

Perhaps the truth is that Milton did not altogether disdain the
idea of a Cabala, however error-laden he may have thought the
work of Agrippa and Fludd to be. The correspondence of the
Jewish Cabala to Christian doctrine that struck Pico and Reuchlin
and all their Christian successors may well have impressed Milton
too. He did not, certainly, try to make *Paradise Lost* a recovery
of the true Mosaical Cabala in the direct, factual-minded way that
Henry More undertook in his *Conjectura Cabalistica,* but he did
think that he was showing a general picture of the angel-world
as it was deducible from the Bible, and he must have recognized
how much it had in common with the angel-world of Platonistic
speculators, despite their excesses. Perhaps in the last analysis
Milton was correcting the occultists on angels at the same time that

he was evading and using them — correcting them by implied rebuke to their curiosity and excessive detail that obscured the essential truths which the Bible imparted, yet finding them, if only by virtue of their biblical roots, worth his attention.

The Puritan theologians — with whom Milton is certainly in sympathy — could never find just the mean they sought between contempt for angelology as a philosophical speculation and the reverence they felt owing to inference from Scripture on angels. Milton plainly is indifferent to angelology as a "science" except for availing himself of fragments that help his narrative along or dress it up or establish him with those of his readers who expect such "science" from him. Yet he had angels on his hands, first in the Bible, where he could not take them as myth or allegory, and then in his epic, where because of the Bible he could not make them simply symbol or machinery. Throughout *Paradise Lost,* then, wherever Milton's path crosses widely-known but dubious theory on angels — that of Dionysius or of Psellus or of More or of the Cabalists — he is in a most complex way at once exploiting, correcting, and evading it. So it is that *Paradise Lost's* angelology may seem, as some recent scholars have suggested, to be borrowed directly from the "Rabbis" or significantly parallel to More's or Fludd's, or a random gathering up of commonplaces.[55] Never, it would seem, is occult angelology a part of *Paradise Lost* which Milton literally believed and which he intended to offer to his reader without great reserve.

Chapter IX

Milton's Heresies on Angels

Howevᴇʀ basically indifferent to angelology as such Milton may have been and however evasively he may have used some of its articles, he did have certain things about angels that he undertook to say explicitly in *Paradise Lost* — or rather, he had certain things to say about God's creation that he undertook to signify partly by passages of daring angelology. When he tells how angels can assimilate human food (V. 401-443; 461-503) and make love with each other (VIII. 615-629), then obviously he is not merely decorating his poem, and certainly he is not validating himself as a poet learned in the lore of his subject or as one making of a well-known theory a convenience for his plot. He is, on the contrary, much nearer to making a nuisance to the plot of almost unheard-of theories that certainly could do no good to his standing as an angelologist. That Milton chose at a cost which many critics have commented on to emphasize these theories of angels suggests, certainly, that they had a calculated part in the whole meaning that he intended his poem to convey. Yet since they are not to be found in the *Christian Doctrine* (are, in fact, obviously angelology more detailed and further from Scripture than Milton could admit to that treatise) they are presumably not themselves doctrine in Milton's eyes. They are, then, a kind of doctrinal indirection; through these angelological heresies Milton speaks of something else. They have place in *Paradise Lost* not so much for their own sake as for the sake of what they point us to.

Milton has in *Paradise Lost* a number of other firmly-made points of heterodox angelology, but only one other for which a structural function is not plain in the story. For instance, to put hell in a place of "utter darkness" instead of at the center was indeed unorthodox of Milton, but of evident service to his story, and the same is true of his asserting the existence of angels long before God's work of the six days.[1] When, however, Milton insists that the elect angels stand by their own strength, he is backing an idea of no service to his plot against the opinion of the vast ma-

jority of angelologists respected in England in his time. The elect
angels, said the majority, were secured by grace from the danger
of lapse, or by a compulsive love of God.[2] Milton had considered
in the *Christian Doctrine* this "opinion that the good angels are
now upheld, not so much by their own strength, as by the grace
of God," and concluded that it is "more agreeable to reason to
suppose that the good angels are upheld by their own strength no
less than man himself was before his fall; that they are called
'elect' in the sense of beloved or excellent. . . ." [3] Since he treats
it in the *Christian Doctrine*, Milton presumably thought that this
question about angels was one on which a man ought to have
some belief, and in *Paradise Lost* he states his point more positively and more fully than in the theological treatise. Can man be
disobedient, asks Adam? Yes, answers Raphael, since God wants
free service and

> ordain'd thy will
> By nature free, not over-rul'd by Fate
> Inextricable, or strict necessity.

Then Raphael adds gratuitously:

> Myself and all th' Angelic Host that stand
> In sight of God enthron'd, our happy state
> Hold, as you yours, while our obedience holds;
> On other surety none; freely we serve,
> Because we freely love, as in our will
> To love or not; in this we stand or fall.
>
> (V. 535-540)

Some angels, Raphael concludes, are already fallen. Plainly he
means to say that those who yet stand may still err if their wills
incline to it.

Milton's purpose, of course, is to emphasize his picture of man's
nature by its parallel in angel's nature. What he has to say here
about angels has importance by virtue of its contribution to his
Arminian doctrine of the human will. Like many a more profes-
sional angelologist, Milton seems to have shaped his doctrine of
angels less by its own intrinsic requirements than by the related
and more important requirements of his anthropology. Arminius
himself makes plain the connection of the angelology and the
anthropology without troubling to express any opinion on the
former. "If you affirm," he retorts to the Cambridge Calvinist,
William Perkins, on the nature of the will, "that the angels obey
God freely, I shall say with confidence, that it is possible that the
angels should not obey God. If, on the other hand, you affirm that

they cannot but obey God, I shall thence boldly infer that they do not obey God freely. For necessity and freedom differ from each other in their entire essence and in genus." [4] Milton did affirm that angels obeyed God freely, and he made Arminius's deduction from it. The opinion is of no importance in *Paradise Lost* as far as the angels alone are concerned; but it does have its weight in the justification to man of God's ways.

Now, as Milton's angelology on the self-dependence of elect angels seems fitted to his anthropology, so on the eating and the love-making of angels, it seems fitted to his metaphysics. As various scholars have suggested in passing, the lines on the eating and the love-making back Milton's conviction of the primacy and goodness of matter. Those who have looked at the angelology as such have either deplored it as needless nonsense or have offered various analogues for it in an effort to show that Milton was writing within a firm tradition. Neither of these approaches fits the facts. Milton's passages are not needless in *Paradise Lost,* and as angelology goes they are not nonsense. But they are basically independent almost to the point of being unique.

II

Those scholars who have looked for analogues to Milton's passages on angels' eating have found much, of course, on the question of whether angels eat and of how they eat, or seem to. Scholars have named Augustine, Tertullian, Scotus, Andrew Willet, Calvin, and Henry More as paralleling Milton,[5] and, of course, Genesis 18, which tells of Abraham's entertainment of three angels. This chapter of Genesis was, in fact, the center of the question on how angels could be said to eat with men, and in Milton's time only two glosses on it were prominent: one developed by Protestant theologians from what seems to have been originally an improvisation of Tertullian's, and the other, much more elaborate, settled in its characteristic form by St. Thomas Aquinas. Neither scheme admitted either the angel's need of any food or his true assimilation of the earthly food he seemed to take.

Tertullian's stand was a by-product of his controversy with Marcion on the Incarnation, of which he urged the "reality" against Marcion's contention that it was but in appearance only. Marcion had offered as similar the apparition of the angels who "did eat" with Abraham, yet must, he thought, have only seemed to do so. Tertullian answered with his widely-cited improvisation on apparition. He will not concede that the angels' flesh was "only putative"; it was "of a true and solid human substance," especially supplied by God, and through its means the angels did "truly converse and eat and work," Tertullian seems to say, "because of the truthfulness of God, who can neither lie nor deceive, and because (angelic beings) cannot be dealt with by men in a human way except in human substance. . . ." [6]

Plainly Tertullian has here little or no interest in angelology as such. He is trying simply to explain away a biblical passage brought against him; to do it he is overturning without scruple — in fact, almost without notice — a "system," a body of "knowledge," on angels to which Marcion has appealed. Tertullian ignores virtually all the angelological points: is this "true flesh" he speaks of in any sense "proper" or permanent to the angels? If not, what becomes of it when their use ends: is it angels' only mode of apparition? And, most important in connection with Milton, is either it or they really nourished by Abraham's hospitality? Plainly Tertullian — like Arminius on the elect angels — shaped his angelology to serve interests larger than its own. And plainly he is saying nothing very closely parallel to Milton, whose angel explicitly does appear in his proper body and does feed on human food, which nourishes him.

All the questions that Tertullian ignores, Aquinas answers circumstantially — totally abandoning, of course, Tertullian's opportunistic position. Aquinas, trying to knit all Christian doctrine into one, was concerned as Tertullian was not with angelology as a branch of theology, with a system of knowledge on angels that needed to be sound in itself. He had, of course, to deal with a much longer Christian tradition than Tertullian did, including many problems hardly present for Tertullian.

One such problem was to reconcile the views of Fathers of the Church who had held angels to be pure spirits with those of Fathers who had held them to have bodies. The solution was the Thomist accommodation on angels as pure spirits able to assume bodies. In such bodies they could not, of course, perform the vital act of digestion and so could not truly eat. [7] This reading agreed with Raphael's statement to Tobit, usually offered as a comment on the Genesis passage: "All these days I did appear unto you; but I did neither eat nor drink, but ye did see a vision." When Duns Scotus contradicted Aquinas with the contention that angels do genuinely eat, he meant no more than that the assumed body chews and swallows.

Some Calvinists — Zanchy most prominently [8] — praised Duns for this contradiction of Aquinas, for like him they wanted to thwart Thomists, and like Tertullian to keep uppermost the assertion that Abraham's angels truly ate. Since Genesis said flatly that the angels "did eat," then, felt the Calvinists, some way must be found to admit that it was so. They reverted, therefore, to Tertullian's stand, only taking care to trim up its angelology a bit. Andrew Willet paraphrases Calvin's well-known opinion on Genesis 18: ". . . as they were endued [by God] with true bodies for the time, so they did verily eate, as they did walke and speake and doe other actions of the bodie truly; yet did they not eate of any necessitie; but like as these bodies by the power of God assumed for the present, were againe disolued and turned into their first nature, so was the meate which they did eate." [9] Calvin and Willet have here rejected the basic Thomistic idea of the body assumed by the angel's ordinary power, but they have not changed — except by Scotus's contrary phrase — the Thomistic conclusion that the angel did not truly eat; for the kind of "true eating" they insist on leaves out the essence of eating: assimilation of the victuals to the eater. Zanchy tries to save the phrase by asking whether Christ's was not a true eating after his resurrection,[10] and by quoting Augustine, who says that Christ's was a true eating and offers the angels as a parallel: "For neither are we to suppose, when men receive them as guests, that the angels eat only in appearance. . . ." But then Augustine goes on: ". . . to any who did not know them to be angels they might seem to eat from the same necessity as ourselves. So these words spoken in the Book of Tobit: 'You saw me eat, but you saw it but in a vision' . . ." [11] Plainly Augustine is no help in getting around the blunt distinction Peter Martyr acknowledges in his criticism of Scotus, who "thinketh that to eate is nothyng else but to chawe meate, and to conueyghte it down into the bellye." To eat, says Peter, "is not only to chawe the meate, or to conueyghte it down into the bellye, but moreouer to conuert it into the substance of hys bodye, by concoction thoroughe the power of vegitacion. Thys, for as muche as the Aungels dyd not, therefore they dyd not eate in very deede." [12]

In fact, then, Augustine and Calvin and Willet are no closer than Tertullian and Scotus to Milton's notion that Raphael ate with "real hunger, and concoctive heat / To transubstantiate . . ." (V. 437-438), since, as the angel explains:

> . . . food alike those pure
> Intelligential substances require
> As doth your Rational; and both contain

> Within them every lower facultie   ·
> Of sense, whereby they hear, see, smell, touch, taste,
> Tasting concoct, digest, assimilate,
> And corporeal to incorporeal turn.
>
> (V. 407-413)

Just as remote from Milton, though in another way, is Henry
More, who did seem to think, indeed, that angels might require
nourishment, but never suggested that they could get it from
earthly food. It is "most natural to conceive," he says, "that partly
by local motion, and partly by the activity of their thoughts, they
set some particles of their Vehicles into a more than usual agitation . . . and that so the vehicle lessens in some measure, and
therefore admits of a recruite. . . ." But the angelic refreshment,
he thinks, must be either by the drawing in of plain air, or by
some sort of heavenly victuals. More's disciple, Joseph Glanville,
agrees that in their *"Heavenly Bodies"* angels "possibly may need
Recruits . . ." so that *"Angel Food* may be more than a *Metaphor:*
But certainly they cannot eat after our Manner, nor feed on our
gross Diet except in appearance only." [13] More and Glanville
hold, then, Milton's heterodox notion that angels require food
from their own realm; but just as certainly they do not go with
him to the more extreme proposition that angels may benefit by
earthly food.

Various scholars have pointed out that More had in his angelology a pre-occupation akin to Milton's; he wanted to establish
the likeness of man to higher creatures, to link the universe into
one chain of being. But More did not want to draw the chain of
being so tight that the function of angelic body would overlap
that of terrestrial body in the conversion of gross matter. He
wanted to keep for the angels a place in the universe parallel to
that of man in this life and equivalent to that of the human soul
in the next life. To admit that an angel could consume human
food would diminish excessively for him the difference between
the condition of the soul in its ethereal or aerial body after death
and that of the soul in its elementary body before death. He had,
of course, already abridged this difference by his Platonistic insistence against the scholastics that angels and separated souls were
animals to the extent of having natural bodies or "vehicles." But
even so, More was almost as near to Aquinas in his conception of
how and why angels ate as to Milton.

The only angelologist who could assert with Milton that angels
profited by earthly food would be one who wanted also to assert

a basic resemblance of man to angel in the whole of their beings.
And this, in fact, appears to be the position and the motive of
Robert Fludd in saying flatly that Abraham's angels received nourishment. If angels "were incorporeal, or if they assumed bodies
accidentally, could they eat and drink with them naturally?"
Surely Abraham, "profound in diuine mysteries," would not have
offered them his food "if he had knowne that it would not naturally haue nourished them?" Plainly Fludd cares little for exegesis as such of Genesis 18; he is simply fixing on the interpretation that seems handiest as a weapon to refute Parson Foster
about the corporeality of angels and the sympathy of body for
body, and through him to baffle the mechanists Mersenne and
Gassendi on the occult links of microcosm and macrocosm and on
the spiritual currents that Fludd contended moved the whole universe. If angels were corporeal the blood of a witch might stay
with the devil that sucked it from her; this blood, infected by the
devil's foul substance, might infect at a distance through the
power of its natural affinity the blood in the witch's body. And
just so, treatment applied to blood on a weapon might be effective
to heal the wound that the weapon had made. So far Fludd's debate with Foster. But that debate was a minor episode in his passionate contentions on how the universe was an organic whole.
God created man, angels, and everything else alike by permeating
prime matter with his essence in different degrees, and his sustaining power flowed into the elementary world through the angels
and shaped all things in their proper forms. For this idea of creation and the cosmos, Fludd argues prodigiously throughout his
chaotic, repetitive, almost endless body of writing, and to its
service he brings all his views on the nature of creatures.

In his explanations of the scale of nature, Milton like Fludd,
is asserting the basic similarity of man and angel, and like Fludd
he is making aggressive use of an item of angelology to support a
contention larger than angelology. The orthodox view that the
soul of man is a separate entity, Milton flatly denied, of course, in
the *Christian Doctrine;*[14] and in Raphael's speeches he conceives
the stages of nature's scale as a sort of telescoping succession in
which the higher comprehends the lower and the whole of the
lower may be translated into the higher. To this conception, the
idea that angels could take man's food was a striking prop, since
it was complementary to the idea that man in his whole being
could rise to take angels' food. And so Raphael encourages Adam:

Wonder not then, what God for you saw good
If I refuse not, but convert, as you,
To proper substance; time may come when men
With Angels may participate, and find
No inconvenient Diet, nor too light Fare:
And from these corporal nutriments perhaps
Your bodies may at last turn all to Spirit,
Improv'd by tract of time, and wingd ascend
Ethereal, as wee, or may at choice
Here or in Heav'nly Paradises dwell;
If ye be found obedient, and retain
Unalterably firm his love entire
Whose progenie you are.

(V. 491-503)

III

Opinion on the loves of the angels is deceptively copious among angelologists. Scholars who read them for something to match Raphael's blushing answer to Adam can find libidinous angels all the way from the Book of Enoch to Henry More and have seemed content to believe that what Milton has to say on angelic amorousness was part of a well-established tradition. And it is true that in some of what Milton says about the dallying of angels with mortal women he is in accord with a well-known though heterodox tradition. Although Milton is orthodox about the nature of the sons of God of Genesis 6 (see above, pp. 129-130), he does have a strongly dissident bit of angelology involved in his very orthodoxy: against the opinion of most Christian authorities, both Protestant and Catholic, Milton seems to say in *Paradise Regained* and certainly to indicate in *Paradise Lost* that fallen angels in their own persons could and would embrace women with desire and even procreate with them. Satan's leering surveillance of Adam's and Eve's delights and his aching words on desire (IV. 502-511) show that Milton's devil was libidinous, whether or not he could impregnate women, and in *Paradise Regained* Satan says flatly that Belial and his "lusty crew" had both the will and the ability; they "Cast wanton eyes on the daughters of men, / And coupl'd with them, and begot a race" (II. 180-181).

Though in thus indicating that devils knew erotic impulse and could genuinely breed with women Milton was counter to most Christian angelologists of his time and of previous times,[15] he did have some authority in St. Augustine, who had expressed a hesitation about whether sylvan spirits and fauns were able to cohabit effectively with women, and more modernly if less reputably in

Paracelsus, who thought that elemental beings could mate effectively with men and women.[16] Henry More, too, speculated that an "airy spirit" acting the male part might be able "to loosen the [female] body into a transmission of such principles and particles as will prove in their conflux in the womb vital and prolifical." [17] More here, like Augustine, was talking of pagan gods and godlets, and so was Milton, for Satan's rebuke to Belial continues:

> Have we not seen, or by relation heard,
> In courts and Royal Chambers how thou lurk'st,
> In Wood or Grove by mossie Fountain-side,
> In Valley or Green Meadow to way-lay
> Some beauty rare, *Calisto, Clymene,*
> *Daphne,* or *Semele, Antiopa*
> Or *Amymone, Syrinx,* many more
> Too long, then lay'st thy scapes on names ador'd,
> *Apollo, Neptune, Jupiter,* or *Pan,*
> *Satyr,* or *Fawn,* or *Silvan?*
>
> (II. 182-191)

For Milton thus to commit himself to the real potency of fallen angels with women was to join a rather free-thinking class of angelologists, but it was as nothing compared with the statement he gives to Raphael in *Paradise Lost;* and none of the angelologists who pace him in the former notion show anything that is really a precedent to the latter. Scholars who examine the tradition of angelic amorousness for predecessors to Milton do not find anywhere that out of a simple ecstasy of affection angel might embrace angel. And that in *Paradise Lost* is the whole point. Milton's angels do not make love with each other for the sake of the sexless reproduction that Gregory of Nyssa is said to ascribe to them,[18] and Adam's question is not of the embraces of women and angels. Adam says:

> Love not the heav'nly Spirits, and how thir Love
> Express they, by looks onely, or do they mix
> Irradiance, virtual or immediate touch?
> To whom the Angel with a smile that glow'd
> Celestial rosie red, Loves proper hue,
> Answer'd. Let it suffice thee that thou know'st
> Us happie, and without Love no happiness.
> Whatever pure thou in the body enjoy'st
> (And pure thou wert created) we enjoy
> In eminence, and obstacle find none
> Of membrane, joynt, or limb, exclusive barrs:
> Easier than Air with Air, if Spirits embrace,
> Total they mix, Union of Pure with Pure

Desiring; nor restrain'd conveyance need
As Flesh to mix with Flesh, or Soul with Soul.
(VIII. 615-629)

One scholar has suggested a parallel to Raphael's embarrassed disclosure in a book of the famous German writer on witchcraft, Johann Wier, whom he paraphrases that "demons have an aerial body which they can change at will into male or female, because of its soft and ductile substance." [19] Wier is here giving the opinions of Psellus, and unquestionably Milton's passage on the total miscibility of angels' substance is a partial echo of his earlier borrowings from Psellus. The Psellian concept of the angelic body gives the physical grounds for the peculiarly intimate embrace that Raphael describes. But neither Wier nor Psellus ever considers the possibility of such an embrace. They are concerned simply with the fact that in apparition demons might seem of either sex.

Another suggestion is that Milton's notion has precedent in Paracelsus' opinion that elemental spirits married not only with men but with each other.[20] Paracelsus' was a widely-noticed idea, of course, scorned by pious angelologists like Boyle and Delrio, and adopted by irresponsibles like Anti-Scot.[21] It was an idea noticed in Talmudical writings by Buxtorf and others and offered in a round-about way by Cardan.[22] But these authorities all differed from Milton drastically, first in that by "demons" they meant not fallen angels as Milton did, but species of invisible beings inhabiting the elements, and second in that they ascribed sex and propagation, whereas Milton speaks only of affectionate embrace, plainly does not intend propagation, and has expressly denied any natural sex among angels.

Aquinas, one scholar notes, tells how angels are attracted to one another. But Aquinas does not have the remotest suggestion that they express their love by caresses. The same scholar mentions too that Joseph Beaumont in his poem *Psyche* speaks of how angels by their looks dart their love each into his fellow's breast.[23] But Milton's Adam asks explicitly whether angels express their love by looks only or by mingling irradiance, and the ultimate answer is of embraces that "obstacle find none / Of membrane, joynt, or limb . . ." (VIII. 624-625).

The fact is that Christian angelologists simply did not speculate on even the possibility that angels embraced each other. The text of Matthew 22.30, which Patrick Hume brings up against Adam's "curious enquiry" — "In heaven is no marrying or giving in mar-

riage" — seemed to everybody a sufficient answer to the question
of whether angels could generate with each other,[24] and few even
thought of the further question of sheer affectionate embrace.

One of those who did think of it was Henry More, for his
scheme of showing that "there are enjoyments attainable after
this earth" of a kind such as we know on this earth compelled him
to acknowledge the question of whether the Genii made love to
each other after their banquets and their dances and their pleasant
converse. His reluctance in *The Immortality of the Soul* either to
admit that the Genii did not experience in their superior bodies
the joys of sensual love or to offend anyone's sensibility by ascribing to them the least grossness apparently hardened in later life
into a decision that angels after all could not be allowed concupis-
cent. In letters written to John Norris of Bemerton in 1684 to
1686 More made very plain that by then, at least, he did not
suppose angels to mingle their substance in any way analogous to
the love which Adam and Eve enjoyed in the flesh. The angels,
he assures Norris, neither marry nor are given in marriage, and
in the "Angellical condition" sexual pleasure is "perfectly silent. . . ." True, when after death we are like the angels, we shall
have "organized bodies" and perhaps we shall taste the food of
angels and shall see, hear, and smell. But the "sixth sense," which
has the stamp of shame upon it, shall not be present.[25] In More's
opinion Raphael could have had nothing to blush for.

More did, it is true, think it possible for spirits to penetrate one
another's substance as well as to penetrate matter, and a modern
editor of *Paradise Lost* comments on the fact in his footnote to
Raphael's answer to Adam.[26] More makes his point, however, without ever a hint that the angels are amorous in such penetration.
Usually when he speaks of spirit penetrating spirit, he is talking
about how God's spirit is in everything. When he spoke of angels'
power to penetrate, More seems to have meant always that the
angel's higher, purely spiritual part, its "soul" had this power, not
the material vehicle. He speaks of angels' spirits permeating their
vehicles, but never of the vehicles as melting into each other. He
was remote, then, from Milton's bold concept.

The thing that restrained More from Milton's boldness was
probably his sense of propriety, as his apology in the Preface to
The Immortality of the Soul indicates. Nothing goes on among
the good Genii, he says, but "might become the most refined spirit
in the World." His project to encourage belief in the next world
by painting it as similar to this, though superior, would not nec-

essarily have been impaired so far as consistency and plausibility went by ascribing embraces to the Genii, and might even have been benefited by it, except in the eyes of those squeamish about the erotic aspects of body. Perhaps More himself was one of these squeamish; at any rate he turned aside from putting the "sixth sense" into heaven. Milton, however, was not the man to hold back upon a mere point of delicacy. He was committed, like More, to paint earth the shadow of heaven (or really the other way around) and things therein each to other like more than most angelologists granted. Matter is good, he had said; so its proper functions are good — all of them. As matter is present throughout the scale of creatures, so its functions are practised by them all, each according to his own form. The form of angels is not suited to procreation, but it is suited in eminence to any kind of joy that man can know, hence to the joys of love.

IV

Perhaps Milton has shown in his lines on angels' eating and making love a certain obduracy; he has insisted on giving answers that his plot did not demand to questions that it did not urgently raise. Simple narrative logic of the events he had to relate did not compel Milton to have Raphael eat with Adam, or if he did have it, to explain the metaphysics of the eating; and if he did explain, the logic of the plot did not forbid the orthodox explanation, which Du Bartas and Heywood had found usable. Milton did not have to let Adam, chastened about his own love, ask his sly question about angels' love, and if he asked it Raphael need not have answered, or might have given the orthodox answer, or at the least might have spared us the physiology of angels' love-making. And above all, many have thought, Raphael need not have blushed.

Milton's justification for giving the general answers he did is, as indicated above, of a kind that had served distinguished, opinionated men before him. Like Tertullian, Arminius, Calvin, and Fludd, he answered the questions so, because answered so they suited his views on a larger and more important question, that of the nature of matter in creatures. The practice of these great men in theology does not help much, however, to justify Milton's in poetry. Why introduce at all into his poem such refractory material as this? What was the importance to the poem of his views on the nature of matter?

The answer is, of course, that those views were close to the heart of the poem. Milton justifies to men the ways that they find in their own beings and in the rest of creation around them, and so justifies the ways of the creator of those created ways. In these passages, often criticized as conveying crabbed and unnecessary dead ideas, Milton is playing the humanist, uniting man to heaven, judiciously exalting the life of God's earth. He is showing the ways of this world as not in themselves defective, as ways primevally free of the basic metaphysical flaw of evil as either co-eternal with good or flowered out of it. The gallant Renaissance faith in man's aboriginal nearness to God and the consequent justification of God's ways, Milton wanted to affirm by as many means as he could — most obviously, of course, through plain his-tory, the traditional events that give his story its general shape. But he made the point, too, with varying success, through the de-tails that add sharpness to the meaning of the well-known story of the fall; through the psychology of the conflict in Adam and Eve and in Satan and Abdiel, through God's blunt theologizing, and through a dozen other means. He could hardly have neglected to indicate his metaphysics to us, and could hardly have come to it better than by way of a comparative angelology and anthropology.

Now, since Milton's lines on the eating and love-making of the angels play such a role in his poem, do such service to the whole scheme of it, his obduracy in them is not that of a poet who stub-bornly writes of extraneous matters, but that of a thinker who clings with an unshaken confidence to opinions that have few en-dorsers. Since this firmness in Milton has not to do so much with angelology as with the grander thought that his angelology here serves, it takes on a dignity that few persons even in Milton's own age would have acknowledged in such extreme angelological spec-ulation retailed for its own sake. In a sense, then, Milton gives least consideration to angelology *per se* in the very passages in which he seems most the angelologist.

It may be that in having Raphael blush, in dropping his prim remark, "No fear lest Dinner coole" (V. 396), and in other details Milton has sinned in a middle-class British way against poetic taste. But that is not a question that really involves the angelology in *Paradise Lost*.

Chapter X

The Significance of Milton's Angelology

IN THE EIGHTEENTH and nineteenth centuries scholars who commented on Milton's angels were usually thinking of him as a Puritan "fundamentalist" who wrote a classical epic, and consequently they seldom looked far beyond the Bible and Mediterranean literature for background to *Paradise Lost's* angelology. Since Milton did indeed rest on Scripture for his angels whenever he possibly could — and sometimes when he could not without taking considerable liberties — and since the action of his work was much governed by conventions of the classical epic, eighteenth and nineteenth-century comment was rarely erroneous as far as it went. The sons of the morning shouted for joy when God laid the foundations of the world; the Dragon drew a third of the stars from heaven and fought with Michael and his angels; Cherubim flourished the flaming sword over fallen Adam and Eve; the chariot of deity was of Wheels and Cherubim; Principalities and Powers were the rulers of the darkness of this world; angels ate with Abraham on the plains of Mamre. Milton's catalogue of devils was like Homer's of ships, and the thousands of spiritual creatures invisible to Adam and Eve were like the unseen daemons of Hesiod.

It was noted, of course, that Milton had misplaced Michael's war with the Dragon, had put the chariot into the work of the six days, though neither Genesis nor Ezekiel does so, and had bestowed on Adam the social honor that Genesis mentioned for Abraham. Occasionally to justify or explain such liberties a commentator went to the Fathers or the Schoolmen, and others detected purely literary parallels to the acts of Milton's angels, such as Satan's use of artillery in Valvasone's *Angeleida;* but so far as theological or philosophical system or tradition on angels went they hardly thought of it in connection with *Paradise Lost*. Bishop Newton in a flash of the curious learning he admiringly ascribed to Milton spotted the first of the two levies on Psellus, but it was a discovery that most commentators after Todd did not bother to notice. In 1850 Thomas Keightley, having written Milton's life, boasted his classical learning and said, too, that he had read through the Old Testament in the original Hebrew, but that he did not hold "it necessary to follow [Milton] into Targums and Mishnas; for I do not think he gathered any poetic fruit in these thickets." Still less did anyone want to enter the jungles of Christian angelology or to believe that Milton himself had explored there. Thus Keightley rejects as of "no authority in Milton's eyes" Johann Wier's once famous *Pseudo-Monarchia Daemonum,* suggested by Todd as giving a precedent for Milton's use of *Belial* as a devil's name.[1] De Quincey and no doubt many others could even suppose that Milton's identification of the fallen angels with pagan gods was a clever device of his own. Walter Raleigh knew De Quincey's error, but still could say flatly in 1900 that Milton on the angels "consigned the Fathers to Limbo and built up his entire system from the words of Scripture." [2]

When the scholars of the twentieth century began to make Milton over in new images, the first to pay much attention to angelology was the learned editor, A. W. Verity, who gave three appendices and many notes to Milton's connections with angelological tradition. He picked various analogues out of Scot, Heywood, the Faust-book, Batman on Bartholomew, and similar general sources. He did not claim that Milton directly used the work of the angelologists he mentioned, but just demonstrated by them more plainly than anyone before him that Milton's ideas about angels were not strange to his own time however unfamiliar to Verity's.[3]

Verity did not look among esoteric writers for Milton's ideas, however, so that M. Denis Saurat found a relation for Milton altogether new when, after turning up some not wholly unsuspected angelological parallels in various Fathers of the Church, he showed Milton to have close correspondence also to Robert Fludd, particularly in questions of the angelic nature, a thing little touched by scholars before him. M. Saurat was enthusiastic over his whole idea of the staid Puritan among the Cabalists, "a gap," he thought, ". . . blown into the very fortress of English literature," through which "much may . . . come in." [4] Wide stretches of this gap were soon plugged by scholars who, though not eager to return Milton to the narrow bounds once laid out for his Puritanism, yet felt that the Cabalists and Fludd were less closely and specially allied to his thought than M. Saurat's supremely stimulating work had purported to show. They made few special attacks against Saurat's findings on the angels, but they did turn up what seemed some of the same angelological notions in the works of many men very different from Fludd: Henry More, Du Bartas, Scot and Anti-Scot, Robert Burton, Tertullian and Aquinas, ancient and medieval Rabbis, and the great commentators on the Bible. The scholarship most inclusive on angelology, Grant McColley's *Paradise Lost: The Birth of an Epic*, offers some sort of parallel for almost every item of Milton's angelology and several, often very diverse, for some. It seems to imply (no doubt against the author's intention) that Milton scratched at random through the literature of the "science" to pick out what nuggets he needed as he needed them, without regard to how they suited one another, either in their origin or in Milton's adaptation. McColley thinks, for instance, that Milton used three different notions of the angelic substance.[5]

Now the fact certainly is that Milton's angelology is syncretic; the parts of it are discernible and seem in their origins more or less incompatible. Milton certainly echoes Cabalists in odds and ends, at least, and he brought some rather positive notions of Platonistic philosophers on angelic nature and operation into a perhaps faintly uneasy union with the reserved and largely negative opinions of Protestant theologians. He retained many ideas usual among Scholastics,[6] though he sneered openly at one most commonly called theirs. He worked into the generally traditional frame of his angelology some notions of his own that are outside any of the traditions which he followed. The warning of a famous Miltonist against incautious talk about Milton's "system" of angelology is obviously sound.[7] But the fact is that it concerns an error of which scholars stand in little danger, for almost no one has ever felt it feasible to attribute an angelological "system" to Milton. A more present danger to our understanding of Milton's methods and results with his angels in *Paradise Lost* seems to be the view that he borrowed everything and did it almost at random, not troubling to achieve even a surface consistency. Modern scholarship has said that Milton has two contradictory conceptions of the angelic substance, or perhaps three; that he made the sons of God who trafficked with the daughters of men either good angels or evil angels or progeny of Seth as suited his narrative moment; that he can be justified out of Dionysius for his most un-Dionysian scrambling of the Dionysian terms of angelic rank; that the angelic eating and loving are commonplaces from authors as disparate as Augustine and Anti-Scot, Aquinas and Paracelsus. Admittedly to cross angelological lines was not hard in the seventeenth century, and certainly Milton crossed them. But he does not contradict himself on the angelic substance or on the sons of God; his obvious shunning of Dionysius is not really a concealed observance of him; what he has to say on angelic eating and loving is an independent stand, not a traditional one, either orthodox or unorthodox, and Milton integrates it with what else he has to say of angels and with his metaphysics generally. Milton does not, it is true, have a full schematic angelology of his own even in the *Christian Doctrine,* and *Paradise Lost* is not based on an unstated one. But the very lack is itself part of Milton's deliberate thinking about angels. His decisions do not amount to a "system" in the sense that Aquinas has a "system," or Henry More, but they do bring a reasonably consistent order into the angelology of *Paradise Lost.*

The order is, of course, principally that sponsored by embattled Protestantism, disdainfully rising above the middle ages, as it thought; hitting its Roman adversary hard where it found it most entangled with out-of-date ways of thought, keeping itself as clear as it could, meanwhile, of the still more embarrassing entanglements that might come with revived Platonistic ways of thought; relaxing not a whit its narrowly biblical insistence on angels. In Milton this combative, half-sceptical tradition of Calvin and Zanchy, Ursinus and Gerhard, is perhaps most conveniently designated Puritan. This cannot mean, of course, that Milton's angelology is Puritan in any sense which implies that the Puritan was an exclusive sort of angelology, but only in the sense that Milton's was, *generally speaking,* the kind of angelology consistently adopted by Puritans as well as by many other sober-minded Protestants. The term *Puritan* can safely distinguish Milton's restricted kind of angelology from the free and up-to-date kind of the Protestant Henry More, and the theosophical kind of the Protestant Robert Fludd. The term signifies that Milton gave unabashed notice to angelology, unlike the Protestant Francis Osborn, who may have found the study unstylish, or the Protestant William Harvey, who found it inconvenient, or the devout Protestant Robert Boyle, who found it embarrassing. It signifies that Milton has no hint of basic sympathy with such consistent and deliberate rationalism as Reginald Scot's, though he shares Scot's stiff disdain of angelological folderol.

Admittedly, of course, Milton's kind of angelology belongs, too, to some men who certainly cannot be brought wholly under any

definition of Puritan, for it was common to many Protestant denominations, both in England and on the continent; bishops of
the Church of England — Hall, Ussher, Bull — speak it as plainly
in general as the Puritan ministers. We may naturally suppose,
however, that Milton would have found this conservative Protestant angelology more appealing in the work of the Puritan, Henry
Lawrence, whom he admired, than in that of his adversary, Bishop
Hall, in spite of a strong coincidence of both tone and substance
between their treatises. Regardless of much overlap between the
Puritan and the Episcopal angelology, if we need a word to apply
to Milton's, a word less inclusive than *Protestant, Puritan* is obviously most serviceable and most accurate. It may be possible that
in angelology, at least, Milton resembled Isaac Ambrose, who
praises Hall's *Invisible World Discovered* with the remark that he
is not offended with the name of Bishop.[8] Ambrose's angelology
was certainly Puritan, however sympathetic to Hall's, and so in
general is Milton's.

The positive characteristics of this Puritan angelology are plain
in *Paradise Lost:* its clinging to the Bible, and its emphasis on
angels as moral beings, as creatures obedient or rebellious to God,
tempters of man or ministers for his salvation. Its negative characteristics, too, — a reserve about whatever it must use that is not to
be fetched direct from the Bible, and a scorn of any gratuitous
speculation — are in *Paradise Lost,* though not always self-evident.
Milton shows the Puritan reserve about hierarchy and guardians,
and about whether or not the angels were dichotomous, about
their power in nature, and about the precise kind of materiality
they had. The scorn of gratuitous speculation is harder to find,
for Milton is speculative occasionally without apology, and he did
not often digress against others. Still, when Raphael is about to
launch Milton's very boldest angelological flight he begins with
a phrase reminiscent of his earlier words on being lowly wise:
"Let it suffice thee . . ." (VIII. 620). Of angels, he seems to say,
Adam ought to know only what concerns him, namely that without love no creature can be happy. By its very nature *Paradise Lost*
had not much scope for expressing contempt of angelological speculation, though Milton did sniff at "Theologians" and at what he
implies is their foolish misstatement of the facts of angelic apparition.

It is true, of course, that after the Puritanesque beginning of his
account of angelic love, Raphael gives Adam a very positive and
rather detailed sketch of an angelological article not easily de-

ducible from the Bible and contradicting what virtually all Christian theologians thought was deducible from it about angelic love. And just before his sneer at the "common gloss of the Theologians" on angels' eating, Milton had stated a notion about it that most of his contemporaries, including Puritans, would have thought much more questionable than that gloss. Certainly, too, Milton's Psellian borrowings were not material that was grateful to the ears of many Puritans. And certainly Milton uses angels' names in common with the Cabala. Does not the case for his predominating Puritanism founder, then, on these plain exceptions, comprising as they do most of the concentrated angelology in *Paradise Lost?*

The answer is, of course, that in writing angelological passages in *Paradise Lost,* Milton was never controlled first by considerations of the "science"; his lines on angels are always poetic fiction before they are angelology, and in them doctrine, conjecture, and fancy coalesce in equal authority as poetic fiction, though separately they remain of very unequal weight as angelology. The fancies, such as Uriel's gliding down the sunbeam, are governed by angelology hardly at all. The conjectures, such as the Psellian material, have no standing as doctrine. Some items, however, do stand as doctrine because though they appear always in the mirror of the epic poetry, shaped by its rhetorical and dramatic requirements, they are shaped, too, by its moral and didactic requirements. When Milton talks of angels, he moulds what he has to say according to ideas of them which he holds to be really true and also according to the needs of effective poetic statement. The Bible was his guide to truth, and the Puritan angelologists were his companions in following it. The Platonistic philosophers and theosophists, however, were not guides or companions to him in the same serious sense. That they were not appears in the fact that they are missing from the only angelology which we may suppose that Milton wrote in accord with the requirements he thought suitable to the "science" proper, the sections in his *Christian Doctrine.* The Platonistic notions appear in *Paradise Lost* because Milton had to consider for his fiction not only the doctrinal truth of what he wanted to say, but the literary truth, the requirements of speaking effectively in the chosen style. These requirements brought about not only Milton's use of Psellus and the Cabalists but his independent expressions on the angelic physiology.

To say, then, that the angelology in *Paradise Lost* is predominantly Puritan is not to deny that ideas from quite other sorts of authorities are prominent in it, but only to decide that the evidence from the *Christian Doctrine* and from *Paradise Lost* itself shows that the angelology which retains in *Paradise Lost* some sort of doctrinal standing is the Puritan, whereas the rest of it is for decoration or the forwarding of the story or for the making of some special point that in itself transcends angelology. As the Psellian material is the clearest case of Milton's connection with Platonistic thought on the angels, so it is the clearest case of the casualness of that connection. Milton adapts the material in such a way as to free himself from the unsuitable rest of Psellus and to give what he uses a wholly different air from that which it has in Psellus. *Paradise Lost* shows no likeness to Psellus' angelology as a whole, in spite of the two definite nuggets of direct debt. Significantly the poem is not thus cut off from the whole angelological scheme and atmosphere of Lawrence, say, or of Ambrose, in spite of divergences from them on some points and in spite of the fact that no direct debt is traceable. In *Paradise Lost* the borrowing from Psellus actually takes on the air that one from Lawrence would have had there, and, similarly, Cabalistic names appear in *Paradise Lost* almost without flavor of the special Cabalistic interest in angels' names; the terms of the Jewish orders appear with only the most shadowy indications of their extra-biblical significations; the placing of the angels in the universe contradicts the prominent occult schemes, and the functions of angels in nature is mentioned hardly at all and then in an equivocal form. Evidently Milton's Platonistic angelology in *Paradise Lost* is controlled to a degree by his Puritan.

In effect, then, Milton is standing with Lawrence on the proposition that though angels may serve God much by virtue of their special talents and their secret offices, yet to inquire too subtly just what angels do and how they do it has in it more danger than instruction.[9] For purposes of fiction, Milton seems to indicate, we may accept a plausible theory that angels can contract and expand, change their shapes, and enter into snakes, and that their names may be of a certain general kind, so that the unknown names resemble those divulged in Scripture. Beyond this, he relies with the Puritans, or at least like them, on biblically secured and morally edifying items of angelology; good angels are the servants of God and ministers to the heirs of salvation and the evil go about like roaring lions. This is the prevailing temper of *Paradise Lost*.

The element in the poem that seems least harmonious with this temper is Milton's insistence on sense in angels and particularly on the pleasures of sense. In this insistence he flatly contradicts both the spirit and the substance of Lawrence and of most other Puritans, who preferred the scholastic idea of angels as devoid of any capacity for earthly appetites or passions, and particularly for the slime-born weakness of concupiscence.

In some of what he has to say on the angelic senses Milton seems to resemble the scientific-minded latitudinarian, Henry More, with his speculation that the genii, like Milton's angels, sing and feast and dance in their own world. The resemblance to More is superficial, however, for Milton's reasons for feast and discourse in heaven and hell lay much more in his literary needs than in his angelology, and his air in speaking of these things is almost as unlike More's as it is unlike that of Psellus, who also tells how daemons take nourishment — by sucking it in through the superficies of their bodies. Whereas More is "demonstrating . . . in dry prose . . . that there are enjoyments attainable after this earth," [10] Milton — particularly in the scene of song and discourse in hell (II. 547-569) — is painting a picture that owes much more to Virgil on Elysium than to any angelologist. From his description of this first social afternoon among devils, Milton passes to the discovery in hell of the conventional infernal rivers and of Medusa on guard over Lethe. Such classical mythology is a far cry from More on how the genii may in the atmosphere around us "sing and play and dance together, reaping the lawful pleasures of the very *Animal life*. . . ." [11] In Milton's heaven the angels dance, but they do it for the honor of God around his awful throne, not for the pleasures of the animal life. Grant that the general idea of delectation and jubilation in the spirit world is one on which Milton and More agree, still it is an idea so suitable and necessary to Milton's fiction that it hardly stands as part of his angelology, of his commonness with reasoned "systems" on angels. A recent book on Satan suggests that Milton could "rely on" Heywood for music in hell;[12] but plainly Milton needed to rely on no one for such a point.

The peak of what Milton has to say about sense in angels is, of course, his heresies on eating and love-making, and here though Milton perhaps resembles More in the extreme speculativeness of his remarks and in their general subject, he goes too far beyond More to be properly referred to him. He goes still farther beyond the Puritans, of course; yet even in these extreme passages a certain conformity to Puritan angelology persists. Thus, Milton's argument for Raphael's genuine eating has its base in secular philosophy in a way not unusual among the Puritans, who often felt a need to sustain themselves briefly with such philosophy. For instance, the widely approved contention among the Puritans that angels could suggest things directly to men's minds was based on faculty psychology and the physiology of the humors. The Puritans did not contend for the details, and neither does Milton in explaining Satan's control of Eve's dream. He merely suggests how such a thing may be as Satan's reaching "The Organs of her Fancie" or tainting "Th' animal spirits" (IV. 802-804). Similarly he merely suggests how the chain of being makes plausible Raphael's assimilation of earthly food, and drops the casual analogy of the "Empiric Alchimist" who turns coal to gold. The fact that Milton has used the idea of nature's scale does not separate him from Puritans, for that idea was in itself agreeable enough to them, and Milton's sweeping use of it is of a sort frequent among them. Too, Milton makes central in his whole exposition of the scale the commonplace dear to Puritan angelologists that in a sense all things, including angels, are bodily save God, though "more spiritous, and pure" the nearer they are placed to him "or neerer tending" (V. 475-476).

None of this ought to obscure the fact, certainly, of Milton's extreme independence on the eating and the loving. But even that, taken in conjunction with the fact that his apparent reasons for it were intrinsic not so much to his angelology as to his governing metaphysics, has a Puritan tang of contempt for speculative angelology. Milton did not care enough for angelology *per se* to forswear a merely angelological heresy, unless it were one that obviously and directly controverted religion as he conceived it. Neither Milton nor the Puritans hesitated to shape angelology to suit more important studies.

Finally, then, the fact that Milton sometimes contradicts the Puritans does not in itself divide him from them. He is against them on other specific points besides the eating and the loving: on the meaning of election in angels, the whereabouts of hell, the time of angels' creation. The thing that shows him a Puritan in angelology is not any undeviating adherence to every item of Puritan doctrine. (Probably no individual Puritan was undeviating, and probably no item-by-item Puritan doctrine could be formulated for one to be undeviating from.) The things that show Milton Puritan in his angelology are the aim and atmosphere of it, his manifest sympathy with the Puritan approach to the "science," together with a *general* conformity of doctrine. Milton's strong-minded independence on particular articles does not cut him off from the Puritans in angelology any more than his similar independence concerning the dissolubility of marriage cuts him off from them about the sacraments. As he believed with the Puritans that marriage was no sacrament and went beyond them to contend for divorce, so analogously he conjectured with them that an angel was not pure spirit in substance and went beyond them to conjecture that an angel might eat man's food and make love with other angels.

Plainly no study of Milton's angelology can say definitely what kind of man and thinker he was. It can only reveal some things about a special part of his background, about some sources and some compositional practices and some intellectual affiliations which, though they may be fairly clear, are certainly very limited. To say at the end of a study of Milton's angelology that it makes him out to be a Puritan is not to deny in him many non-Puritan characteristics, some perhaps more powerful than the Puritan. Milton's humanism, for instance, gets little chance to show itself in his angelology, for angelology was not by his time any longer the humanistic study that it had been for such men as Ficino, Agrippa, and Colet. The hope that Ficino and Agrippa held to enhance humanity by theurgical communion with angels had been lost in black doubts about the theurgical method, and the purer mysticism that Colet grounded on Dionysius had thinned to nothing with the destruction among Protestants of faith in Dionysius and the association of authoritative angelology with scholastic aridity.[13] Milton does, of course, retain here and there echoes of humanistic angelology, such as the guardian spirit in *Comus* and the lines in *Il Penseroso* that speak of unsphering the spirit of Plato concerning

> . . . those *Daemons that are found*
> In fire, air, flood, or underground,
> Whose power hath a true consent
> With Planet or with Element.

But the judgment which a great Milton scholar made more than twenty-five years ago still is sound that these "translunary dreams of Plato" and of Hermes, Iamblichus, and Psellus afforded Milton only "a fascinating realm for curiosity to explore"; he "could hardly allow in these fantastic writings more than a small residuum of truth to challenge his more sober thought." [14] Milton's

serious humanism shows itself very little in his angelology anywhere.

It appears most strongly, of course, in the passages on the scale
of nature, where angelology is hardly more than an excuse to
assert the basic holiness of man in his entire being, the positive
linkage, not only moral but metaphysical, of this world to heaven,
and the worth of this world as God's and of God. The humanistic
spirit in those passages does not rest upon Agrippa's Neo-Platonic
notion that by cultivating angels man might rise beyond them in
power and understanding, but on Milton's own unconventional
one, suggesting no theurgical operations, that man and angel were
throughout of one common stuff. To the extent that Milton's
improvised angelology supports his humanism, it may be called
humanistic, of course, just as it may be called Puritanistic from
the fact that Milton regards it lightly in itself, or scholastic from
the fact that Milton embodies some scholastic notions in it. The
chief point here is that the angelology as such is secondary. A
passage which as angelology shows strong though concealed Puritan and scholastic characteristics may yet serve humanistic uses.

This means in part, certainly that, as many scholars have shown,
humanism and Puritanism were not such opposite poles of culture
in Milton or in others as was once supposed. The cleavage between a Puritan angelology and a Platonistic one, true, is rather
marked; but either one might serve either a humanist or a Puritan, as appears in the works of Sir Thomas Browne, for instance,
and of Peter Sterry. It may be true of Milton, and the study of
his angelology may help to show, that a stern Protestant conviction
was the pulsing heart of all that he said and did. But it seems true
also that he expanded that conviction with the understanding of
a learned humanist and ornamented all that he said and did out
of that understanding. No study of his angelology could diminish
these facts.

Notes

*Numbers in brackets at the top of the following pages indicate the pages
in the text to which these notes refer.*

CHAPTER I

1. Aldous Huxley, *Ape and Essence* (New York, 1948); Thomas Mann, *Doctor Faustus* (New York, 1948); C. E. M. Joad, *God and Evil* (London, 1942).
2. C. S. Lewis, *The Screwtape Letters* (London, 1944); Denis de Rougemont, *The Devil's Share* (Washington, 1944); C. S. Lewis, *Out of the Silent Planet* (London, 1943), and *Perelandra* (New York, 1944).
3. Summers' most recent remarks on this theme that are known to me are in his introduction to the reprint of Richard Bovet's *Pandaemonium* (Aldington, Kent, 1951).
4. See the second part of *Absalom and Achitophel*. Pordage there figures as "Lame Mephibosheth, the wizard's son."
5. Scores of pamphlets on apparitions and other demonic marvels streamed from the press of Milton's time, such as *Strange Relation of a Young Woman Possest with a Devill* (London, 1647), and *Strange and Terrible News from Cambridge* (London, 1659). See the bibliography appended to Montague Summers, *The History of Witchcraft and Demonology* (London, 1926) or the notes to G. L. Kittredge, *Witchcraft in Old and New England* (Cambridge, 1928).
6. Christopher Fowler, *Daemonium Meridianum* (London, 1655), pp. 98-100.
7. Henry More, *The Immortality of the Soul* (London, 1659), Preface, Section 6.
8. Pierre Le Loyer, *Discours et Histoires des Spectres* (Paris, 1605), I, iv, 21-32, refutes the Peripatetics but spares Aristotle, and Strozzio Cicogna, *Magiae Omnifariae* (Cologne, 1607), II, v. 182-188, does about the same. R. P. P. Valderama, *Histoire General du Monde* (Paris, 1618), is a little harder on Aristotle. Robert Burton, *Anatomy of Melancholy*, ed. A. R. Shilleto (London, 1912), I, II, I, II, 206, notices that like the Sadducees the Peripatetics denied spirits, "even *Aristotle himself*, as *Pomponatius* stoutly maintains, and *Scaliger* in some sort grants; though *Dandinus* the Jesuit . . . stiffly denies it."
9. *Laws* in *The Dialogues of Plato*, trans. B. Jowett (New York, 1937), XII, 701.
10. *Metaphysics* in *The Basic Works of Aristotle*, ed. Richard McKeon (New York, 1941), XII, viii, 882. *De Caelo* in *The Works of Aristotle*, under ed. W. D. Ross, trans. J. L. Stocks (Oxford, 1930), II, 12, 292ᵃ.
11. "On the Cessation of Oracles," *Plutarch's Morals. Theosophical Essays*, trans. C. W. King (London, 1908), p. 83 and p. 132.
12. For a bibliography see William George Heidt, *Angelology of the Old Testament* (Washington, 1949). I have not drawn my sketch of the attitude toward angels shown in the Old Testament from Heidt, though I believe his work confirms some points of it.
13. See W. O. E. Oesterley and G. H. Box, *A Short Survey of the Literature of Rabbinical and Medieval Judaism* (London, 1920), p. 55 n.; Alfred Edersheim, *The Life and Times of Jesus the Messiah* (New York, 1927), II, 748-754; Louis Ginzburg, *The Legends of the Jews* (Philadelphia, 1909), I, 53 ff.; *The Jewish Encyclopedia* on *angels* and *demons*; Bernard J. Bamburger, *Fallen Angels* (Philadelphia, 1952), pp. 92-93.
14. The readiest source book of Neo-Platonic daemonology is the celebrated anthology of Ficino, containing his translations *De Mysteriis Aegyptiorum, Chaldaeorum, Assyriorum* attributed to Iamblichus, and the *Pimander* attributed to Trismegistus, and excerpts of Proclus, *In Platonicum Alcibiadem de Anima,*

atque Daemone, Porphyry, *De Diuinus atque Daemonibus* and *De Sacrificio et Magia,* and Psellus, *De Daemonibus.* This work appeared in many editions, of which I have one of Lyons, 1577. It was very largely from this work that sixteenth and seventeenth-century writers took their ideas of Neo-Platonists on daemons. Modern authorities on the Neo-Platonists have not had much to say about their daemonology. E. R. Dodds does have some long notes in his translation of Proclus' *The Elements of Theology,* 2nd ed. (Oxford, 1933), pp. 294-295, 308. Karel Svoboda, *La Demonologie de Michel Psellos* (Brno, 1927), traces the ideas of Psellus, many of them, to Neo-Platonic sources and gives ample reference and full discussion.

15. St. Augustine, *The City of God* in *The Basic Writings of St. Augustine,* ed. Whitney J. Oates (New York, 1948), XV, xxiii, 307.

16. Michael Psellus, *De Operatione Daemonum Dialogus,* trans. Pierre Moreau (Paris, 1615). This translation was reprinted four times between 1615 and 1654. Equally available is Ficino's translation mentioned in note 14 above. It appeared at least six times between 1497 and 1641. For Psellus' opinions see below pp. 70-72 and 145-148. For the Talmudist notion see Johann Buxtorf, *Lexicon Chaldaicum, Talmudicum, et Rabbinicum* (Basle, 1639), p. 2339.

17. Jerome Cardan, *De Rerum Varietate* (Avignon, 1558), XVI, vcii, 802-814. On Paracelsus see *Paracelsus of the Supreme Mysteries of Nature,* trans. Robert Turner (London, 1655), pp. 51-54; *A Book on Nymphs, Sylphs, Pigmies, Salamanders, and other Spirits* in *Four Treatises of Theophrastus von Hohenheim,* ed. Henry Sigerist (Baltimore, 1941); Franz Hartman, *The Life of Paracelsus* (London, n.d.), pp. 116-127.

18. Henry More, *The Immortality of the Soul* (London, 1659), and other works as treated below, pp. 81-90, and elsewhere.

19. John Pordage, *Theologia Mystica* (London, 1683), pp. 78-79, 87-93.

20. Augustine treats the problem in several places very inconclusively, now quoting Apuleius' definition of daemons as airy (a quotation of which those made much who wanted St. Augustine to have declared for proper body in angels), again pointing to passages in the Bible that seem to imply that angels have not bodies. Probably Augustine most accurately declares his own opinion when he says "To ask questions like these . . . is a useful exercise . . . if we avoid the error of supposing ourselves to know what we do not know." See *The Enchiridion* in *The Works of Aurelius Augustine,* trans. Marcus Dodds, vol. IX, lviii, 217. For a sixteenth-century Protestant opinion on Augustine's opinion see Peter Martyr, *The Common Places* (London, 1574), I, x, 81, or Jerome Zanchy, *De Operibus Dei* in *Operum Theologicorum* (Geneva, 1613), II, iii, 67. Zanchy depends in part for his interpretation on Augustine's use of Apuleius's definition in *The City of God,* VIII, xvi. It is a reed to lean on, since Augustine does not speak very favorably of Apuleius. Both Peter Martyr and Zanchy were extremely influential in England on angelology.

21. For Anselm I rely on Edward Langton, *Supernatural: the Doctrine of Spirits, Angels, and Demons, from the Middle Ages until the Present Time* (London, 1934), pp. 34-38, and a cursory check in the *Patrologia.* For St. Bernard see *Sermones in Cantica Canticorum* in *Opera Omnia* (Paris, 1719), vol. I, sermon v, p. 1284e. In other places Bernard is equally indifferent.

22. See Langton, *Supernatural,* pp. 43-59. Langton does not touch the angelology of Bonaventure, which was outside the tradition made dominant by Aquinas in that it ascribed body of a sort to angels. Bonaventure's ideas did not, however, fit at all with those of the grosser Platonists, such as Apuleius and Psellus. See Etienne Gilson, *The Philosophy of St. Bonaventure* (London, 1938), pp. 238-271, for an unsurpassed account of the saint's angelology, especially as it varies from that of Aquinas. Some seventeenth-century Catholic angelologists turned toward a doctrine of proper bodies for angels. See, for instance, Ludovico Maria Sinistrari, *Demoniality,* trans. Montague Summers (London, n.d.), pp. 28-31

This work was not published until 1875, though written in the seventeenth century.

23. As Professor George L. Burr pointed out long ago in connection with the literature of witchcraft, the fact that an age has no surviving literature of scepticism does not necessarily mean that it was entirely without scepticism, but perhaps that in that age scepticism was neither stylish nor healthful. Professor Burr thought that the existence of a certain scepticism might be inferred from the constant complaints of the witchmongers against unbelievers. Medieval angelologists did not attack Sadducees and Epicureans as often as their Renaissance successors did, but they did feel an impulsion to give rational "proofs" of the existence of angels and to show how angels might rationally be thought equal to the marvels ascribed to them. See James Collins, *The Thomistic Philosophy of Angels* (Washington, 1947), pp. 1-40, especially pp. 15, 16. For Professor Burr's views see his "The Literature of Witchcraft," *Papers of the American Historical Association*, IV, (New York, 1890), 56.

24. Agrippa's tremendously influential *Occult Philosophy* is the chief monument to this revival of theurgy. For an account of Agrippa's theories of elevated magic see my *Invisible World* (Athens, Georgia, 1939), pp. 39-48.

25. Lambert Daneau, *A Dialogue of Witches* (London, 1575), Introduction, sig. B4.

26. *D. Erasmi in Novum Testamentum . . . Annotationes* (Basle, 1660), note on Acts 17.34. Erasmus follows Grocyn and Valla in marshaling some of the evidence against the belief that the author of the *Celestial Hierarchy* was the Areopagite. Many Protestants took up the battle. For one in the seventeenth century see Archbishop James Ussher, *Dissertatio de Pseudo-Dionysii Scriptis* in *The Whole Works* (London, 1847), XII, 499-520.

27. Calvin, *The Institution of Christian Religion*, 6th ed. (London, 1580), I, xiv, 44b; Peter Martyr, *The Common Places* (London, 1574), I, xii, 120.

28. Jerome Zanchy, *De Operibus Dei* in *Operum Theologicorum* (Geneva, 1613), II, xiv, 92-96.

29. *The Institution*, I, xiv, 44 and 44b.

30. *The Holy Gospel of Jesus Christ, according to John with the Commentary of M. John Calvin*, trans. Christopher Teetherstone (London, 1584), on chapter 5, verse 4; and *A Commentarie upon the Prophecie of Isaiah by Mr. John Calvin*, trans. by C. C. (London, 1609), on chapter 37, verse 36.

31. *Commentary on Isaiah*, 63.9.

32. *Purchas his Pilgrimage*, 2nd ed. (London, 1614), p. 10, as quoted in Francis R. Johnson, *Astronomical Thought in Renaissance England* (Baltimore, 1937), p. 260. Johnson notices Calvin's "relatively liberal attitude toward the interpretation of the scriptural references to scientific matters," under his listing of Calvin's *Commentarie upon Genesis* in his bibliography.

33. *Galileus Galileus His System of the World in Mathematical Collections and Translations . . . by Thomas Salusbury* (London, 1661), Dialogue I, pp. 11, 12, 19. See also H. Butterfield, *The Origins of Modern Science*, 1300-1800 (London, 1950), p. 125.

34. See Edwin A. Burtt, *The Metaphysical Foundations of Modern Physical Science*, 2nd ed. (London, 1949), p. 78 ff.

35. Mersenne's *Questiones Celeberrimae in Genesim* (Paris, 1623) is full of believing entries on angels, but he does not indicate that he supposed them regularly active in controlling nature. Gassendi, who wrote against Robert Fludd partly on Mersenne's behalf, opposed Fludd's theories of angelic control of the cosmos and in other works maintained reserve about the activities of angels. He says, for instance, that Aristotle supposed them to control the spheres, but never says whether Aristotle was right. See his *Syntagmata Philosophici* II, I, IV, viii, 293, in vol. I of the *Opera Omnia* (Florence, 1727), and his *Fluddanae Philosophiae Examen*, in vol. III, pp. 222 ff.

36. See the correspondence between Spinoza and Hugo Boxel (Letters LV-LX) as given in *The Chief Works of Benedict de Spinoza*, trans. R. H. M. Elwes (New York, 1951), pp. 375-388.

37. See Pope's *First Epistle of the Second Book of Horace, To Augustus*, 1, 101; *Essay on Man*, I, 237. On the fate of "machinery" in Pope's time and his work see Mark Schorer, *William Blake, The Politics of Vision* (New York, 1946), p. 31.

38. See "On the Partial Attempts that Have Been Made to Reform the Abuses of Human Reason," which is Section IV of *Essay the Second* in *The Works of Henry St. John, Lord Viscount Bolingbroke* (London, 1809), VI, 180-184.

39. See David Hume, *The Natural History of Religion* in *Philosophical Essays* (Philadelphia, 1817), II, 380, for the briefest and most nominal acknowledgment that "we" believe in a supreme God who uses the agency of "angels and subordinate ministers."

40. For Wesley's views see Langton, *Supernatural*, pp. 91-98 and 242-246. For Swedenborg's see pp. 98-109.

41. John Leland, *View of the Principal Deistical Writers that Have Appeared in the Last and Present Century* (London, 1757), I, 427.

42. Augustine Calmet, *The Phantom World*, trans. Henry Christmas, from ed. of 1751 (Philadelphia, 1850).

43. Samuel Hibbert, *Sketches of the Philosophy of Apparitions* (London, 1824).

44. See, for instance, Ernest Renan, *Vie de Jesus* (Paris, 1895), xvi, 264-280, on miracles.

45. For the views of Schleiermacher and Dorner I have depended chiefly on Edward Langton, *Satan, a Portrait* (London, 1945), pp. 96-99 and 108-110.

46. See, for instance, John Fiske, *Outline of Cosmic Philosophy Based on the Doctrine of Evolution* (Boston, 1875), p. 379, on how "The contemporaries of Bodin were so thoroughly predisposed by their general theory of things to believe in the continual intervention of the Devil, that it needed but the slightest evidence to make them credit any particular act of intervention," whereas "to the educated man of today such intervention seems too improbable to be admitted on any amount of testimony."

47. William James, *A Pluralistic Universe* (New York, 1943), pp. 153-164.

CHAPTER II

1. "An Hydrostatical Discourse," in *The Works* (London, 1744), III, II, i, 276 and III, II, v, 288.

2. The original treatise on the demon of Mascon was the work of a Swiss minister, Francois Perrault (or Perraud) in whose house the poltergeist was active. It was printed with Perrault's *Demonologie ou Traitte des Demons et Sorciers* (Geneva, 1653) forty years after the occurrence it recorded. Boyle met and talked with Perrault and was so persuaded of the truth of his account that he got Dr. Peter Du Moulin to translate it into English (See the letter from Boyle to Du Moulin prefixed to *The Divell of Mascon*, 5th ed., Oxford, 1679). Earlier, in correspondence with Glanville on the latter's project, Boyle asserted his continued faith in the tale of the demon of Mascon as a whole. See his letters to Glanville of Sept. 18, 1677 and Feb. 10, 1677-78 in *The Works*, V, 244-245. Henry More made a great point of Boyle's conviction in his *Antidote against Atheism* in *Several Philosophical Writings* (London, 1712), III, iii, 95.

3. Theosophy and mysticism persisted in England, of course, through the "age of reason," and not all its representatives were inferior persons. William Law, for instance, is certainly worthy of his master, Boehme. Yet obviously Law was isolated in his time.

4. See Wallace Notestein, *A History of Witchcraft in England* (Washington, 1911), pp. 160-162.

5. See C. L'Estrange Ewen, *Witchcraft and Demonianism* (London, 1933), p. 250.

6. William Harvey, "Exercitatio Altera, ad J. Riolanum," in *Opera Omnia* (London, 1766), I, 116. Harvey is concerned chiefly with the bodily spirits, but seems to declare against the lore of "cacodemons" too.

7. *John Selden and his Table Talk*, ed. Robert Waters (New York, 1899), pp. 98-100.

8. Samuel Butler, "Magique," in *Satires and Miscellaneous Poetry and Prose*, ed. René Lamar (Cambridge, 1928), p. 199.

9. Francis Osborn, "Essay on Such as Condemn All they Understand not a Reason for," in *The Works* (London, 1673), p. 551. See also *Advice to a Son, The Works*, 118.

10. John Selden, *De Diis Syriis* (London, 1617), II, v, 214.

11. "A Contemplation on Adam's Fall," *Works*, pp. 563-565.

12. Alexander Ross, *Leviathan Drawn out with a Hook* (London, 1653), p. 38.

13. *Leviathan*, Everyman's Library (New York, 1914), III, xxxiv, 214, 217.

14. John Locke, *An Essay Concerning Human Understanding* in *The English Philosophers from Bacon to Mill*, ed. for The Modern Library by Edwin A. Burtt (New York, 1939), IV, iii, 340-341. Subsequent references to this work will appear in the text. Locke's scrupulous though short acknowledgment of angels appears again in his *Some Thoughts Concerning Education* in *The Works* (London, 1824), VIII, 182-183, where he makes the existence and nature of non-human spirits a large though briefly-treated division of his elaborate scheme for the education of the young.

15. Robert Boyle, "The Christian Virtuoso," in *The Works* (London, 1744), V, The Preface, 38-39. I take my brief account of Boyle on angels from a number of his essays, with, necessarily, a continuity in my text that does not always reflect the skipping about that I have done in his. I have accurately indicated this skipping in my references, however, and I am sure that I have done no violence to Boyle's views on angels, which are consistent throughout his work. All my references will be to the 1744 edition of *The Works*.

16. "The Excellency of Theology," III, 410, 515. For another account of angels backed by biblical texts see "Of the High Veneration Man's Intellect Owes to God," IV, 350-351.

17. "The Christian Virtuoso," Appendix to Part I, V, 662-663.

18. "The Christian Virtuoso," Part II, V, 721.

19. "Of the High Veneration Man's Intellect Owes to God," IV, 347, 351-352.

20. "The Excellency of Theology," III, 417.

21. Letter to Joseph Glanville, Feb. 10, 1677-78, in V, 245. See also the letter of Sept. 18, 1677.

22. "Some Considerations about the Reconcileableness of Reason and Religion," Part I, sect. viii, in III, 529.

23. Letter to Dr. Peter Du Moulin prefacing *The Divell of Mascon*, 5th ed. (Oxford, 1679).

24. John Dryden, "A Discourse Concerning the Original and Progress of Satire," in *Essays of John Dryden*, ed. W. P. Ker (Oxford, 1926), II, 34.

25. See letter of Samuel Hartlib to John Worthington, August 26, 1661, in *The Diary and Correspondence of Dr. John Worthington*, ed. James Crossley (Manchester, 1847), p. 369. All my references to the letters of Worthington, Beal, and Hartlib are from this work unless otherwise noted.

26. Joseph Mede, *Discourse X* in *The Works*, 4th ed. (London, 1677), p. 40.

27. Francis Bacon, *The Advancement of Learning*, Everyman's Library (New York, 1915), II, 89.

28. J. A. Comenius, *Naturall Philosophie Reformed by Divine Light* (London, 1651). See especially chapt. xii, pp. 228-238, which is entirely on angels.

29. For Beal on Digby and Bacon see Hartlib to Worthington as given in note 25 above. Digby has occasional random mention of angels scattered through his

NOTES [32-39]

192

writings, as, for instance, in his *Observations on the Twenty-second Stanza of the Ninth Canto of the Second Book of Spenser's Faerie Queene* (London, 1643). He says in his *Private Memoirs* (London, 1827), pp. 130-153, that he was both curious and industrious to have experience with spirits but could never do so until he met a "Brachman" who by use of a magical book showed him a spirit in the likeness of Venetia. Whether or not this is to be taken seriously, Digby was certainly just the sort of man who would have pined to meet the supernatural. He was, nevertheless, most cool and level-headed about witches, as is shown in his famous rebuke to Sir Thomas Browne.

30. See letter of Beal to Robert Boyle, Oct. 31, 1666, in Boyle's *Works*, p. 488.
31. Letter of Hartlib to Worthington, August 20, 1661, *The Diary and Correspondence*, I, 356-364.
32. Letter of Worthington to Hartlib, Sept. 5, 1661, *Diary*, II, 1-12.
33. *Conway Letters*, ed. Marjorie Hope Nicolson (New Haven, 1930), pp. 329, 220, 249.
34. See the *Antidote* in *Several Philosophical Writings* (London, 1712), p. 6. All my references to this work are from this edition and will henceforth appear in the text.
35. *The Immortality of the Soul* (London, 1659), Preface. All my references to this work will be to this edition unless otherwise indicated and henceforth will appear in the text.
36. *An Answer to a Letter of a Learned Psychopyrist* in *Sadducismus Triumphatus* (London, 1726), p. 149.
37. *An Explanation of the Grand Mystery of Godliness* (London, 1660), III, xviii, 94.
38. *Immortality of the Soul,* in *Several Philosophical Writings* (London, 1712), Preface, p. vii. This bow to the Platonists first appeared in the edition of 1662.
39. *Enthusiasmus Triumphatus* (London, 1656), pp. 41-46.
40. Samuel Parker, *A Free and Impartial Censure of the Platonick Philosophie* (Oxford, 1666), pp. 79-80.
41. *The Second Lash of Alazonomastix* (London, 1655), p. 204. This work was part of More's controversy with Thomas Vaughan and is bound with More's *Enthusiasmus Triumphatus* and *Observations upon Anthroposophia Theomagica,* and upon *Anima Magica Abscondita.*
42. Francis Osborn, "Essay on All Such as Condemn All they Understand not a Reason for," *Works*, p. 550.
43. John Webster, *The Displaying of Supposed Witchcraft* (London, 1677), pp. 3-9. See also Webster's earlier book, *Academiarum Examen* (London, 1654), for praise of Fludd and other progressive thinkers.
44. Richard Baxter, *Of the Nature of Spirits* (London, 1682), pp. 4, 5.
45. *A Key for Catholics* (London, 1839, 1st ed. 1659), p. 383.
46. *The Reasons of the Christian Religion . . . Also an Appendix, Defending the Soul's Immortality* (London, 1667), p. 579. This Appendix contains one of Baxter's most extensive accounts of angels.
47. *The Saints Everlasting Rest,* 8th ed. (London, 1659), II, vii, 266.
48. Henry Lawrence, *Militia Spiritualis. Or a Treatise of Angels,* 4th ed. (London, 1652). The Epistle Dedicatory. This edition seems to be identical in pagination with earlier ones. Subsequent references to this book will be in the text.
49. Isaac Ambrose, *Ministration of and Communion with Angels* in *The Compleat Works* (London, 1674), the Prolegomena. Subsequent references to Ambrose on angels will be to *The Works* (London, 1829), which omits the Prolegomena, and will be in the text.
50. In this, it must be noticed, the Puritans were not very different from many other Protestants. Bishop Joseph Hall, for instance, treads the same narrow path in *The Invisible World Discovered* (London, 1652), I, 87 ff.; I, 103 ff.
51. *Saints Rest,* II, vii, 266.

52. John Gaule, *The Magastromancer or the Magicall-Astrological Diviner Posed and Puzzled* (London, 1652), viii, 81.
53. Baxter, *The Reasons of the Christian Religion,* Appendix, p. 572.

CHAPTER III

1. George Hakewill, *An Apologie or Declaration of the Power and Providence of God in the Government of the World,* 2nd ed. (London, 1630), p. 235 and the Third Advertisement.
2. John Wollebius, *The Abridgment of Christian Divinitie . . . in some obscure places cleared and enlarged by Alexander Ross,* 2nd ed. (London, 1656), p. 51.
3. For their books see the bibliography below. For a sketch of their views see my *Invisible World* (Athens, Georgia, 1939), and for a full account of Aquinas' angelology see James Collins, *The Thomistic Philosophy of the Angels* (Washington, 1947).
4. John Salkeld, *A Treatise of Angels* (London, 1613), p. 23 ff. Subsequent references to this work will appear in the text.
5. Andrew Willet, *Synopsis Papismi,* 4th ed. (London, 1614), II, viii, 385 ff.
6. Salkeld notices that "Some doe gather prayer unto the Angels" from Genesis 48, but says that he will not discuss so sore a question (p. 239).
7. Jeremy Taylor, "The Insecurity of the Roman Religion," *The Works* (London, 1850), II, 910.
8. Joseph Mede, *The Apostasy of These Latter Times, or The Gentiles Theology of Daemons,* in *The Works,* 4th ed. (London, 1677), p. 626 ff.
9. John Gumbledon, *Christ Tempted: the Divel Conquered* (London, 1657), p. 70.
10. Ussher preached against worship of angels before the House of Commons in 1620; see his *Whole Works* (London, 1847), II, 439-40. Edward Leigh emphasized the danger of worship in his comment on Revelations 19.9 in *Annotations upon all the New Testament* (London, 1650). Henry More touches it often; for instance, in his *Antidote against Idolatry* (London, 1669), pp. 10, 20, ff. Stillingfleet attacked worship in his *Discourse Concerning the Idolatry Practised in the Church of Rome,* 4th ed. (London, 1676), p. 152 ff. George Bull devoted a sermon largely to it, "The Existence of Angels and their Nature," *Sermons and Other Discourses* (London, 1713), II, 432 ff. These Church of England luminaries were as ardent against worship of angels as was the dissenter, Richard Baxter, who cites Ussher's sermon in *Forty Popish Frauds Detected and Disclosed,* 1st American ed. (New York, 1835), pp. 164-5.
11. Robert Dingley, *The Deputation of Angels* (London, 1654), p. 76.
12. King James I, *Daemonologie* (Edinburgh, 1597), p. 21.
13. Henry Lawrence, *Militia Spiritualis, Or a Treatise of Angels,* 4th ed., (London, 1652), p. 9. This edition seems to be identical in pagination with earlier ones. Subsequent references to this book will be in the text.
14. Isaac Ambrose, *Ministration of and Communion with Angels* in *The Works* (London, 1829), p. 479. All my references to this work will be from this edition except those to the Prolegomena, which will be from *The Compleat Works* of 1674 or of 1689 as specified in the accompanying notes. All subsequent references to the *Works* of 1829 will be given in the text.
15. Ambrose, *Communion with Angels* in *The Compleat Works* (London, 1674), p. 94.
16. See *The Compleat Works.*
17. Not even the strictest Scholastic, of course, thought the angels totally without composition. See John Maldonat, *Traicté des Anges et Demons* (Paris, 1605) IV, iii, 31 ff. for a discussion of eight kinds of composition and of the question of which may be said to be in angels. Protestants, even those who deny body to the angels, allow composition of "being and essence," of "act and capability," and of "subject and inherent accident." See Arminius, "Disputation XXV. On

Angels in General and Particular," trans. James Nichols, in *The Works* (London, 1828), II, 359.

18. The continental writers here named were all influential in England on angelology, though Vossius less so than the rest. Meric Casaubon in *The Original and Cause of Temporal Evils* (London, 1645), p. 19, refers his reader interested in the details of theory on apparitions to Vossius' *De Origine Idolatriae*. For Vossius' view of angelic substance, see the *De Origine Idolatriae* (Amsterdam, 1668), I, vi, 20 ff. The kindred opinions of the others listed appear in various places in this volume, or see my article "The Substance of Milton's Angels," *South Atlantic Modern Language Association Studies in Milton* (Gainesville, Florida, 1953).

19. See the Conclusion to the Prolegomena in *The Compleat Works*, 1674.

20. *Summa Theologica* Q. 50. Art. I, in *The Basic Writings of Saint Thomas Aquinas*, ed. Anton C. Pegis (New York, 1945).

21. Otho Casman, *Angelographia* (Frankfurt, 1605), I, iii, 62, 63; Strozzio Cicogna, *Magia Omnifariae* (Cologne, 1607), II, viii, 195; Maldonat, *Traicté des Anges*, IV, i, 20.

22. Thomas Heywood, *The Hierarchie of the Blessed Angels* (London, 1635), p. 210; William Foster, *A Sponge to Wipe Away the Weapon Salve* (London, 1629), p. 50.

23. *Most Fruitful and Learned Commentaries upon Judges of Dr. Peter Martyr*, (London, 1564), on Judges 13. See also Peter Martyr, *The Common Places* (London, 1574), I, xiii, 113; Jerome Zanchy, *De Operibus Dei Spacium Sex Dierum Creato* in *Operum Theologicorum* (Geneva, 1613), II, iv, 70. No doctrine was more turned about than this one. Peter sneers at the Scholastics' use of it to establish the immateriality of angels, but in another place uses it himself for exactly that purpose (*Common Places*, I, x, 81). Benjamin Camfield, who follows Henry More in contending that angels have bodies, and also in contending that the angels' "soul" is pure spirit, uses the doctrine to explain away Fathers whom he supposed to think that angels *are* bodies. See *A Discourse of Angels* (London, 1678), p. 21. The heterodox Catholic, Pierre Charron, uses it to show that angels — and of more interest to him, the soul — are material in just about the way Camfield opposes. See *Of Wisedom* (London, 1630), I, vii, 25, 26.

24. Tertullian, *Against Marcion* in *The Ante-Nicene Fathers*, trans. Alexander Roberts and James Donaldson (New York, 1903), III, ix, 328-9.

25. Peter Martyr, *Commentaries* xiii, 209, 210; Zanchy, *De Operibus Dei* II, iii, 67 and II, viii, 81.

26. John Calvin, *Commentaries on the First Book of Moses Called Genesis*, trans. John King (Edinburgh, 1847), on Genesis 18.2.

27. *Commentaries*, p. 209.

28. Lawrence does depart from Calvin's view by implying that assumption of body is entirely by an "Angelicall power" (p. 16) rather than being a direct act of God. Protestant opinion was shadowy on the subject because the authorities did not want to ascribe the bodies of fallen angels to God. Andrew Willet says, "But I note a difference between the apparition of good and bad angels, that these never appeared with true bodies, and therefore were called *phantasmata*, visions, fancies, Marke 6.49. But unto the other God gave the use of true bodies for a time. . . ." See his *Hexapla in Genesin* (Cambridge, 1605), on Genesis 6.2. Willet is not inclined to force the point, but shrugs it off with the conclusion that "howsoever spirits may assume bodies" they cannot generate with women.

29. Reginald Scot, *A Discourse of Devils and Spirits*, ed. Brinsley Nicholson (London, 1886), 413. All subsequent references to this work will be given in the text. One seventeenth-century contender for a rationalistic view of witchcraft who recognized the extremeness of Scot's position was Balthasar Bekker, *The World Bewitched* (London, 1695), xxii, 234. The great Dutchman, who perhaps more

than anyone else gave witchcraft its *coup de grace,* states flatly that Scot went further than anyone else in denying the physical powers of the devil.

CHAPTER IV

1. E. M. Butler, *Ritual Magic* (Cambridge, England, 1949), p. 242.
2. *A Discourse Concerning Devils and Spirits,* Book II, Append. II to Reginald Scot, *The Discoverie of Witchcraft,* ed. Brinsley Nicholson (London, 1886), p. 493. All my subsequent references to the work of Anti-Scot will be given in the text and will be from this edition.
3. See Aquinas, *Summa Theologica Q.* 64, a. 4. Anti-Scot, p. 519.
4. See Butler, *Ritual Magic,* pp. 47-100, and my *Invisible World* (Athens, Georgia, 1939), chs. iii and vii.
5. *Paracelsus of the Supreme Mysteries of Nature,* trans. R. Turner (London, 1655), pp. 51-53, and Franz Hartman, *The Life of Paracelsus,* 2nd ed. (London, n. d.), pp. 116, 120 ff.
6. Martin Delrio, *Les Controverses et Recherches Magiques,* trans. Andre Du Chesne (Paris, 1611), II, xxvii, 302. Campanella notices on Galileo's behalf this "insanity of Paracelsus," which, Campanella insists, has no relation to Galileo's idea that stars may be other worlds with people of their own, and backs his attack on Paracelsus by citing Delrio. See Thomas Campanella, *The Defense of Galileo,* trans. Grant McColley, *Smith College Studies in History,* Vol XXII, Nos. 3-4, Apr.-July, 1937, pp. 8-67.
7. See *Paracelsus of the Supreme Mysteries,* p. 51; Hartman, *Life of Paracelsus,* p. 120.
8. Hartman, p. 124.
9. Samuel Pordage, *Mundorum Explicatio* (London, 1661), p. 88 marginal note; John Pordage, *Innocencie Appearing through the Dark Mists of Pretended Guilt* (London, 1655), p. 73. Samuel Pordage also talks some of "elementals" in much the Paracelsan vein. See p. 32.
10. For an exposition of Agrippa's theories of magic see my *Invisible World,* pp. 39-48 and elsewhere as given in the index.
11. Lambert Daneau, *A Dialogue of Witches* (London, 1575) sig. Bv.
12. Meric Casaubon, Preface to *A True and Faithful Relation of What Passed for Many Years between Dr. John Dee . . . and Some Spirits* (London, 1659), sig. E3.
13. J. F. to the Judicious Reader, *Occult Philosophy* (London, 1651). All my references to the *Occult Philosophy* are to this translation and will henceforth appear in the text.
14. Thomas Vaughan, *Anthroposophia Theomagica* in *The Works,* ed. A. E. Waite (London, 1909), p. 50. G. G. Coulton, *Five Centuries of Religion* (London, 1929), II, 418.
15. The Council of Rome under Pope Zachary in 745 recognized only Michael, Gabriel, and Raphael as angels with known names. It forbade the invocation of others by name. Many orthodox demonologists mention this ban. See, for instance, Delrio, *Les Controverses Magique,* p. 81, and Thomas Heywood, *The Hierarchie of the Blessed Angels* (London, 1635), p. 216.
16. Christopher Love, *The Ministry of Angels to the Heirs of Salvation* (London, 1657), p. 19.
17. Benjamin Camfield, *A Theological Discourse of Angels* (London, 1678), p. 67.
18. Camfield, *Discourse of Angels,* p. 46.
19. Robert Burton, *The Anatomy of Melancholy,* ed. A. R. Shilleto (London, 1912), I, 214; Heywood, *The Hierarchie of the Blessed Angels,* p. 436.
20. Marsilio Ficino, *Ex Secundo Libro Porphyrii De Sacrificiis, et Diis, atque Daemonibus* bound with his trans. of *Iamblichus De Mysteriis Aegyptiorum, Chaldaeorum, Assyriorum* (Lyons, 1577), p. 311. The first ed. of Agrippa's

Occulta Philosophia (Cologne, 1533), quotes and misquotes Porphyry on p. 242.

21. See my article "Milton and Michael Psellus," *Philological Quarterly*, XXVIII (October, 1949), 477-489.

22. Daneau, *Dialogue of Witches*, sig. Bv.

23. John Deacon and John Walker, *A Dialogicall Discourse of Spirits and Devils* (London, 1601), p. 83.

24. Richard Baxter, *The Reasons of the Christian Religion . . . Also an Appendix Defending the Soul's Immortality* (London, 1667), p. 528.

25. George Pictorius, *An Introductory Discourse of the Nature of Spirits*, trans. Robert Turner (London, 1655), pp. 154-155; Jerome Cardan, *De Rerum Varietate* (Avinione, 1580), XVI, xcii, 805 ff.

26. John Salkeld, *A Treatise of Angels* (London, 1613), p. 31.

27. Jean Wier, *Histoires Disputes et Discours des Illusions et Impostures des Diables*, as reprinted for Bibliotheque Diabolique (Paris, 1885), I, 2, 67.

28. Jerome Zanchy, *De Operibus Dei* in *Operum Theologicorum* (Geneva, 1613), IV, xvii, 205; xix, 208.

29. Reginald Scot, *A Discourse Concerning Devils and Spirits*, chs. iii, iv.

30. J. F.'s literal translation of Agrippa is inaccurate once or twice in this passage and I have altered it to fit the literal sense of Agrippa's Latin. J. F. gives "*Psellus* the *Platonist*, and *Christianus* do think that the nature of spirits is not without body . . ." for "Psellus Platonicus & Christianis, daemonum naturam non putat esse sine corpore. . . ." and "neither can any of the *Demons* . . ." for "neque tamen unumquodque daemonum genus. . . ."

31. See Marsilio Ficino, *Ex Michael Psello De Daemonibus, Interpres Marsilius Ficinus* (Lyons, 1577), ii, 337, and *Traicte Par Dialogue de L'Energie ou Operations des Diables, Traduit en Francoys du Grec de Michel Psellus* (Paris, c. 1576), p. 20. The French is a trans. of τιμονεος η περι δαιμονων, Psellus' principal work on daemons and Ficino's excerpts seem probably from the same work, though they show some puzzling variations.

32. See the places cited in note 31 above. The linking of angelic eating with angelic procreation appears in various seventeenth-century authors, usually with the absurdity of one assumed as part of a demonstration of the absurdity of the other. See, for instance, Abraham Ross, *An Exposition on the Fourteene First Chapters of Genesis* (London, 1626), p. 96.

33. Ficino, iii, 349.

34. See Karel Svoboda, *La Démonologie de Michel Psellos* (Brno, 1927), p. 11.

35. See *Occulta Philosophia* (1533), III, xviii, 245; Ficino's *De Daemonibus*, p. 339; and John Trithemius, *Octo Quaestionum Libellus* bound with *Occulta Philosophia* (Paris, 1567), p. 657.

36. See Svoboda, p. 6. For the views of Paracelsus and Anti-Scot see above p. 63. For those of Cardan see *De Rerum Varietate*, XVI, xciii, 802-814, and *Hyperchen* in *Opera Omnia* (Lyons, 1563), I, 287; and for those of the Talmudists see Johan Buxtorf, *Lexicon Chaldaicum, Talmudicum, et Rabbinicum* (Basle, 1640), on the word *Daemon*, p. 2339.

37. Montfaucon de Villars, *Comte de Gabalis*, trans. by "The Brothers" (London, 1913), II, 43. Andrew Willet, *Hexapla in Genesin* (Cambridge, 1605), on Gen. 6.

38. William Foster, *A Sponge to Wipe away the Weapon-Salve* (London, 1629), pp. 47-52. Subsequent references to this work will be in the text.

39. Robert Fludd, *Doctor Fludd's Answer unto M. Foster or the Squeezing of Parson Fosters Sponge* (London, 1631), p. 42 ff. Subsequent references to this work will be in the text.

40. In his discussion of efficient causes in his physics Gassendi considers the agency of angels perfunctorily with the admission that it is a very difficult question what their substance is and the note that the faith holds them incorporeal. See his *Syntagmata Philosophici* II, I, IV, viii, 292-293, in *Opera Omnia* (Florence, 1727), ii. In his writing against Fludd he has to take considerable adverse notice

of Fludd's angelology. See *Fluddanae Philosophiae Examen* in the *Opera*, III, 222 ff. Foster's reference to the work against Fludd is III, xiii, 121.

41. *Responsum ad Hoplocrisma Spongum* (Gouda, 1638), 28.

42. See Robert Fludd, *Philosophia Sacra* (Frankfort, 1626), p. 268. Fludd's larger works have so many divisions and subdivisions that references which noticed them all would be intolerably tedious. The above reference, for instance, would be Sect. I, Port. IV, Part II, Lib. IV, Memb. II, ch. viii. Although the pagination in some of Fludd's works is in two or more series, I have thought it most serviceable to give a simple page reference. None of his books, so far as I know, were printed more than once, except that the work against Foster was translated into Latin and the *Mosaicall Philosophy* from the Latin.

43. *Philosophia Sacra*, p. 214.

44. Robert Fludd, *Mosaicall Philosophy* (London, 1659), pp. 172-188; *Philosophia Sacra*, 254-257.

45. *Mosaicall Philosophy*, p. 180; *Philosophia Sacra*, p. 254; *Medicina Catholica* (Frankfort, 1629), 76; *Integrum Morborum Mysterium* (no place, 1631), p. 40. Agrippa gives the same scheme with a few variations in *Occult Philosophy*, III, x, 368-369.

46. *Sancti Dionysii Areopagitae Operum Omnium* (Paris, 1644), chs. ix, x, xi, pp. 107-129.

47. Fludd's ideas about the winds and their angels appear plentifully in nearly all his works. For Azazel and his associates see *Mosaicall Philosophy*, p. 189; *Anatomiae Amphitheatrum* (Frankfurt, 1623), p. 204; *Philosophia Sacra*, p. 225; *Medicina Catholica*, p. 81; *Integrum Morborum Mysterium*, p. 173.

CHAPTER V

1. See Richard Burthogge, *An Essay upon Reason and the Nature of Spirits* (London, 1694), p. 41, where a passage from Fludd is quoted as an example of what Burthogge means by nonsense.

2. This was not an extraordinary number for a demonologist, though as Burton names them in staccato succession they seem myriad. Reginald Scot uses almost twice as many and Zanchy twice that many.

3. Robert Burton, *The Anatomy of Melancholy*, ed. A. R. Shilleto (London, 1912), I, 214-215. Subsequent references to *The Anatomy* will be in the text.

4. Campanella in defending Galileo had felt it necessary to deny that the putative inhabitants of other worlds were identifiable with Paracelsus' elementals. The idea that angels literally lived in the heavens was commonplace. Robert Boyle, *A Disquisition about the Final Causes of Natural Things* in *The Works* (London, 1744), IV, 536, says: ". . . since the angels are a nobler order of intellectual creatures than men . . . how do we know but that in the system of that part of heaven, of which we need telescopes to know, that there is such a thing *in rerum natura*. . . ." Professor Merritt Y. Hughes points out in the Introduction to his edition of *Paradise Lost*, p. xxiv, that the astronomer Thomas Digges had thought the fixed stars literally the residences of holy angels.

5. *The Diary and Correspondence of Dr. John Worthington*, ed. James Crossley (Manchester, 1847), I, 120.

6. *Conway Letters*, ed. Marjorie Hope Nicolson (New Haven, 1930), p. 149.

7. Robert Bolton, *Of the Foure Last Things, Death, Iudgement, Hell, and Heaven*. 4th ed. (London, 1639), pp. 111-151; Richard Baxter, *The Saints Everlasting Rest*, 8th ed. (London, 1659), p. 93. Another man besides More who tried to demonstrate the immortality of the soul with some acknowledgment of the new science was Walter Charleton, *The Immortality of the Human Soul Demonstrated by the Light of Nature* (London, 1657). Charleton did not, however, sketch any such pictures of the after life as More did.

8. Henry More, *The Immortality of the Soul so Farre Forth as it is Demonstrable*

from the Knowledge of Nature and the Light of Reason (London, 1659), The Preface, sect. 7. See also p. 415. Subsequent references to this work will be in the text.

9. *Philosophical Writings of Henry More,* ed. Flora Isabel MacKinnon (New York, 1925), note, p. 284.

10. *Observations upon Religio Medici Occasionally Written by Sir Kenelm Digby, Knight,* printed with *Pseudodoxia Epidemica . . . Together with Religio Medici,* 5th ed. (London, 1672), p. 122.

11. More was neither the first to attribute extension to spirit nor the only one of his time to do so. But he seems to have been more decided about it than his contemporaries, to have depended more on it, and to have linked it as most of them did not to the new science. See MacKinnon, note, pp. 284-285.

12. In fact, by the time he wrote the Preface General to his *Collection of Several Philosophical Writings,* (London, 1662), p. xv, More could say: "I have demonstrated with evidence no less than the Mathematical, That there are Substances incorporeal, and that all Substance is in some sense extentional. . . ."

13. *The Antidote Against Atheism* in *A Collection of Several Philosophical Writings of Dr. Henry More,* 4th ed. (London, 1712), III, xiv, 131. This was a point of orthodoxy that More's conservative friend, John Worthington, seems to have valued in him.

14. Andrew Willet, *Hexapla in Genesin: that is, A Sixfold Commentarie upon Genesis* (Cambridge, 1605), on Genesis 6.

15. John Webster, *The Displaying of Supposed Witchcraft* (London, 1677), pp. 197 ff., and p. 207. Subsequent references to this work will be in the text.

16. Benjamin Camfield, *A Theological Discourse of Angels* (London, 1678), p. 195.

17. Henry More, *Conjectura Cabbalistica, or a Conjectural Essay of Interpreting the Mind of Moses according to a Threefold Cabbala: Literal, Philosophical, Mystical, or, Divinely Moral* (London, 1653), pp. 173 and 132.

18. Henry More, *An Explanation of the Grand Mystery of Godliness* (London, 1660), II, iii-iv, 34-36.

19. *Conjectura Cabbalistica,* pp. 42-46. See also the account given by More's follower Henry Hallywell, *Melampronoea, or a Discourse of the Polity and Kingdom of Darkness* (London, 1681), pp. 1-15, of the fall of angels, which was all but the same as the fall of man.

20. Richard Baxter, *The Reasons of the Christian Religion . . . an Appendix, Defending the Soul's Immortality* (London, 1667), pp. 528-533. Subsequent references to this work will appear in the text.

21. *The Diary and Correspondence of Dr. John Worthington,* ed. James Crossley (Manchester, 1886), vol. II, pt. ii, Worthington to Edward Fowler, Sept. 26, 1671.

22. Richard Baxter, *The Certainty of the World of Spirits* (London, 1691), p. 125.

23. Richard Baxter, *Of the Nature of Spirits* (London, 1682), pp. 1, 2. Subsequent references to this work will appear in the text.

24. See the annotations (presumably More's) to George Rust, *A Discourse of the Use of Reason in Matters of Religion* bound with Joseph Glanville, *Lux Orientalis* under the title *Two Choice and Useful Treatises* (London, 1682), p. 202. More writes in his "Digression" against Baxter as though he were a third person. Subsequent references to this "Digression" will appear in the text.

25. John Beaumont, *Treatise of Spirits* (London, 1705).

26. Bodin's story of his friend's good angel was much cited, probably because it was one of the comparatively few "well-attested" stories of the apparition of a good angel. See *De la Demonomanie des Sorciers,* 4th ed. (Paris, 1598), I, ii, 21-26. Bodin's opinion on angelic substance is hard to be sure of though he seems to incline to some sort of body. In the Preface to the *Demonomanie* he enlarges on the difficulty of the question. In I, i, 12-13 he quotes and rejects Apuleius that demons have bodies of air, but will himself say only that they are of a quintessence like the sky. In the *Colloquium Heptaplomeres* is much

talk about demons as corporeal, but it is in the mouths of characters by defini-tion heretical. In the *Refutation des Opinions de Iean Wier* attached to *La Demonomanie* Bodin seems to yield to the scholastic opinion. See p. 502.

27. Henry More, *An Antidote Against Atheism* in *Collected Philosophical Writings* (London, 1712), III, xi, 124.

28. Robert Boyle, *The Usefulness of Natural Philosophy* in *The Works* (London, 1744), I, 430. Boyle recurs to the idea in *A Disquisition about the Final Causes of Natural Things,* IV, 536.

29. J. A. Comenius, *Naturall Philosophie Reformed by Divine Light* (London, 1651), pp. 10, 18.

30. Joseph Glanville, *Sadducismus Triumphatus,* 4th ed. (London, 1726), p. 5.

31. John Beal to Robert Boyle, November 9, 1663, in Boyle's *Works,* V, 456.

32. Robert Fludd, *Mosaicall Philosophy* (London, 1659), p. 195.

CHAPTER VI

1. *The Seventh Prolusion,* XII, 265.

2. *The Christian Doctrine,* I, vii, 37. For quotations from this work I give the book and chapter together with the page number in the Columbia edition. Subsequent references will be in the text.

3. James Holly Hanford, "The Chronology of Milton's Private Studies," *Publica-tions of the Modern Language Association,* XXXVI (1921), 308-309.

4. See Louis I. Bredvold, "Milton and Bodin's *Heptaplomeres,*" *Studies in Philology,* XXI (1924), 399-402.

5. See the Preface to *Female Pre-eminence: or the Dignity and Excellency of that Sex above the Male . . . Written Originally in Latin by Henry Cornelius Agrippa . . . Done into English with additional Advantages by H. C.* (London, 1670).

6. For Aquinas' sources see Etienne Gilson, *The Philosophy of St. Thomas Aquinas,* trans. Edward Bullough (Cambridge, 1924), pp. 141-146.

7. For the case that Milton used Psellus (or if not Psellus one of his many sum-marizers, such as Cardan) see below, pp. 145-148, or for more detail my article "Milton and Michael Psellus," *Philological Quarterly,* XXVIII (1949), 477-489. The truth is, of course, that when we speak of astronomy or of angelology in a poem we speak equivocally in somewhat the same way in which we speak of a "man" or a "mountain" in a photograph. They are not there, certainly, though recognizable reproductions of them are. The "angelology" in *Paradise Lost* is not of the body of the "science" itself, but a partial facsimile of it, a fictional reproduction according to the terms set by the story and its epic form. It is recognizable for what it represents, its kin and kind may be known, its implications and affiliations; but because *Paradise Lost* is not dominated as a whole nor entirely in any of its parts by either the methods or the findings of angelology but merely shows the sign of them for poetical purposes, *Paradise Lost* is not at any point quite angelology. Still, the reader may recognize its representation of angelology, and if he does not feel its implications and affili-ations he has missed some of the poem.

8. Rex Clements, "The Angels in *Paradise Lost,*" *Quarterly Review,* CCLXIV (1935), 285, says that the stripling Cherub "suggests comparison with the cre-ations of Cimabue." Henry More snorts that artists often picture angels "like good plump cherry-cheek'd Lads." See *The Antidote Against Atheism* in *Several Philosophical Writings* (London, 1712), III, xiv, 131.

9. John Bakeless, *The Tragicall History of Christopher Marlowe* (Cambridge, Mass., 1942), I, 314, says: "*Doctor Faustus* provides one of the clearest Marlowe-Milton parallels — the idea, common to both poets, that the individual soul can be its own hell. Even this is not an undoubted parallel, for the conception is one which Milton was quite capable of evolving himself. . . ." No doubt Milton

was quite capable of originating the idea or of borrowing it from Marlowe. But since it was stock medieval and Renaissance theology, that he invented it seems unlikely and that his use of it links him to Marlowe still more unlikely. A Miltonist who notices the same evident resemblance between *Paradise Lost* and *Dr. Faustus* is N. Bogholm, *Milton and Paradise Lost* (London, 1932), pp. 50, note, and 61.

10. Commentators had not missed the possibility that the Cherubim of Genesis 3.24 were other than angels. For a digest of opinion see John Salkeld, *A Treatise of Paradise* (London, 1617), chapter li, and particularly p. 233.

11. Henry More, *The Grande Mystery of Godliness* (London, 1660), V, vi, 147; Cornelius Agrippa, *Three Books of Occult Philosophy*, trans. J. F. (London, 1651), III, xxviii, 436. Jean Bodin refers to the *Gigantomachia* as a clouded pagan version of the war in Heaven. See *La Demonomanie des Sorciers* (Paris, 1598), I, i, 4. Bodin's contemporary, Pierre Le Loyer, *Histoires des Spectres* (Paris, 1605), III, iii, 184, says the same thing more fully. See my note, "Milton's 'Giant Angels'" *Modern Language Notes* LXVII (1952), 21-23.

12. See, for instance, James Holly Hanford, *A Milton Handbook*, 4th ed. (New York, 1947), pp. 206-207; A. J. A. Waldock, *Paradise Lost and its Critics* (Cambridge, Eng., 1947), pp. 101, 104; R. J. Zwi Werblowsky, *Lucifer and Prometheus: A Study of Milton's Satan* (London, 1952), p. 22; John Bailey, *Milton* (London, 1947, 1st pub. 1915), pp. 155-156. Many other writers on *Paradise Lost* have expressed similar views.

13. Isaac Ambrose, *The Ministration of and Communion with Angels* in *The Works* (London, 1829), vi, 482. Ambrose says that angels "minister for the saints" because God wills and commands it. Sin God wills but does not command; hence, though devils may operate at his will they do so against his orders.

14. See Dr. Johnson's life of Milton in his *Lives of the English Poets*. My references to this essay will appear in the text and are all to the excerpt in the convenient *Milton Criticism: Selections from Four Centuries*, ed. James Thorpe (New York, 1950).

15. Waldock, *Paradise Lost and its Critics*, pp. 108, 111. Subsequent references to this work will appear in the text.

16. T. S. Eliot, "Milton," in *Milton Criticism*, ed. James Thorpe, p. 323.

17. Douglas Bush, *Paradise Lost in Our Time* (Ithaca, 1945), p. 60.

18. P. L. Carver, "The Angels in *Paradise Lost*," *Review of English Studies*, XVI (1940), p. 415.

19. *The Jerusalem Delivered of Torquato Tasso*, trans. J. H. Wiffen (New York, 1849), I, xiii, 72 and VII, xcix, 255.

20. E. M. W. Tillyard, *The Miltonic Setting* (London, 1947), p. 173.

21. For statements of this view of the poet's obligations as including the didactic and of Milton's performance in accord with it see C. M. Bowra, *From Virgil to Milton* (London, 1948), pp. 238, 243, and specifically as it applies to Milton's picture of the angels C. S. Lewis, *A Preface to Paradise Lost* (London, 1942), pp. 105, 111.

22. E. M. W. Tillyard, *Studies in Milton* (New York, 1951), p. 143.

23. He does imply, of course, that Satan, Raphael, and Uriel cannot transfer instantaneously from place to place. But he never makes any overtly angelological comment to call attention to the problem of place.

24. Richard Bovet, *Pandaemonium*, ed. Montague Summers (Aldington, Kent, 1951), I, ii, 9. Subsequent references to this work will appear in the text.

25. See Marjorie H. Nicolson, "Milton and Hobbes," *Studies in Philology*, XXIII (1926), pp. 411-412; and William B. Hunter, Jr., "Eve's Demonic Dream," *ELH*, XIII (1946), 257.

26. Sir Samuel Morland, *The Urim of Conscience* (London, 1695), pp. 13, 14. Subsequent references to this work will be in the text.

27. See Richard Garnett, *Life of Milton* (London, 1890), p. 163.

28. George Puttenham, *The Arte of English Poesie,* ed. Gladys Doidge Willock and Alice Walker (Cambridge, Eng., 1936), I, iii, 7.
29. John Dryden, "A Discourse Concerning the Original and Progress of Satire," in *Essays of John Dryden,* ed. W. P. Ker (Oxford, 1926), II, 34.
30. Charles Gildon, "To Mr. T. S. in Vindication of Mr. Milton's Paradise Lost," in *Miscellaneous Letters and Essays on Several Subjects* (London, 1694), p. 42.
31. John Dennis, *Remarks on a Book Entituled, Prince Arthur, an Heroick Poem* (London, 1696), p. 129.
32. See *The Poetical Works of Mr. John Milton . . . Together with Explanatory Notes on each Book of the Paradise Lost . . .* (London, 1695).

CHAPTER VII

1. John Milton, the *Christian Doctrine,* the Preface, p. 5. All subsequent references to the *Christian Doctrine* will appear in the text. To facilitate reference for those using other editions, I shall give not the volume of the Columbia edition, but the book and chapter of the *Christian Doctrine* with the page of the Columbia edition.
2. B. Rajan, *Paradise Lost and the Seventeenth Century Reader* (London, 1947), pp. 32, 33.
3. Rajan, p. 35.
4. Andrew Willet, *Synopsis Papismi,* 4th ed., (London, 1614), pp. 385-387; George Hakewill, *An Apologie or Declaration of the Power and Providence of God in the Government of the World,* 2nd ed. (London, 1630), III, vii, 235.
5. M. L. Bailey, *Milton and Jakob Boehme* (New York, 1914), p. 158, seems to think that the placing of hell is a matter of poetic necessity. Maurice Kelley, *This Great Argument* (Princeton, 1941), p. 192, holds otherwise.
6. A kindred divergence is that Milton uses *Lucifer* in *Paradise Lost* as an alternate name for Satan, though he never mentions it in the *Christian Doctrine.* The nearest thing that *Paradise Lost* shows to a direct contradiction of the angelology in the *Christian Doctrine* is the line that spirits "cannot but by annihilating die" (VI. 347), which seems by implication to be against the contention in the *Christian Doctrine* that not even God can annihilate anything. But the line of *Paradise Lost* does not say that God can annihilate but only that spirits could die no other way. See the earlier speech of Belial on God's power to annihilate the devils: "how he can / Is doubtful; that he never will is sure" (II. 153-154). It tallies as exactly as a speech in the mouth of a character need with the conclusion of the *Christian Doctrine* that "God is neither willing, nor, properly speaking, able to annihilate anything altogether" (I. vi. 27). For a contemporary statement of the orthodox view see Walter Charleton, *The Immortality of the Human Soul* (London, 1657), pp. 80, 81.
7. See William B. Hunter, Jr., "Eve's Demonic Dream," *ELH, A Journal of English Literary History,* XIII (1946), 255-265, and Murray W. Bundy, "Eve's Dream and the Temptation in Paradise Lost," *Research Studies, State College of Washington,* X (1942), 274-291.
8. This question of how angels spoke was considered by most Protestants too intricate and doubtful to be worth debate. For one version of how Satan "abused the tongue and mouth of the serpent," see William Perkins, *Discourse of the Damned Art of Witchcraft* in *The Works* (Cambridge, 1613), I, 612. John Gumbledon, *Christ Tempted: the Divel Conquered,* p. 21, gives curt notice to the means of Satan's speech. The Catholic witchmongers treat it at a little greater length; see Henry Boguet, *An Examen of Witches,* ed. Montague Summers, trans. E. A. Ashwin (London, 1929), x, 26-29; Martin Delrio, *Les Controverses et Recherches Magique* (Paris, 1611), II, xxviii, 314. Occultists also had their comparatively elaborate say on this question. See Cornelius Agrippa, *Occult Philosophy* (London, 1651), III, xxiii, 412-414.

9. Du Bartas, it has been noted, does not choose between the theories on how Satan ruled the snake. See N. Bogholm, *Milton and Paradise Lost* (London, 1932), p. 103. Du Bartas, of course, had not the problems of Milton's tight-knit story.

10. John Deacon and John Walker, the Church of England eristics who took over from Samuel Harsnett the contest against the Puritan exorcist, John Darrel, labored prodigiously to deny a local entrance in possession without denying possession itself. See their *Dialogicall Discourse of Spirits and Devils* (London, 1601), II, 40-41. They deny flatly that there is any question of a natural serpent in the Genesis story; *serpent* there signifies Satan, *op. cit.* IV, 110. The Church of England was extremely reserved about exorcism and hence about contemporary possession. See Wallace Notestein, *A History of Witchcraft in England* (Washington, 1911), p. 87, note 36.

11. John Salkeld, *A Treatise of Paradise* (London, 1617), pp. 222-223.

12. See Arnold Williams, *The Common Expositor: An Account of the Commentaries on Genesis, 1527-1623* (Chapel Hill, 1948), p. 128. For an authoritative statement of the medieval view see Aquinas, *Summa Contra Gentiles* in *The Basic Writings,* ed. Anton C. Pegis (New York, 1945), vol. II, cxii, 220.

13. See Williams, p. 128.

14. See Williams, p. 117, and Don Cameron Allen, "Milton and the Sons of God," *Modern Language Notes,* LXI (1946), 73-79.

15. Hakewill, *An Apologie,* III, vii, 235.

16. See *Of Reformation,* III, 21.

17. See the annotations in *Paradise Lost,* ed. Merritt Y. Hughes (New York, 1935), and in *Paradise Regained,* ed. Merritt Y. Hughes (New York, 1937). For the similar views of other scholars and for the details of my own opposed reading see my note "Milton's Sons of God," *Modern Language Notes,* LXV (1950), 187-191.

18. *The Institution of Christian Religion,* 6th ed. (London, 1580), I, xiv, 45-46.

19. C. S. Lewis, *A Preface to Paradise Lost* (London, 1942), p. 108.

20. "To Leonora Singing in Rome," I, 229.

21. See Thomas Peyton, *The Glass of Time in the Second Age* (London, 1620), stan. 28, p. 114, for a poet who does use Raziel as Adam's angel, assisted by Michael and Gabriel.

22. Clara Starrett Gage in her unpublished dissertation "The Sources of Milton's Concepts of Angels and the Angelic World" (Cornell, 1936), p. 80, calls attention to the fact that *Virtues* is not in the English Bible as the name of a hierarchy, but that Eph. 1.21 in the Greek New Testament is δυναμεις, translated in the Vulgate and by Junius-Tremellius as *virtutes*. English translations usually give *might.*

23. E. M. W. Tillyard, for instance, in *The Elizabethan World Picture* (New York, 1944), p. 39, says that Milton diverges from the Dionysian tradition to make Archangels the highest order.

24. *Discourse X* in *The Works,* 4th ed. (London, 1677); p. 43.

25. Gervase Babington, *An Exposition of the Catholike Faith* in *The Works,* 3rd ed. (London, 1622), p. 186.

26. Heinrich Bullinger, "Sermon on the Good Spirits," in *The Decades,* ed. for the Parker Society by Thomas Harding (Cambridge, England, 1851), IV, 337.

27. Harris Fletcher, *Milton's Rabbinical Readings* (Urbana, 1930), p. 221 ff., thinks that Milton intended Gabriel also for an archangel. But Milton never actually applies the term to Gabriel and I cannot quite see the "very real need" Mr. Fletcher thinks Milton was under "to secure equal rank for . . . Satan, Raphael, Michael, Gabriel, and Uriel."

28. Protestants were inclined to consider such terms as these to have as much claim as any to be hierarchical. Zanchy, *De Operibus Dei,* in *Operum Theologicorum* (Geneva, 1613), II, xiv, 95, suggests an order of Warriors and another of

Watchers. Some Fathers had, in fact, included such terms as *Aeons, Armies.* See Fernand Prat, *The Theology of Saint Paul,* trans. J. L. Stoddard (London, 1927), II, 414. John Salkeld, *A Treatise of Angels* (London, 1613), p. 294, suggests the possibility of other orders than Dionysius had given.

29. *Synopsis Papismi,* II, viii, 387. Willet denies that Michael is head on the ground that by the name *Michael* Scripture signifies Christ whenever it ascribes command of angels. On this point Milton is, of course, opposed to Willet.

30. See Rex Clements, "The Angels in *Paradise Lost," Quarterly Review,* CCLXIV (1935), 291; and Gage, "Sources of Milton's Concepts of Angels," p. 129. Professor Harris Fletcher, *Milton's Rabbinical Readings,* pp. 216, 221, seems to suggest a similar opinion. For these ideas in Dionysius see *De Caelesti Hierarchia* in *Sancti Dionysii Areopagitae Operum Omnium* (Paris, 1644), v. 60, 61.

31. Mede, *Discourse* X, p. 40.

32. Salkeld, *A Treatise of Angels,* pp. 302, 312, 313; Zanchy, II, xiv, 94, 95.

33. Zanchy, *loc. cit.;* Babington, pp. 185-186; Deacon and Walker, *A Summary Answer to all the Material Points in any of Master Darel, his Books* (London, 1601), II, 141-144; Willett, II, viii, 385. Other Protestants did allow Seraphim and Cherubim as of orders. See, for instance, William Perkins, *The Second Treatise on the Duties and Dignities of the Ministerie* in *The Works* (London, 1631), III, 452.

34. For a summary of scholarly opinion see my article "The Substance of Milton's Angels," in *The South Atlantic Modern Language Studies in Milton* (Gainesville, Fla., 1953), pp. 20-24.

35. Henry More, *An Explanation of the Grand Mystery of Godliness* (London, 1660), I, iii, 6.

36. P. L. Carver, "The Angels in *Paradise Lost," Review of English Studies,* XVI (1940), p. 430, seems to think that when Adam "acknowledges" Raphael to be pure spirit that expresses, for the time being, Milton's stand on angelic substance. A. W. Verity had quoted "incorporeal spirits" (I, 789) with the same implication. See his edition of *Paradise Lost,* note to I, 777-780. See also the unpublished dissertation "Some Scholastic Elements in *Paradise Lost"* by Alfred Henry Deutsch, University of Illinois, 1945, p. 121.

37. Psellus' *Dialogue on the Operation of Daemons,* trans. Marcus Collison (Sidney, 1848), p. 29; *Dr. Fludd's Answer unto M. Foster* (London, 1631), p. 54.

38. Appendix to *The Antidote Against Atheism* in *Several Philosophical Writings* (London, 1712), xiii, 223.

39. Zanchy, II, i, 59.

40. James Ussher, *A Body of Divinitie* (London, 1645), p. 98; Richard Baxter, *Appendix Defending the Soul's Immortality against the Somatists or Epicureans, and other Pseudo-Philosophers* in *The Reasons of the Christian Religion* (London, 1667), p. 530.

41. *Occult Philosophy* (London, 1651), III, xxx, 444.

42. *An Answer to a Letter of a Learned Psychopyrist* in *Sadducismus Triumphatus* (London, 1726), p. 135.

43. C. S. Lewis, *A Preface to Paradise Lost* (London, 1942), p. 108, considers this probability.

44. Mr. Carver, p. 417, suggests that "nor in mist" may be explained by an obscure point in Duns Scotus that earthly food taken by angelic apparitions was dissipated in "fumes." Mr. Carver's conjecture seems perhaps far-fetched. See my article "The Substance of Milton's Angels," pp. 27-28.

45. Clements, p. 284.

46. For a discussion of the connections of this passage with Aristotelianism and Thomism see William B. Hunter, Jr., "Milton's Power of Matter," *The Journal of the History of Ideas,* XIII (1952), 551-562.

47. Carver, pp. 423-425.

48. Peter Martyr, *The Common Places* (London, 1574), I, xiii, 112, and *The Com-*

mentary on Judges (London, 1564), 208. See, too, Zanchy, III, vi, 114, and Henry Lawrence, *Militia Spiritualis,* 4th ed. (London, 1652), p. 30.

49. See Walter Clyde Curry, "The Genesis of Milton's World," *Anglia,* LXX (1951), 129-149.

50. Henry Vane, *The Retired Mans Meditations, of the Mysterie and Power of Godliness* (London, 1655), pp. 42-43.

51. Zanchy, II, iii; Bullinger, 328; Peter Martyr, *The Commonplaces,* I, xiii.

52. See Augustine, *Enchiridion* in *The Works of Aurelius Augustine,* trans. Marcus Dodds (Edinburgh, 1892), IX, lix, 217; Bernard, *De Consideratione,* V, iv, 453 and *Sermones in Cantica Canticorum,* v. 1284, in *Opera Omnia* (Paris, 1719), vol. I. Aquinas, too, says that knowledge of the substance of angels is not vital to salvation, noting Augustine on it; but that did not prevent him from detailed speculation. See *De Malo,* Q. XVI, art. I, *Opera Omnia* in the American reprint of the Parma ed. (New York, 1949), VIII, 888.

CHAPTER VIII

1. *A True and Faithful Relation of What Passed for many years between Dr. John Dee . . . and Some Spirits . . . With a Preface Confirming the Reality (as to the point of Spirits) of this Relation. . . . By Meric Casaubon* (London, 1659), Preface sig. F.

2. *Ex Michaele Psello De Daemonibus, Interpres Marsilius Ficinus* (Lyons, 1577), iii, 348. The Latin: . . . nullus daemon suapte natura mas est, vel foemina. Compositorum enim sunt huiusmodi passiones: corpora vero daemonum simplicia sunt ductu, flexuque; facilia, ad omnemque configurationem naturaliter apta. Sicut enim nubes suspicimus nunc hominum, nunc ursorum, nunc draconum, aliorumque praeferre figuras, sic & corpora daemonum; sed hoc interest, quod nubes externis agitatae ventis figuras varias agunt, daemones autem proprio concilio, prout ipsi volunt, corporum formas in se variant, & modo in breviorem molem contrahuntur, modo rursus in longiorem se extendunt. Quemadmodum lumbricis videtur accidere ob substantiam meliorem, ductuque facillimam; neque solum magnitudine in eis diversitas accidit, verum etiam figuras, coloresque; variant multiformes: corpus enim daemonis ad utrumque est natura paratum. qua enim ratione est natura facile cedens, sic in varias figurarum species transformatur. qua vero aereum est, diversos aeris instar colores subit. Sed aer quidem ab extrinseco coloratur, corpus vero daemonis ab intima phantasiem actione species colorum accipit, quemadmodum nobis expavescentibus genae pallescunt, verecundia vero affectis rubescunt. . . .

   On the relation of Milton and Psellus see my article "Milton and Michael Psellus," *Philological Quarterly,* XXVIII (1949), 477-489.

3. Milton means, of course, only that angels can appear as of either sex, not that they have proper sex. Angels have in his scheme certain erotic abilities that we associate with sex, but these abilities do not seem to express essential sex in his angels.

4. Milton does not reproduce Psellus' analogy of the earthworm, but in the passage at the end of Book I that explains how the devils shrink to crowd into Pandaemonium, "they but now who seem'd / In bigness to surpass Earth's Giant Sons / Now less than smallest Dwarfs, in narrow room / Throng numberless, like that Pigmean Race / Beyond the *Indian Mount.* . . ." (I. 777-781), Milton shares the analogy to giants and pigmies with Agrippa, who expounded how demons varied in appearance, ". . . heightning themselves to the length of a giant's body, and again shrinking themselves up to the smallness of the Pigmies and changing themselves into divers forms. . . ." See *Occult Philosophy* (London, 1651), III, xviii, 400.

5. See "Mr. Addison's Criticism on The Paradise Lost" in *The Poetical Works of John Milton,* ed. Henry John Todd (London, 1801), I, 78.

6. Walter Raleigh, *Milton* (London, 1900), p. 115.

7. *De Daemonibus*, vi, 360-361. The Latin: . . . quae sentiunt non nervus ipse est, qui sentit, sed qui eis spiritus inest. . . . Nempe compositum nunquam per se doleret, sed quando participat spiritum, quo quidem privatum privatur & sensu. Daemonicum itaque corpus per totum se naturaliter sensuale secundum partes singulas absque medio videt, audit, tangit, patiturque; tangendo, & divisum dolet, sicut & corpora solida. Sed hoc interest, quod corpora quidem solida, divisa cum sunt, aut vix, aut nunquam restituuntur, corpus vero daemonum, ubi secatur mox in se iterum recreatur, & coalescit, sicut aquae, aerisque. . . . Dolet tamen interea, dum dividitur, quamobrem aciem ferri metuit. . . .

8. These ideas are scattered throughout Ficino's *De Daemonibus* and also through-out Pierre Moreau's full-length and more exact translation of Psellus' τιμονεος η περι δαιμονον, published as *De Operatione Daemonum Dialogus* (Paris, 1615), with the Greek on facing pages. This work was printed four times between 1615 and 1654. According to James Holly Hanford, "The Chronology of Milton's Private Studies," *PMLA*, XXXVI (1921), 290, Milton did have "some material ascribed to Psellus" in his library. It was, says Mr. Hanford, bound with Milton's copy of Heraclitus the Mythographer, Gesner's edition of 1544. Accord-ing to the British Museum Catalogue of Printed Books it must, then, have been Ιαμβοι εις αρετας και κακιας.

9. *Doctor Fludd's Answer unto M. Foster* (London, 1631), p. 52.

10. *Answer*, p. 54.

11. *Answer*, p. 55.

12. *Answer*, p. 54.

13. Henry More, *An Answer to a Letter of a Learned Psychopyrist* in *Sadducismus Triumphatus* (London, 1726), p. 135.

14. Richard Baxter, *Of the Nature of Spirits* (London, 1682), pp. 66, 67, 4.

15. See, for instance, Walter Clyde Curry, "Milton's Scale of Nature," *Stanford Studies in Language and Literature* (1941), p. 176, and Marjorie Nicolson, "The Spirit World of Milton and More," *Studies in Philology* XXII (1925), 435. See my discussion of Milton and dichotomy in "The Substance of Milton's Angels," *South Atlantic Modern Language Association Studies in Milton* (Gainesville, Fla., 1953), pp. 42-48.

16. Henry More, *The Immortality of the Soul* (London, 1659), The Preface 6.

17. *The Christian Doctrine*, I, vii, 41. The other brief quotes from Milton in this paragraph and in that preceding are from this same page of the *Christian Doctrine* or from p. 23.

18. See Denis Saurat, *Milton Man and Thinker* (New York, 1925), pp. 301-310 and A. S. P. Woodhouse, "Milton's Views on the Creation," *Philological Quarterly*, XXVIII (1949), pp. 220-229 for Milton and Fludd. Milton's resemblances to Agrippa, which are many — and random — have never been pointed out in detail. Of the angelological ones I give some intimation in this work. There are many others. Agrippa (like many others) speaks, for instance, of the dark fire of hell, *Occult Philosophy* I, v. 9 and xlix, 98. For details on Milton's obscure angels' names see my article, "The Names of Milton's Angels," *Studies in Philology*, XLVII (1950), 211-223.

19. See Masson's note on *Paradise Lost* VI. 371-372 in his *The Poetical Works of John Milton* (London, 1874).

20. *Occult Philosophy*, III, xxviii, 435-437. Fludd says exactly the same in several places, for instance in *Philosophia Sacra* (Frankfort, 1626), p. 210, as does Caesare Longinus, *Trinum Magicum* (Frankfort, 1630), III, V, 476. Reginald Scot, *A Discourse of Divells and Spirits*, ed. Brinsley Nicholson (London, 1886), xix, 436, mentions reverently that we find in Scripture that devils take their names sometimes from wicked men or places.

21. Harris Francis Fletcher, *Milton's Rabbinical Readings* (Urbana, 1930), pp.

272, 273. Professor Fletcher notes that it is impossible that the *Pistis Sophia* could have been directly known to Milton.

22. "The Testament of Solomon," trans. F. C. Conybeare, *Jewish Quarterly Review* X (1898), p. 35.

23. "The Wisdom of the Chaldeans: An Old Hebrew Astrological Text," *Studies and Texts in Folklore, Magic, Medieval Romance, Hebrew Apocrypha, and Samaritan Archaeology,* by Moses Gaster (London, 1925-28), I, 348.

24. *Occult Philosophy*, III, xxiv, 416; Fludd, *Utriusque Cosmi Historia* (Oppenheim, 1617-18, Tome II, p. 93; Kircher, *Oedipus Aegyptiacus* (Rome, 1653), II, ix, 331.

25. *The Key of Solomon the King*, trans. and ed. by S. Liddell MacGregor Mathers (London, 1909), p. 74. Mathers used seven mss., only two antedating Milton, and gives no way to tell from which of them he takes this pentacle of the sun. But the name was certainly in circulation on such magical figures long before *Paradise Lost.*

26. *Hierarchie* (London, 1635), pp. 216-217.

27. *Onomasticon Urbium et Locorum Sacrae Scripturae* (Amsterdam, 1704), under the entry *Arina*. This edition has the Greek of Eusebius in one column, a literal translation in another, and St. Jerome's free translation and his comments in another. Milton does not mention the *Onomasticon,* though he does, of course, mention Eusebius and Jerome often. The *Onomasticon* was easily available to Milton.

28. *Occult Philosophy* III, xxviii, 436.

29. *Of Reformation*, III, 34.

30. *Onomasticon,* as cited.

31. See Fletcher, *Milton's Rabbinical Readings*, pp. 209-300, and my article, "The Names of Milton's Angels," *Studies in Philology*, XLVII (1950), 211-223.

32. Allan H. Gilbert, *On the Composition of Paradise Lost* (Chapel Hill, 1947), p. 123, reports *Abdiel.* For Uzziel (Usiel) in the *Sepher Raziel* as among the seven angels before the throne of God and among nine set over die vier Wenden des Jahres," see Eric Bischoff, *Die Elemente der Kabbalah* (Berlin, 1920), III, 175-176. See also Moise Schwab, *Vocabulaire de l'Angelologie* (Paris, 1897), who gives Uzziel as from *Raziel* f. 34b and 40a. Schwab notes the name, too, from *Hekalôth Rabbati. The Jewish Encyclopedia* notices it in the *Masseket Azilut,* an early work of Jewish mysticism, as chief of the Malakim, an order of angels usually matched with the Dionysian Virtues. None of these works was in print in Milton's time.

33. Thomas Nashe, *Pierce Penniless* in *The Works,* ed. Ronald B. McKerrow (London, 1908), the notes, IV, 140, where it is shown that Nashe's entire demonological passage is a translation from the *Isagogae* of George Pictorius of Villingen. See *A Discourse on the Nature of Spirits,* trans. Robert Turner (London, 1655), p. 140. Pictorius' Latin was often printed with Agrippa's *De Occulta Philosophia* and other occult works.

34. John Selden, *De Diis Syriis* (London, 1617), I, iii, 43.

35. *Occult Philosophy*, III, xxvii, 432.

36. *The Key of Solomon,* p. 71.

37. *Vocabulaire de l'Angelologie* lists "ζπηργ Cofeh El 'Dieu surveille,'" from *Raziel* f. 42b. Professor S. I. Feigin of the Oriental Institute, the University of Chicago, tells me that ζπιηργ, the exact spelling of Thomas Keightley's transliteration of *Zophiel,* appears in an incantation in *Raziel* (Vienna, 1873), p. 66. For Keightley's transliterations see his *An Account of the Life, Opinions, and Writings of John Milton* (London, 1855), pp. 469-473.

38. *Mosaical Philosophy* (London, 1659), p. 180. The Latin version of 1638 also has *Zophiel.*

39. See my article, "The Names of Milton's Angels." *Studies in Philology*, XLVII (1950), note 33.

40. Fludd mentions this line-up at least seven times; see, for instance, *Philosophia Sacra*, p. 225. In some books he has elaborate cuts showing the four evil standard bearers attacking man; see, for instance, the mystical figure that opens *Medicina Catholica* (Frankfort, 1629.)

41. Professor Merritt Y. Hughes in his note on Azazel in his edition of *Paradise Lost*, p. 28, calls attention to Azazel as a standard bearer in John Reuchlin's *De Arte Cabalistica*. In *Integrum Morborum Mysterium* (Frankfort, 1631), p. 173, Fludd acknowledges Reuchlin as his source. In *Anatomiae Amphitheatrum* (Frankfort, 1623), p. 267, Fludd refers the item to "Archangel, in Cabal," and in the *Mosaical Philosophy* (p. 188) acknowledges "Mnahem Racanat." Reuchlin himself in *De Arte Cabalistica* (Basle, 1550), III, 887, credits Recanati.

42. Samuel Bochart, *Hierozoicon sive Bipertitum Opus de Animalibus Sacrae Scripturae* (London, 1663), as quoted in Fletcher, *Milton's Rabbinical Readings*, p. 292. Bochart notices Recanati on the four devils, though he does not give them the standards. Selden, *De Diis Syriis* II, v. 214.

43. In his notes on *Paradise Lost* I. 81, I, 361, and elsewhere, Professor Hughes points out that Milton could have known this scheme from Robert Burton's *Anatomy of Melancholy*. He could have had it from a dozen other authors, too, of whom Burton names five—Agrippa, Zanchy, Pictorius, Pererius, and Cicogna. Closer to Milton in date and place were Heywood, *Hierarchie*, p. 436, and Fludd, *Utriusque Cosmi Historia* (Oppenheim, 1617-18), 114, 115. The scheme seems to be late Scholastic, but it is often associated by Protestants with the extravagances of Jewish classifications of angels.

44. See the *Christian Doctrine* I, ix, 109.

45. Clara Starrett Gage, "Sources of Milton's Concepts of Angels and the Angelic World," unpublished dissertation, Cornell University (1936), pp. 25, 26.

46. See Frederic N. Lindsay, *Kerubim in Semitic Religion and Art*, dissertation, Columbia University (1912), p. 6.

47. *Occult Philosophy*, III, x, 368. Fludd, *Mosaical Philosophy*, pp. 179-181, (see above, p. 77), Kircher, *Oedipus Aegyptiacus*, II, IV, viii, 292, and others recite the same scheme. It was undoubtedly well known among those who read theosophy. John Heydon, *Theomagia* (London, 1663), p. 144 ff. has a garbled version of it.

48. E. C. Dewick, *Primitive Christian Eschatology* (Cambridge, 1913), p. 93, on angels in Enoch, The Testament of the Twelve Patriarchs, the Assumption of Moses, and other such works, finds them foreign to normal Hebrew development, but admits that they "figure largely," as in Enoch 55.15-21 spirits of sea, thunder, mist, rain, etc. are designated. Certainly this foreign element became extremely common in later Jewish mystical writings.

49. Reuchlin, *De Arte Cabalistica*, I, 741; Kircher, *Oedipus Aegyptiacus*, II, IV, ii, 221; Fludd, *Utriusque Cosmi Historia*, II, 109; Jacob Boissard, *De Divinatione et Magicis Praestigiis* (Oppenheim, 1616), II, ii, 37.

50. See Fludd, op. cit., II, 108; *John Tritemius, Abbott of Spanheim, of the Heavenly Intelligences, Governing the Orbes under God,* trans. Elias Ashmole, in William Lilly, *The World's Catastrophe* (London, 1647); Kircher, op. cit., II, IV, iii, 227; Jerome Cardan, *De Subtilitate* (Lyons, 1580), XX, 695.

51. See Fletcher, *Milton's Rabbinical Readings*, p. 247.

52. See Agrippa, *Occult Philosophy*, III, xxiv, 416; Fludd, *Utriusque Cosmi Historia*, II, 93; Christopher Love, *The Ministry of Angels to the Heirs of Salvation*, (London, 1657), p. 19. Heywood, Cicogna, Valderama, Zanchy, and other orthodox authors sneer at the Jewish distribution of the angels.

53. The chief effort to connect Milton's placing of angels with Jewish lore has been Professor Fletcher's. He thinks that he finds Milton's source for Uriel in the sun in the Midrasch Rabba to the Book of Numbers, which says: "For

the Holy One blessed-be-He through Uriel (as through the Sun) spreads his light over Israel . . ." *(Rabbinical Readings,* p. 244.) It may very well be, of course, that this or some similar passage gave Milton the hint that made him choose Uriel, though the passage itself certainly does not place Uriel in the sun or say that he is angel of the sun. Uriel sometimes appears in Jewish writings as "with countenance flaming all around" (see Gaster, *The Wisdom of the Chaldeans,* p. 353), and is often, too, the angel of the south and so, as Henry More notes, "He that rules in the power of the Meridian Sunne" and darts "fiery scorching shafts." (See "Psychozoia" in More's *Philosophical Poems* (Cambridge, 1647), Canto III, stanze i, and the note on verse 5.)

54. See the note by Pearce in Todd's edition of *Paradise Lost,* X, 664 ff.
55. See the books of Saurat, Fletcher, Taylor, McColley, Whiting, and the articles of Nicolson, Curry, Carver, *et al.,* as cited in my bibliography and in appropriate places in my notes.

CHAPTER IX

1. Milton argues for both these items in the *Christian Doctrine* and we may suppose with Mr. Maurice Kelley, *This Great Argument* (Princeton, 1941), p. 192, that he believed what he said. On the other hand M. L. Bailey, *Milton and Jakob Boehme* (New York, 1914), p. 158, is obviously partly right; if Milton's placing of hell is not a poetic necessity in *Paradise Lost* it is at least a convenience. Bentley changes Milton's "utter darkness" in the Argument to Book I of *Paradise Lost* to "outer darkness" to suit the more usual translation of Matt. 8.2—*"tenebrae exteriores"* in the *Christian Doctrine,* I, 33, 372. See Richard Bentley, *Milton's Paradise Lost* (London, 1732).

2. See, for instance, William Ames, *The Marrow of Sacred Divinity* (London, 1639), x, 46; Zacharias Ursinus, *The Summe of Christian Religion* (London, 1633), p. 190; Henry Lawrence, *Militia Spiritualis,* 4th ed. (London, 1652), pp. 29, 33; John Salkeld, *A Treatise of Angels* (London, 1613), p. 217 ff.; John Gumbledon, *Two Sermons: First An Angel in a Vision Appeareth to a Souldier . . .* (London, 1657), p. 5.

3. *Christian Doctrine,* I, ix, 98-99.

4. *An Examination of the Treatise of William Perkins concerning the Order and Mode of Predestination* in *The Works of James Arminius,* trans. by W. R. Bagnall (Buffalo, 1853), III, 417.

5. See Grant McColley, *Paradise Lost: An Account of its Growth and Major Origins* (Chicago, 1940), p. 70, P. L. Carver, "The Angels in *Paradise Lost,*" *Review of English Studies,* XVI (1940), 419; Marjorie Nicolson, "The Spirit World of Milton and More," *Studies in Philology,* XXII (1925), 442; C. S. Lewis, *A Preface to Paradise Lost* (London, 1942), p. 107. For my attempt at a detailed refutation of these authorities see my "Milton's Angelological Heresies," *Journal of the History of Ideas,* XIV (1953), 116-123.

6. *Against Marcion* in *The Ante-Nicene Fathers,* trans. Alexander Roberts and James Donaldson (New York, 1903), III, ix, 328-329.

7. See *Summa Theologica,* I, Q. LI, art. 2, 3.

8. Jerome Zanchy, *De Operibus Dei* in *Operum Theologicorum* (Geneva, 1613), II, ix, 83.

9. Andrew Willet, *Hexapla in Genesin,* (London, 1605), on Genesis 18.8.

10. Zanchy as cited above.

11. *The City of God* in *Basic Writings of Saint Augustine,* ed. Whitney J. Oates (New York, 1948), XIII, xxii, 230.

12. *Most Fruitfull & Learned Commentaries on Judges of Dr. Peter Martyr* (London, 1564), 209. M. Rajan, *Paradise Lost and the Seventeenth Century Reader* (London, 1947), note 5, p. 149, rightly cites this passage in Peter Martyr as containing the heart of the question about the eating of Milton's angels.

13. Henry More, *The Immortality of the Soul* (London, 1659), III, ix, 423; Joseph Glanville, *Sadducismus Triumphatus* (London, 1726), p. 234.

14. *Christian Doctrine*, I, vii, 41-43.

15. See Aquinas, *Summa Theologica*, I, Q. 51, art. 3. Virtually all Catholic authorities respected in Milton's time follow Aquinas: Maldonat, Cicogna, the eight or ten writers in the anthology going under the name of the *Malleus Maleficarum*, and dozens of others. See, for instance, Laurentio Beyerlinck's monumental *Magnum Theatrum Vitae Humanae* (Lyons, 1666) under *Angelus*, p. 433, which seems to be a detailed popularization of orthodox Catholic thought on the subject. On this point Protestant orthodoxy had no quarrel with Catholic.

16. Augustine, *City of God*, XV, xxiii, 307. On Paracelsus, see Franz Hartman, *The Life of Paracelsus,* 2nd ed. (London, n.d.), p. 124.

17. Henry More, *An Explanation of the Grand Mystery of Godliness* (London, 1660), III, xviii, 94.

18. Gregory, Bishop of Nyssa, *On the Making of Man* in *A Select Library of Nicene and Post-Nicene Fathers,* trans. Henry Austin Wilson (New York, 1893), 2nd Series, V, p. 407. Debating how humanity would have been propagated if there had been no fall and so no "procreation," Gregory cites Luke 20.35.36 about how the saved shall be as angels with no marrying or giving in marriage. Sinless man, he says, would have multiplied as angels do, however that is. Clara Starrett Gage, "Sources of Milton's Concepts of Angels and the Angelic World," an unpublished dissertation (Cornell, 1936), p. 123, suggests that Gregory's opinion "may have had some little bearing on the passage in which Adam and Raphael discuss the love of angels one for another."

19. C. S. Lewis, *A Preface to Paradise Lost,* p. 107. See Jean Wier, *Histories Disputes et Discours des Illusions et Impostures des Diables,* as reprinted for Bibliotheque Diabolique (Paris, 1885), I, xiv, 67.

20. Lewis, as cited above.

21. Robert Boyle, *The Christian Virtuoso, The Second Part* in *The Works* (London, 1744), V, 721; Martin Delrio, *Les Controverses et Recherches Magiques,* trans. Andre Du Chesne (Paris, 1611), II, xxvii, 302. Anti-Scot, *A Discourse Concerning Devils and Spirits,* Book II, Appendix II to Reginald Scot, *The Discoverie of Witchcraft,* ed. Brinsley Nicholson (London, 1886), p. 495. See above p. 63.

22. Jerome Carden, *De Rerum Varietate* (Avignon, 1558), XVI, xcii, 808-809. Willet, *Hexapla in Genesin,* on Gen. 6 sneers at Cardan's idea. Henry More links Cardan's tale of these elementals who visited his father not to angelic loves but to the question of mortality. According to it, he says, "Aerial Genii" would be held born at set times as well as we. "Not that any she-*Daemons* are brought to bed of them, but that they seem to have a beginning to their existence . . ." (*Immortality of the Soul* [London, 1659] III, xvii, 512). Johann Buxtorf, *Lexicon Chaldaicum, Talmudicum, et Rabbinicum* (Basle, 1639), p. 2339, cites the Rabbinical notion of the demons as like angels in having wings, swiftness, and knowledge of the future, and like men in that they eat, beget, and die. Various Christian demonologists rebuke the notion that this is an acceptable description of fallen angels. See, for instance, R. P. Maldonat, *Traicté des Anges et Demons* (Paris, 1605), p. 164, and John Heywood, *Hierarchie of the Blessed Angels* (London, 1635), pp. 230-231.

23. Grant McColley, *Paradise Lost,* p. 85.

24. Patrick Hume, *Annotations of Milton's Paradise Lost* (London, 1695). See also Willet, *Hexapla in Genesin* on Gen. 6; J. A. Comenius, *Naturall Philosophie Reformed by Divine Light* (London, 1651), p. 233; Johann Gerhard, *Meditations,* trans. and revised Ralph Winterton (Cambridge, 1635), p. 297. Even Franciscus Mercurius Van Helmont in the "enthusiasm" of his *Two Hundred Queries* (London, 1684), does not waver from the orthodox notion that "as the Angels neither marry nor give in Marriage," they have no "incli-

nation to a carnal propagation, as betwixt Male and Female among mankind."
See Query 182.

25. John Norris, *The Theory and Regulation of Love . . . to which are Added Letters Philosophical and Moral between the Author and Dr. Henry More* (Oxford, 1688), pp. 172, 173, 190, 191.

26. See *Paradise Lost,* ed. Merritt Y. Hughes (New York, 1935), note on VIII, 627.

CHAPTER X

1. Thomas Keightley, *An Account of the Life, Opinions, and Writings of John Milton* (London, 1855), p. vi. For Keightley's rejection of Wier on Belial, see his *The Poems of John Milton* (London, 1859), note on *Paradise Lost* I. 490.

2. Thomas De Quincey, "On Milton," *Collected Writings,* ed. David Masson (London, 1897), X, 406. Walter Raleigh, *Milton* (London, 1900), pp. 107, 113-114.

3. *Paradise Lost,* ed. by A. W. Verity (Cambridge, England, 1910), Appendices B. C. and F.

4. Denis Saurat, *Milton Man and Thinker* (New York, 1925), p. 299.

5. Grant McColley, *Paradise Lost: An Account of its Growth and Major Origins* (Chicago, 1940), pp. 112-113.

6. See P. L. Carver, "The Angels in *Paradise Lost,*" *Review of English Studies,* XVI (1940), pp. 415 ff.; and the unpublished dissertation of Alfred Henry Deutsch, "Some Scholastic Elements in *Paradise Lost,*" University of Illinois, 1945, pp. 110-169.

7. Harris Francis Fletcher, *Milton's Rabbinical Readings* (Urbana, 1930), p. 216.

8. Isaac Ambrose, *Ministrations of and Communion with Angels* in *The Compleat Works,* 3rd ed. (London, 1689), Prolegomena, p. 730.

9. Henry Lawrence, *A Treatise of Angels,* 4th ed. (London, 1652), p. 48.

10. *Conway Letters,* ed. Marjorie Hope Nicolson (New Haven, 1930), p. 149.

11. Henry More, *Immortality of the Soul* in *A Collection of Several Philosophical Writings* (London, 1712), III, ix, 200; quoted in Marjorie H. Nicolson, "The Spirit World of Milton and More," *Studies in Philology,* XXII (1925), p. 442.

12. R. J. Zwi Werblowsky, *Lucifer and Prometheus* (London, 1952), p. 24. In all justice, Mr. Werblowsky does not seem to take Milton's reliance on Heywood too seriously.

13. See John Colet, *Two Treatises on the Hierarchies of Dionysius,* trans. J. H. Lupton (London, 1869).

14. James Holly Hanford, "The Youth of Milton," *Studies in Shakespeare, Milton, and Donne.* University of Michigan Publications, vol. I (New York, 1925), pp. 150-151.

Bibliography

The following list of short titles is limited to those given in text or notes and directly concerned with either angelology or Milton.

ANGELOLOGY

Anania, Giovanni Lorenzo d', *De Natura Daemonum,* Venice, 1589.

Agrippa, Cornelius von Nettesheim, *Occult Philosophy,* trans. J. F., London, 1651.

——————, *Occulta Philosophia,* Cologne?, 1533.

——————, *Female Pre-eminence: or the Dignity and Excellency of that Sex above the Male,* trans. H. C., London, 1670.

Ambrose, Isaac, *Ministration of and Communion with Angels* in *The Compleat Works,* London, 1674, 1689, and in *The Works,* London, 1829.

Ames, William, *The Marrow of Sacred Divinity,* London, 1638.

Aquinas, St. Thomas, *Summa Theologica* in *The Basic Writings,* ed. Anton C. Pegis, New York, 1945.

——————, *De Malo,* in *Opera Omnia,* American reprint of the Parma Edition, New York, 1949, vol. VIII.

Arminius, James, *An Examination of the Treatise of William Perkins concerning the Order and Mode of Predestination* in *The Works,* trans. W. R. Bagnall, Buffalo, 1853, vol. III.

Augustine, Saint, *The City of God,* in *The Basic Writings of St. Augustine,* ed. Whitney J. Oates, New York, 1948.

——————, *The Enchiridion* in *The Works of Aurelius Augustine,* trans. Marcus Dods, vol. IX, Edinburgh, 1892.

Babington, Gervase, *An Exposition of the Catholike Faith* in *The Works,* 3rd edition, London, 1622.

Bacon, Francis, *The Advancement of Learning,* Everyman's Library, New York, 1915.

Bamburger, Bernard J., *Fallen Angels,* Philadelphia, 1952.

Baxter, Richard, *Of the Nature of Spirits,* London, 1682.

——————, *The Reasons of the Christian Religion . . . Also an Appendix, Defending the Soul's Immortality,* London, 1667.

——————, *The Saints' Everlasting Rest,* 8th ed., London, 1659.

——————, *The Certainty of the World of Spirits,* London, 1691.

——————, *A key for Catholics,* London, 1839 [1st ed. 1659].

Beaumont, John, *A Treatise of Spirits,* London, 1705.

Bernard, Saint, *De Consideratione* and *Sermones in Cantica Canticorum* in *Opera Omnia,* Paris, 1719.

Beyerlinck, Laurentio, *Magnum Theatrum Vitae Humanae,* 3rd ed., Lyons, 1666.

211

Binsfield, Peter, *Tractatus de Confessionibus Maleficorum*, Treves, 1591.

Bischoff, Eric, *Die Elemente der Kabbalah*, Berlin, 1920.

Bodin, Jean, *De la Demonomanie des Sorciers*, 4th ed., Paris, 1598.

——————, *Colloque de Jean Bodin Des Secrets Cachez des Choses Sublimes entre Sept Scavans*, trans. Roger Chauvire, Paris, 1914.

Boguet, Henry, *An Examen of Witches*, ed. Montague Summers, trans. E. A. Ashwin, London, 1929, [1st ed. of French, 1590].

Bolton, Robert, *Of the Foure Last Things, Death, Iudgement, Hell, and Heaven*, 4th ed., London, 1639.

Boissard, Jacob, *De Divinatione et Magicis Praestigiis*, Oppenheim, 1611.

Bovet, Richard, *Pandaemonium, or the Devil's Cloyster*, ed. Montague Summers, Aldington, Kent, 1951 [1st pub. 1684].

Boyle, Robert, *The Works of*, London, 1744.
    An Hydrostatical Discourse, vol. III.
    The Christian Virtuoso, vol. V.
    The Excellency of Theology, vol. III.
    Of the High Veneration Man's Intellect Owes to God, vol. IV.
    Some Considerations about the Reconcileableness of Reason and Religion, vol. III.

Bromhall, Thomas, *A Treatise of Specters*, London, 1658.

Bullinger, Heinrich, "Sermon on the Good Spirits," in *The Decades*, ed. for the Parker Society by Thomas Harding, Cambridge, 1851 [from the ed. of 1587].

Burr, George L., "The Literature of Witchcraft," *Papers of the American Historical Association*, IV, New York, 1890.

Burthogge, Richard, *An Essay upon Reason and the Nature of Spirits*, London, 1694.

Burton, Robert, *Anatomy of Melancholy*, ed. A. R. Shilleto, London, 1912.

Butler, E. M., *Ritual Magic*, Cambridge, England, 1949.

Butler, Samuel, "Magique," in *Satires and Miscellaneous Poetry and Prose*, ed. René Lamar, Cambridge, 1928.

Buxtorf, Johann, *Lexicon Chaldaicum, Talmudicum, et Rabbinicum*, Basle, 1639.

Calmet, Augustin, *The Phantom World*, trans. Henry Christmas, Philadelphia, 1850 [from ed. of 1751].

Calvin, John, *The Institution of the Christian Religion*, 6th ed., London, 1580.

——————, *The Holy Gospel of Jesus Christ, according to John with the Commentary of M. John Calvin*, trans. Christopher Teetherstone, London, 1584.

——————, *A Commentarie upon the Prophecie of Isaiah by Mr. John Calvin*, trans. C. C., London, 1609.

—————, *Commentarie on the First Book of Moses Called Genesis,* trans. John King, Edinburgh, 1847.

Camfield, Benjamin, *A Discourse of Angels,* London, 1678.

Campanella, Thomas, *The Defense of Galileo,* trans. Grant McColley, *Smith College Studies in History,* Vol. XXII, Nos. 3-4, Apr.-July, 1937.

Cardan, Jerome, *De Rerum Varietate,* Avignon, 1558.

—————, *Hyperchen* in *Opera Omnia,* Lyons, 1563, vol. I.

—————, *De Subtilitate,* Lyons, 1580.

Casaubon, Meric, *The Original and Cause of Temporal Evils,* London, 1645.

Casman, Otho, *Angelographia,* Frankfurt, 1605.

Charleton, Walter, *The Immortality of the Human Soul Demonstrated by the Light of Nature,* London, 1657.

Charron, Pierre, *Of Wisedom,* trans. Samson Lennard, 4th ed., London, 1630.

Cicogna, Strozzio, *Magiae Omnifariae,* Cologne, 1607.

Colet, John, *Two Treatises on the Hierarchies of Dionysius,* trans. J. H. Lupton, London, 1869 [1st publication].

Collins, James, *The Thomistic Philosophy of Angels,* Washington, 1947.

Comenius, J. A., *Natural Philosophie Reformed by Divine Light,* London, 1651.

Conway Letters, ed. Marjorie Hope Nicolson, New Haven, 1930.

Daneau, Lambert, *A Dialogue of Witches,* London, 1575.

Deacon, John, and Walker, John, *A Dialogicall Discourse of Spirits and Devils,* London, 1601.

Dee, John, *A True and Faithful Relation of What Passed for Many Years between Dr. John Dee . . . and Some Spirits,* London, 1659.

De Lancre, Pierre, *Tableau de l'Inconstance des Mauvais Anges et Demons,* Paris, 1612.

Delrio, Martin, *Les Controverses et Recherches Magiques,* trans. Andre Du Chesne, Paris, 1611.

Dewick, E. C., *Primitive Christian Eschatology,* Cambridge, England, 1913.

Digby, Sir Kenelm, *Private Memoirs of,* London, 1827.

—————, *Observations upon Religio Medici,* printed with *Pseudodoxia Epidemica . . . Together with Religio Medici,* 5th ed., London, 1672.

Dingley, Robert, *The Deputation of Angels,* London, 1654.

Dionysius the Areopagite (Pseudo-), *De Caelesti Hierarchia* in *Operum Omnium,* Paris, 1644.

Edersheim, Alfred, *The Life and Times of Jesus the Messiah,* New York, 1927.

Eusebius of Caesarea, *Onomasticon Urbium et Locorum Sacrae Scripturae,* trans. St. Jerome, Amsterdam, 1704.

Ewen, C. L'Estrange, *Witchcraft and Demonianism,* London, 1933.

Fludd, Robert, *Dr. Fludd's Answer unto M. Foster or the Squeezing of Parson Foster's Sponge,* London, 1631.

——————, *Responsum ad Hoplocrisma-Spongum,* Gouda, 1638.

——————, *Philosophia Sacra,* Frankfurt, 1626.

——————, *Mosaicall Philosophy,* London, 1659.

——————, *Medicina Catholica,* Frankfurt, 1629.

——————, *Integrum Morborum Mysterium,* no place, 1631.

——————, *Anatomiae Amphitheatrum,* Frankfurt, 1623.

——————, *Utriusque Cosmi Maioris scilicet et Minoris Metaphysica, Physica atque Technica Historia,* Oppenheim, 1617-18.

Foster, William, *A Sponge to Wipe away the Weapon Salve,* London, 1629.

Fowler, Christopher, *Daemonium Meridianum,* London, 1655.

Gassendi, Pierre, *Fluddanae Philosophiae Examen,* in *Opera Omnia,* Florence, 1727, vol. III.

Gaule, John, *The Magastromancer or the Magicall-Astrological Diviner Posed and Puzzled,* London, 1652.

——————, *Select Cases of Conscience Touching Witches and Witchcraft,* London, 1666.

Gilpin, Richard, *Daemonologia Sacra, or a Treatise of Satan's Temptations,* London, 1677.

Gilson, Etienne, *The Philosophy of St. Thomas Aquinas,* trans. Edward Bullough, Cambridge, 1924.

——————, *The Philosophy of St. Bonaventure,* trans. Dom Illtyd Trethowan and F. J. Sheed, London, 1938.

Ginzburg, Louis, *The Legends of the Jews,* Philadelphia, 1900.

Glanville, Joseph, *Sadducismus Triumphatus,* 4th ed., London, 1726.

Gregory, Bishop of Nyssa, *On the Making of Man* in *A Select Library of Nicene and Post-Nicene Fathers,* trans. Henry Austin Wilson, New York, 1893, 2nd series, vol. V.

Gumbledon, John, *Christ Tempted: the Divel Conquered,* London, 1657.

——————, *Two Sermones: First An Angel in a Vision Appeareth to a Souldier . . . ,* London, 1657.

Hakewill, George, *An Apologie or Declaration of the Power and Providence of God in the Government of the World,* 2nd ed., London, 1630.

Hall, Joseph, *The Invisible World Discovered,* London, 1652.

Hallywell, Henry, *Melampronoea, or a Discourse of the Polity and Kingdom of Darkness,* London, 1681.

Hammond, George, *A Discourse of Angels; also Something Touching Devils, Apparitions, and Impulses,* London, 1701.

Hartman, Franz, *The Life of Paracelsus*, 2nd ed., London, n.d.

Harvey, William, *Exercitatio Altera, ad J. Riolanum,* in *Opera Omnia,* London, 1766.

Heidt, William George, *Angelology of the Old Testament,* Washington, 1949.

Heydon, John, *Theomagia, or the Temple of Wisdom,* London, 1663.

Heywood, Thomas, *The Hierarchie of the Blessed Angels,* London, 1635.

Hobbes, Thomas, *Leviathan,* Everyman's Library, New York, 1914.

Iamblichus, (Pseudo-) *De Mysteriis Aegyptiorum, Chaldaeorum, Assyriorum,* trans. Marsilio Ficino, Lyons, 1577.

James I, *Daemonologie,* Edinburgh, 1597.

Key of Solomon the King, The, trans. and ed. S. Liddell MacGregor Mathers, London, 1909.

Kircher, Athanasius, *Oedipus Aegyptiacus,* Rome, 1653.

Kittredge, G. L., *Witchcraft in Old and New England,* Cambridge, Mass., 1928.

Langton, Edward, *Supernatural: The Doctrine of Spirits, Angels, and Demons, from the Middle Ages until the Present Time,* London, 1934.

——————, *Satan, a Portrait,* London, 1945.

Lawrence, Henry, *Militia Spiritualis, Or a Treatise of Angels,* 4th ed., London, 1652.

Le Loyer, Pierre, *Discours et Histoires des Spectres,* Paris, 1605.

Lindsay, Frederic N., *Kerubim in Semitic Religion and Art,* dissertation, Columbia University, 1912.

Locke, John, *An Essay Concerning Human Understanding,* in *The English Philosophers from Bacon to Mill,* ed. for The Modern Library by Edwin A. Burtt, New York, 1939.

Longinus, Caesare, *Trinum Magicum,* Frankfurt, 1616.

Love, Christopher, *The Ministry of Angels to the Heirs of Salvation,* London, 1657.

Maldonat, John, *Traicté des Anges et Demons,* Paris, 1605.

Mather, Increase, *Angelographia, or a Discourse Concerning the Nature and Power of the Holy Angels,* Boston, 1696.

Mede, John, *The Works of,* ed. John Worthington, 4th ed., London, 1677. *Discourse* X, pp. 40-43. *The Apostasy of these Latter Times, or The Gentiles Theology of Daemons,* pp. 623-693.

Mersenne, Marin, *Questiones Celeberrimae in Genesim,* Paris, 1623.

Michaelis, Sebastien, *Discours des Esprit,* Douay, 1613.

More, Henry, *The Immortality of the Soul,* London, 1659.

——————, *Antidote against Atheism* in *Several Philosophical Writings,* London, 1712.

——————, *An Answer to a Letter of a Learned Psychopyrist* in *Sadducismus Triumphatus,* London, 1726.

—————, *An Explanation of the Grand Mystery of Godliness,* London, 1660.

—————, *Enthusiasmus Triumphatus,* London, 1656.

—————, *The Second Lash of Alazonomastix,* London, 1655.

—————, *Antidote against Idolatry,* London, 1669.

—————, *Philosophical Writings of,* ed. Flora Isabel MacKinnon, New York, 1925.

—————, *Conjectura Cabbalistica, or a Conjectural Essay of Interpreting the Mind of Moses according to a Threefold Cabbala: Literal, Philosophical, Mystical or Divinely Moral,* London, 1653.

—————, "Psychozoia," in *Philosophical Poems,* Cambridge, 1647.

Nashe, Thomas, *Pierce Penniless, his Supplication to the Divell* in *The Works,* ed. Ronald B. McKerrow, London, 1908, vol. IV.

Notestein, Wallace, *A History of Witchcraft in England,* 1558-1718, Washington, D. C., 1911.

Oesterley, W. O. E., and Box, G. H., *A Short Survey of the Literature of Rabbinical and Medieval Judaism,* London, 1920.

Osborn, Francis, *The Works of,* London, 1673.
   "Essay on Such as Condemn All they Understand not a Reason for," pp. 549-553.
   "Advice to a Son," pp. 1-250.
   "A contemplation on Adam's Fall," pp. 561-573.

Papini, Giovanni, *The Devil,* trans. by Adrienne Foulke, New York, 1954.

Paracelsus, *A Book on Nymphs, Sylphs, Pigmies, Salamanders and other Spirits,* trans. Henry Sigerist, in *Four Treatises of Theophrastus von Hohenheim,* ed. Henry Sigerist, Baltimore, 1941.

—————, *Paracelsus of the Supreme Mysteries of Nature,* trans. Robert Turner, London, 1655.

Parker, Samuel, *A Free and Impartial Censure of the Platonick Philosophie,* Oxford, 1666.

Perkins, William, *Discourse of the Damned Art of Witchcraft* in *The Works,* Cambridge, 1613, vol. III.

—————, *The Second Treatise on the Duties and Dignities of the Ministerie* in *The Works,* London, 1631, vol. III.

Perraud, Francois, *Demologie ou Traitte des Demons et Sorciers,* Geneva, 1653.

—————, *The Divell of Mascon,* trans. Peter Du Moulin, 5th ed., Oxford, 1679.

Peter Martyr, *The Common Places,* London, 1574.

—————, *Most Fruitful and Learned Commentaries upon Judges of Dr. Peter Martyr,* London, 1564.

Peyton, Thomas, *The Glass of Time in the Second Age,* London, 1620.

Pictorius, George, *An Introductory Discourse of the Nature of Spirits,* trans. Robert Turner, London, 1655.

Plutarch, "On the Cessation of Oracles," *Morals*, trans. C. W. King, London, 1908.

Pordage, John, *Theologia Mystica*, London, 1683.

——————, *Innocencie Appearing through the Dark Mists of Pretended Guilt*, London, 1655.

Pordage, Samuel, *Mundorum Explicatio, or the Explanation of an Hieroglyphical Figure: Wherein are couched the Mysteries of the External, Internal, and Eternal Worlds*, London, 1661.

Porphyry, *Ex Secundo Libro Porphyrii De Sacrificiis, et Diis, atque Daemonibus*, trans. Marsilio Ficino, Lyons, 1577.

Prat, Fernand, *The Theology of Saint Paul*, trans. J. L. Stoddard, London, 1927.

Psellus, Michael, *De Operatione Daemonum Dialogus*, trans. Pierre Moreau, Paris, 1615.

——————, *De Daemonibus*, trans. Marsilio Ficino, Lyons, 1577.

——————, *Traicté par Dialogue de L'Energie ou Operations des Diables*, Paris, c. 1576.

——————, *Dialogue on the Operation of Daemons*, trans. Marcus Collison, Sidney, 1848.

Remy, Nicholas, *Daemonolatreiae Libri Tres*, Cologne, 1596.

Reuchlin, John, *De Arte Cabalistica*, Basle, 1550.

Ross, Abraham, *An Exposition of the Fourteene First Chapters of Genesis*, London, 1626.

Ross, Alexander, *Leviathan Drawn out with a Hook*, London, 1653.

Salkeld, John, *A Treatise of Angels*, London, 1613.

——————, *A Treatise of Paradise*, London, 1617.

Schwab, Moise, *Vocabulaire de l'Angelologie*, Paris, 1897.

Scot, Reginald, *The Discoverie of Witchcraft*, ed. Brinsley Nicholson, London, 1886.

——————, *A Discourse of Devils and Spirits*, ed. Brinsley Nicholson, London, 1886.

Selden, John, *De Diis Syriis*, London, 1617.

——————, *John Selden and his Table Talk*, ed. Robert Waters, New York, 1899.

Sibbes, Richard, *Light from Heaven . . . in Foure Treatises*, London, 1638.

Sinistrari, Ludovico Maria, *Demoniality*, trans. Montague Summers, London, n.d.

Spinoza, Benedict de, "Letters LV-LX," in *The Chief Works of Benedict de Spinoza*, trans. R. H. M. Elwes, New York, 1951.

Strange and Terrible News from Cambridge, London, 1659.

Strange Relation of a Young Woman Possest with a Devill, London, 1647.

Summers, Montague, *The History of Witchcraft and Demonology*, London, 1926.

Svoboda, Karel, *La Demonologie de Michel Psellos*, Brno, 1927.

Tertullian, *Against Marcion* in *The Ante-Nicene Fathers*, trans. Alexander Roberts and James Donaldson, New York, 1903.

Testament of Solomon, The, trans. F. C. Conybeare, *Jewish Quarterly Review*, X (1898), pp. 1-45.

Trithemius, John, *Of the Heavenly Intelligences, Governing the Orbes under God*, trans. Elias Ashmole, bound with William Lilly, *The World's Catastrophe*, London, 1647.

————, *Steganographia*, Frankfurt, 1606.

————, *Octo Quaestionum Libellus* bound with Agrippa, *De Occulta Philosophia*, Paris, 1567.

Ursinus, Zacharias, *The Summe of Christian Religion*, trans. D. Henry Parry, 8th ed., London, 1633.

Ussher, James, *A Body of Divinitie*, London, 1645.

Valderama, R. P. P., *Histoire General du Monde*, Paris, 1618.

Vane, Henry, *The Retired Mans Meditations, or The Mysterie and Power of Godliness*, London, 1655.

Van Helmont, Franciscus Mercurius, *Two Hundred Queries*, London, 1684.

Vaughan, Thomas, *Anthroposophia Theomagica* in *The Works*, ed A. E. Waite, London, 1909.

Villars, De Montfaucon de, *Comte de Gabalis*, trans. "The Brothers," London, 1913.

Vossius, Gerardus Joannes, *De Origine et Progressu Idolatriae*, 2nd ed., Amsterdam, 1668.

Webster, John, *Academiarum Examen*, London, 1654.

————, *The Displaying of Supposed Witchcraft*, London, 1677.

West, Robert H., *The Invisible World: A Study of Pneumatology in Elizabethan Drama*, Athens, Ga., 1939.

Wier, Jean, *Histoires Disputes et Discours des Illusions et Impostures des Diables*, Paris, 1579.

Willet, Andrew, *Synopsis Papismi*, 4th ed., London, 1614.

————, *Hexapla in Genesin*, Cambridge, 1605.

"Wisdom of the Chaldeans: An Old Hebrew Astrological Text," trans. Moses Gaster, *Studies and Texts in Folk-lore, Magic, Medieval Romance, Hebrew Apocrypha, and Samaritan Archaeology*, London, 1925, I, 338-355.

Wolleb, John, *The Abridgment of Christian Divinitie . . . in some Obscure Places Cleared and Enlarged by Alexander Ross*, 2nd ed., London, 1656.

Worthington, John, *The Diary and Correspondence of*, ed. James Crossley, Manchester, 1847.

Zanchy, Jerome, *De Operibus Dei* in *Operum Theologicorum*, Geneva, 1613.

MILTON

Allen, Don Cameron, "Milton and the Sons of God," *Modern Language Notes*, LXI (1946), 73-79.

Bailey, M. L., *Milton and Jakob Boehme*, New York, 1914.

Bailey, John, *Milton*, London, 1915.

Bogholm, N., *Milton and Paradise Lost*, London, 1932.

Bowra, C. M., *From Virgil to Milton*, London, 1948.

Bredvold, Louis I., "Milton and Bodin's *Heptaplomeres*," *Studies in Philology*, XXI (1924), 399-402.

Bundy, Murray W., "Eve's Dream and the Temptation in *Paradise Lost*," *Research Studies, State College of Washington*, X (1942), 274-91.

Bush, Douglas, *Paradise Lost in Our Time*, Ithaca, 1945.

Carver, P. L., "The Angels in *Paradise Lost*," *Review of English Studies*, XVI (1940), 415-431.

Clements, Rex, "The Angels in *Paradise Lost*," *Quarterly Review*, CCLXIV (1935), 284-293.

Curry, Walter Clyde, "The Genesis of Milton's World," *Anglia*, LXX (1951), 129-149.

——————, "Milton's Scale of Nature," *Stanford Studies in Language and Literature*, (1941), 173-192.

Dennis, John, *Remarks on a Book Entituled, Prince Arthur, an Heroic Poem*, London, 1696.

De Quincey, Thomas, "On Milton," in *Collected Writings*, ed. David Masson, London, 1897, vol. X.

Deutsch, Alfred Henry, "Some Scholastic Elements in *Paradise Lost*," unpublished dissertation, University of Illinois, 1945.

Dryden, John, *A Discourse Concerning the Original and Progress of Satire* in *Essays of John Dryden*, ed. W. P. Ker, Oxford, 1926.

Fletcher, Harris, *Milton's Rabbinical Readings*, Urbana, 1930.

Gage, Clara Starrett, "The Sources of Milton's Concepts of Angels and the Angelic World," unpublished dissertation, Cornell University, 1936.

Garnett, Richard, *The Life of Milton*, London, 1890.

Gilbert, Allan H., *On the Composition of Paradise Lost*, Chapel Hill, 1947.

Gildon, Charles, "To Mr. T. S. in Vindication of Mr. Milton's Paradise Lost," in *Miscellaneous Letters and Essays on Several Subjects*, London, 1694.

Hanford, James Holly, "The Chronology of Milton's Private Studies," *PMLA*, XXXVI (1921), 251-315.

——————, "The Youth of Milton," *Studies in Shakespeare, Milton, and Donne*, University of Michigan Publications, I (1925), 87-165.

——————, *A Milton Handbook*, 4th ed., New York, 1947.

Hunter, William B., "Eve's Demonic Dream," *ELH*, XIII (1946), 255-265.

——————, "Milton and the Power of Matter," *The Journal of the History of Ideas*, XIII (1952), 551-562.

Keightley, Thomas, *An Account of the Life, Opinions, and Writings of John Milton*, London, 1855.

Kelley, Maurice, *This Great Argument*, Princeton, 1941.

Lewis, C. S., *A Preface to Paradise Lost*, London, 1942.

McColley, Grant, *Paradise Lost: An Account of its Growth and Major Origins*, Chicago, 1940.

Milton, John, *The Works*, Frank Allen Patterson, General Ed., New York, 1931-38.

——————, *The Poetical Works . . . Together with Explanatory Notes on Each Book of the Paradise Lost*, London, 1695.

——————, *Paradise Lost*, ed. Merritt Y. Hughes, New York, 1935.

——————, *Paradise Regained*, ed. Merritt Y. Hughes, New York, 1937.

——————, *Paradise Lost*, ed. A. W. Verity, Cambridge, England, 1910.

——————, *The Poetical Works*, ed. Henry John Todd, London, 1801.

——————, *The Poetical Works*, ed. David Masson, London, 1874.

——————, *Paradise Lost*, ed. Richard Bentley, London, 1732.

——————, *Paradise Lost*, ed. Thomas Newton, London, 1749.

——————, *The Poems*, with notes by T. Keightley, London, 1859.

Milton Criticism: Selections from Four Centuries, ed. James Thorpe, New York, 1950.

Morland, Sir Samuel, *The Urim of Conscience*, London, 1695.

Nicolson, Marjorie H., "Milton and Hobbes," *Studies in Philology*, XXIII (1926), 405-433.

——————, "The Spirit World of Milton and More," *Studies in Philology*, XXII (1925), 433-452.

Raleigh, Walter, *Milton*, London, 1900.

Rajan, B., *Paradise Lost and the Seventeenth Century Reader*, London, 1947.

Saurat, Denis, *Milton Man and Thinker*, New York, 1925.

Taylor, George Coffin, *Milton's Use of Du Bartas*, Cambridge, Mass., 1934.

Tillyard, E. M. W., *The Miltonic Setting*, London, 1947.

——————, *Studies in Milton*, New York, 1951.

——————, *The Elizabethan World Picture*, New York, 1944.

Waldock, A. J. A., *Paradise Lost and its Critics*, Cambridge, England, 1947.

Werblowsky, R. J. Zwi, *Lucifer and Prometheus: A Study of Milton's Satan*, London, 1952.

West, Robert H., "The Terms of Angelic Rank in *Paradise Lost*," *Essays in Honor of Walter Clyde Curry*, Nashville, 1954.   —

——————, "Milton and Michael Psellus," *Philological Quarterly*, XXVIII (October, 1949), 477-489.

——————, "Milton's Sons of God," *Modern Language Notes*, LXV (1950), 187-191.

——————, "The Substance of Milton's Angels," in *The South Atlantic Modern Language Association Studies in Milton*, Gainesville, Florida, 1953.

——————, "The Names of Milton's Angels," *Studies in Philology*, XLVII (1950), 211-253.

——————, "Milton's 'Giant Angels,'" *Modern Language Notes*, LXVII (1952), 21-23.

Whiting, George Wesley, *Milton's Literary Milieu*, Chapel Hill, 1939.

Williams, Arnold, *The Common Expositor: An Account of the Commentaries on Genesis, 1527-1623*, Chapel Hill, 1948.

Woodhouse, A. S. P., "Milton's Views on the Creation," *Philological Quarterly*, XXVIII (1949), 222-229.

Index

223